D0548623

Since He Went Away

BY THE SAME AUTHOR

Ring A-Roses
Maggie Craig
A Leaf in the Wind
Emma Sparrow
Gemini Girls
The Listening Silence
Lisa Logan
Polly Pilgrim
Clogger's Child
A Better World Than This
Passing Strangers
A World Apart
The Travelling Man
When Love Was Like That
Marie Joseph Omnibus

SINCE HE WENT AWAY

Marie Joseph

BCA

LONDON · NEW YORK · SYDNEY · TORONTO

Copyright © Marie Joseph 1992

All rights reserved

The right of Marie Joseph to be identified as the author of this work has been asserted by her in accordance with the Copyright, Designs and Patents Act 1988.

This edition published 1992 by
BCA
by arrangement with
Random Century Group

CN 2426

Typeset by Deltatype Ltd, Ellesmere Port
Printed and bound in Great Britain by
Mackays of Chatham PLC, Chatham, Kent

For Muriel

Prologue

Amy Battersby was a well-respected, cheery girl. Everybody liked her and often said they felt better for seeing her. It was obvious she adored her husband Wesley, who was tall, dark and handsome. Like a film star, some said. Like a tailor's dummy, others muttered.

Amy was quite pretty in a nondescript way, with toffee-brown hair and a neat little figure. She could easily have passed for twenty-seven instead of ten years older. She laughed a lot, but never at other folk's misfortunes, and if she could be faulted it was that she lived in a fantasy world where everything in the garden was perpetually lovely, where families talked to each other like characters in *Little Women*.

It was true to say there wasn't a mean bone in Amy Battersby's body, yet on the New Year's Eve following the Abdication in the December of 1936, Wesley went out of their house into the street to bring in the New Year. He carried a cob of coal in his hand, according to northern tradition. Amy closed the door behind him quite happily.

At the hour of midnight clocks chimed and guns boomed, but there was no knock on the door, no smiling Wesley bringing in the New Year with kisses all round and a chorus of 'Auld Lang Syne'.

Wesley had disappeared. Vanished. Gone. Leaving a slab of coal on the doorstep and the smell of his last Wills's Capstan cigarette lingering in the vestibule.

1

Amy always had Wesley's parents and her own mother round on New Year's Eve for a bite to eat and a bit of a sing-song round the piano. Wesley, who possessed a rather fine light baritone voice, was a member of the local operatic society, and had played the Red Shadow more times than most folks in the town had had hot dinners.

Gladys Renshawe, Amy's mother, wasn't much of a mixer, but she wouldn't have missed the little get-together for all the tea in China. She considered the Battersbys to be very much her social superiors, and thought it a privilege to be there to see in the New Year with them.

Phyllis and Edgar Battersby lived in a red-brick detached house called The Cedars, up by the Corporation Park. They had a telephone and a car, and went all the way down to Bournemouth every year for their holidays, which set them well apart from the likes of Gladys, whose husband, before he died, had been a warehouseman in a local cotton mill.

Gladys was very proud of the way her daughter had gone up in the world when she married into the Battersby family. Edgar, who called himself a cigar and tobacco *merchant*, owned no less than three shops, one in Blackburn, one in Darwen and another in Preston, catering, as he said himself, only for the better class of customer.

Yes, Amy had done well for herself, but her mother couldn't help wishing that she would brighten herself up a bit. Perhaps wear something that picked out the colour of her blue eyes instead of that brown dress with the cream organdie collar and cuffs. It only needed a frilly pinny and Amy could have been taken for a waitress in a tea shop. Gladys felt like ordering a toasted teacake and a pot of tea for one every time she looked at her.

Phyllis Battersby never wore brown, except for her furs, of course. She wondered why her daughter-in-law thought the colour suited her. There was no accounting for tastes.

Her husband Edgar wondered how soon they could get away. Wesley was obviously in one of his moods, not that his mother would notice. She thought the sun shone out of his backside, always had. Edgar narrowed his eyes and hid a small belch behind a hand. He wondered who Wesley took after with his flashy dark good looks and his musical leanings. His hair was so black you would think there was a touch of the tarbrush in him; though how could there be when there'd been Lancashire Battersbys for generations – right back to Cromwell and Marston Moor.

It was very hot in the small living room with the flames from the fire leaping up the chimney back. Edgar watched a fleece of soot hang quivering. He would have to go down the yard again to the lavatory for the third time. The salmon sandwiches, sherry trifle and rich fruit cake were playing his stomach up, and when he stood up and saw his face all lopsided in the scalloped mirror over the fireplace, he almost recoiled. Was he really as ruddy-complexioned as that?

'Best be quick, Mr Battersby,' Amy's mother called out as he tried to leave the room unnoticed. 'Only five minutes to go before your Wesley goes outside to fetch the New Year in.'

Amy saw the way her husband's lip curled. She'd been trying to jolly him out of his black mood all evening, but he wasn't having any. He'd played the piano and sung 'One Alone', then for some reason started to play cross-hands, thumping a foot down so hard on the loud pedal that a photograph of him dressed as the Red Shadow jumped at least six inches in the air.

'Come on, love,' she said, half pushing him down the lobby and through the front door. 'You'll have to go now if you want to be outside before midnight.'

Back from his trip down the yard Edgar advanced on the glasses of ginger wine set out ready on a tray. 'Are your glasses *charged* ?' he boomed, being a big Mason and knowing the right phraseology.

From the wireless Big Ben chimed the last seconds of the old year away. Amy started for the door to let Wesley in.

4

'He's not knocked yet,' her mother shouted after her. 'Wait till he's knocked.'

'Come on, lad.' Edgar needed to sit down. He'd got shocking indigestion, and a pain underneath his right ribs, which had troubled him a lot lately. He considered the ginger wine in his glass to be a decidedly funny colour. Why they all had to pretend to be teetotal he had never understood and never would. Wesley could sup a reservoir and still sing God Save the King backwards, and his mother was partial to a drop or two of sherry – a drop or three at times.

Phyllis was smiling now. 'Wesley's playing one of his little jokes on us,' she was saying, neat as a doll-in-a-box in her mauve knitted two-piece. She put up a hand to her grey hair, fussing with her marcel wave. 'He doesn't usually miss his cue.'

'Come on, lad,' Edgar said again. 'It's coming down like stair-rods outside. What's he playing at?'

Amy put her glass down on the table and said she'd go and see.

When she opened the door Wesley wasn't there. The long street was deserted, its pavements black-wet and shiny from the falling rain. All the other husbands and fathers had gone inside to kiss their wives and mothers and sing 'Auld Lang Syne'. She could see one lot across the street through their front window, jumping about and acting daft, wearing paper hats and throwing coloured streamers about the room.

She shivered, rubbed the tops of her arms, moved from the doorstep and felt the rain on her head. The houses either side of her were in darkness, their occupants obviously gone to bed. Amy hesitated at the door on her left.

Last year Wesley had invited Dora Ellis to join their little party, but it hadn't been a good idea. How could it have worked when Dora cleaned part time for Phyllis, doing her rough for sixpence an hour? The atmosphere had been filled with embarrassment, what with Dora trying to act posh, Phyllis ignoring her and Edgar overdoing the mateyness. Wesley had thought it a scream to see his mother struggling to treat her char as her social equal.

5

This year Dora had gone to bed alone. Amy looked up and saw a light was on in the front bedroom, so there would be no point in knocking to ask if Dora had seen Wesley.

'Wesley?' Amy turned and walked back to the doorway. 'Wesley?' Feeling foolish, she called his name again.

The Battersby Rover saloon car was parked at the kerb. Amy walked over to it and peered inside. Wesley was a great one for practical jokes. As long as they weren't played on him, Amy muttered to herself, angry now.

'Wesley?' Her voice was louder this time.

Maybe he was hiding round the corner, listening to her calling his name and laughing. He'd been in a strange mood all evening.

'Wesley?'

Amy *knew* that he wouldn't be round the corner, hiding from her. That was a childish game, not his style at all. Besides, he hated getting wet, hated discomfort of any kind. He'd told her once, a long time ago, that he had an umbrella with him out in France during the war.

'*Wesley?*' She could hear the panic in her voice. 'I'm getting wet through.'

A street lamp flickered and went out, and a man loomed up in front of her as suddenly as if he'd popped out of a hole. Amy gave a small scream and backed away, a hand to her throat.

'Mrs Battersby! It's only me – Bernard Dale. I didn't mean to frighten you . . .'

Amy wished her neighbour from further along the street would just keep on walking and go inside his own house. Beneath the brim of his trilby his thin face looked shadowed and sinister, threatening almost, though Wesley had always said Bernard Dale was a pansy.

'A happy New Year, Mrs Battersby!'

Just as though it was three o'clock on a fine afternoon and Amy was wearing her hat and coat, he raised his trilby and walked on, his rubber-soled shoes silent on the shiny pavement. Not a word about what was she doing out there in the dark and the pouring rain, running about like a wild woman calling her husband's name.

'And to you, Mr Dale!' Amy shouted after him, waiting till she

6

heard him go inside his own house and close the front door before she called out again.

'Wesley? Stop playing silly beggars. They're waiting for you an' I'm getting wet through!'

Bernard Dale had never liked Wesley Battersby. Everything about him was too *much*. His hair was too black, the waves in it too deep, his glance too bold, his smile too flash. Besides which, he wore a camelhair coat swathed round him like a dressing gown, and suede shoes. Bernard took off his trilby, shook the raindrops from it and carried it through into the living room. He put his raincoat on a hanger and hung it on the picture rail to dry. A sluggish fire, needing no more than a touch of a poker to bring it to life, sulked in the grate. The room was as tidy as if set out for visitors.

A solitary man, an orderly man, Bernard liked living alone. He knew some considered him to be something of an old woman, set in his ways, but he wasn't going to lose any sleep over that. He accepted, too, that coming from London marked him down as a foreigner in this East Lancashire town, and although he could never get used to what he saw as the overfamiliarity of some of his neighbours, their open-hearted kindness and friendliness never ceased to amaze him. Take this street for instance. Let someone fall ill and it was as though a switch had been clicked on. Basins of hot food passed over backyard walls, errands run, bottles of tonic fetched from the chemist. Two years ago when he'd had flu he'd had at least three offers to rub his chest with goose grease and camphorated oil.

Bernard sat down in his fireside chair, leaned his head back and closed his eyes. It had been a good evening with friends of like minds, listening to gramophone records. Inside his head the music still soared. Debussy never failed him. He waved a finger in time. In a moment he would wind up the clock on the mantelpiece, take off his shoes, leaving them there on the rug with their laces spread, and go up to bed.

He wished to God he hadn't seen Wesley Battersby walking quickly down Balaclava Street carrying a suitcase; wished to God he hadn't heard Wesley's wife calling her husband's name with blind panic in her voice. Even in the darkness it had been possible to glimpse the fear in her eyes and to sense her terrible anxiety, and now he was implicated, and that was the last thing he wanted to be.

Why hadn't he told her what he'd seen? He half rose from his chair then sat down again, knowing full well why he'd kept quiet.

Telling would be construed as kindness, not interference, because all his neighbours interfered. Bernard's fingers beat a tattoo on the wooden arms of his chair. And kindness could rebound. Oh, dear God, how it could rebound. No one knew that better than he. Show sympathy to someone who needed it badly and they latched on. Fast.

If he went to bed now he would never sleep. For all he knew that bonny lass could still be outside searching for her husband, while he . . . Battersby had been walking so quickly, with his head down, was it possible that he could have made a mistake? Bernard picked up a book from the wine table set by his chair and took out a leather-thonged marker. It had been Battersby all right.

By now Amy was past caring that she was shouting aloud in the street, acting common, as her mother would say. Any minute now and doors would open, heads bob out to see what was going on. She was wet, cold and blazing mad, though anger didn't come easily to Amy Battersby. On the rare occasions when she had lost her temper Wesley had laughed so much she had ended up laughing with him.

Slowly she turned and walked back to the house, hearing the rainwater flowing along the gutter, gurgling like a mountain stream.

'What's going on?' Amy almost collided with her mother shooting out of the door as if she'd been pinged from a catapult. 'You're like a drowned rat.' Gladys shook her daughter's arm. 'Where's Wesley?'

Phyllis came out, holding an umbrella over her marcel wave, keeping her voice low in case the neighbours heard.

'Where's Wesley? You're like a drowned rat, Amy. I think we ought to go inside.'

In single file they went into the house, three anxious women, needing to tell the older Mr Battersby that Wesley seemed to have disappeared. Sure that he would come up with the answer.

8

Edgar was as red as a beetroot, having managed in the last few minutes to swig at least half the whisky in the silver flask he carried around in his inside pocket. For medicinal purposes, he told himself.

'You're very red, Father,' Phyllis told him in her high, haughty voice.

'Boozer's flush,' Gladys sniffed, smelling the drink on him right away.

'Wesley's playing one of his little jokes on us,' Phyllis said when Edgar failed to come up with anything worth while.

'*I* don't think it's all that funny,' Amy said, steaming away in front of the roaring fire.

'He'll come in through the door when he thinks we've worried enough.' Phyllis smiled.

'I call that cruel, not funny.'

Gladys was shocked to hear her daughter speak like that to Wesley's mother. Amy had gone to sit on the piano stool now, with her damp skirt rucked up, showing her knees.

'Sit decent,' Gladys told her, averting her eyes from the sight of her daughter with her hair hanging over her face in wet ropes and her lipstick all chewed off.

'He didn't look well to me,' Phyllis suddenly said. 'He didn't look well over Christmas.'

'I'll go outside and see if I can find him.' Edgar prised himself up from the settee, patted his pocket to make sure the flask was still there and trod with careful tread down the lobby.

'I'll go after him,' Amy said in a distracted way. 'He's not fit to be out in the rain.'

'An' *you'll* be fit for nothing if you don't go upstairs and get those wet things off.' Gladys turned to Phyllis. 'Wesley's not the type to do away with himself,' she comforted, oblivious to the look of blank amazement on Mrs Battersby's face. 'I'll go through and put the kettle on.'

Phyllis would have followed Amy upstairs if breeding hadn't indicated that she sat still where she was, discreet as a mother-in-

9

law should always be. She sat on the settee, apparently withdrawn and unconcerned, hearing the gas burner pop in the kitchen as Amy's dreadful mother put the kettle on. What on earth had she meant about Wesley not being the type to do away with himself? Phyllis shivered in spite of the overwhelming heat from the fire.

Wesley wasn't in any trouble, was he? Edgar had said something about the turnover at the Preston shop not being up to expectations. Edgar had spared no expense in the fittings, had taken on a second assistant, and only the week before Christmas he'd congratulated Wesley on a most tasteful window display of every conceivable type of pocket requisites for smokers. No one could dress a window quite like Wesley. It was the artistic side in him coming out, the talented side that had been nipped in the bud by that dreadful war and his enforced marriage to a girl who had done nothing to help him express himself. Encouraged, Wesley could have stormed the West End stage down in London. Sung on the wireless. Painted a masterpiece.

'The tea's nobbut ready, Mrs Battersby,' Gladys called brightly from the kitchen.

Phyllis shuddered, straining her ears for sounds from upstairs, staring into the fire till her eyes went dry.

Amy had seen the note the minute she went into the front bedroom. It was held in place by Wesley's leather stud box, a single sheet of notepaper, folded once. She gave a little cry as she read it and her face went as white as milk. Her legs went to nothing, and she caught at the kidney-shaped dressing table for support. She closed her eyes and when she opened them the baskets of flowers repeated all over the wallpaper blurred into each other.

'My son would *never* take his own life. He's made of sterner stuff.' Phyllis glared at Gladys coming innocently through from the back with a tray of cups and saucers.

'Sorry if I spoke out of turn,' Gladys said, humble and contrite, putting the tray down on the table, going back for the teapot.

'He'd have to be driven to it,' Phyllis said, anxiety sharpening her voice.

'I hope you don't mean by my daughter!' Gladys wasn't going to stand for that. 'She's waited on him hand and foot, been a slave to him.'

Amy heard her mother say that as she stumbled, sickened, down the stairs. It was no good. She couldn't face them, not yet, even though she was very quiet inside her head, hardly feeling anything at all.

Turning right instead of left at the foot of the stairs she went down the lobby and out through the open front door. She saw her father-in-law sitting inside his car at the kerb, his head sunk deep on his chest as if he were asleep. She had no clear idea of where she was going, knowing only that she had to get away from the house, away from the time when she would have to tell them what Wesley had done.

'Mrs Battersby?'

For the second time in less than an hour, Mr Dale from four doors down appeared before her.

'I was coming along to see you,' he said, and gave a slight embarrassed cough. 'I think I can shed some light . . .'

But Amy was in total shock – gone, he could see, into some far-off place where mercifully, for a little while, nothing could touch her. Bernard had seen that same rigid expression on the faces of men in the trenches when news came from home that a loved one had died. Taking her arm he led her gently into his house, not in the least surprised when she made no objection. Gently he led her to the chair by the fire, pushed her down into it, knelt by her side, took both her hands in his, rubbed them between his own.

'Nothing bad has happened to your husband,' he told her. 'I should have said before . . .' Even now, wanting to spare her, he hesitated. 'I saw him walking down Balaclava Street, carrying a case. He seemed to be . . .'

'He was going to *her*,' Amy interrupted in a cold, matter-of-fact voice. 'Here. Look at this. See for yourself.' Withdrawing her hands from his grasp, she took a sheet of paper from a pocket in the side of her skirt and handed it to him. 'Go on. I want you to read it. I *need* you to read it. Please . . .'

11

At once Bernard stood up, first pushing the letter back at her. He hadn't bargained for this. She looked terrible with her hair hanging like wet string down each side of her face. Her eyes were dead eyes, looking at him but not seeing him. The sweet damp smell of April violets rose from her, and he knew that deep inside her she was crying bitterly, the worst kind of crying there is.

He liked Mrs Battersby. They were comparative strangers, doing no more than pass the time of day, but he liked her. She had been born to be happy. How did he know that? Once he had seen her holding a kitten up to her cheek, but when he stopped and asked was it hers, she had explained that her husband was allergic to fur, so that wouldn't be possible.

He knelt down again by her side. 'You're not yourself, lassie. You've had a shock.' He touched her hand. 'I'm sure you don't really want me to read a very private letter . . .'

'You *have* to read it!' For a moment she came alive with the force of her emotions. 'Can't you see, I have to tell *someone*. I can't tell the others. Not yet. An' you don't know me very well, an' I don't know you hardly at all, so please read it.' There was the wail of desolation in her voice. 'Share it with me, please.'

Bernard was used to reading reports at speed, skimming down the page, taking in the salient points. He had already guessed the gist of it, but phrases jumped out at him, as if they'd been underlined in red ink. It was strange indeed the way some of the words sounded familiar:

At long last I have come to the time when I can keep quiet no longer, a time at the very beginning of a New Year when to carry on without the woman I love beside me would be too heavy a burden . . .

And more, much on the same lines. A letter to be read aloud, phrases so well turned they were meaningless:

Clara is my life. Without her I am nothing . . . never knew such happiness could be . . . try to understand . . . she is filled with

12

sadness for this hurt she is giving you . . . And for the hurt she is giving Charlie . . .

Bernard handed the flimsy sheet of paper back, only just curbing an urge to screw it into a ball and throw it into the fire. He stroked his chin thoughtfully, at a loss for words. It was unbelievable, but it was true. Battersby had culled part of his farewell letter to his wife from Edward's abdication speech on the radio and followed it up by a dramatic exit as the church bells rang in the New Year. He deserved an Oscar for a performance like that – he deserved his name in bloody great lights in London's West End.

Amy was putting the letter away in her pocket. She seemed calmer now. 'Wesley is just play-acting, he's like that.' She stood up. 'I'm all right now, but I'm not going to tell them yet. Thank you for helping me. You've earned an extra jewel in your heavenly crown tonight.'

She was trying to smile, but she didn't fool him for a minute. Her composure was nature's way of holding back the unacceptable until she was ready to absorb it.

Outside the rain had stopped and the air felt fresh and clean. At the front of Amy's house an elderly man was getting out of his car, walking stiffly across the pavement as if his legs were paining him.

'My father-in-law,' Amy explained as they parted.

'Who was that chap?' Edgar blinked in the light. 'Do I know him? For a minute I thought it was Wesley back again.'

'What chap?' Phyllis's voice was as brittle as set toffee, only needing a tap to break into little pieces.

From the look on their faces Amy could see that there had been words between them. Phyllis sat poker straight in her chair, while Amy's mother stood in the doorway running a teacloth through her hands, her face flushed and defiant.

'Going off like that.' She glared at Amy. 'Without saying. I nearly had a pink fit when I went upstairs and found you not there.'

'What in the name of God is going on?' Edgar had a red mark down the side of his face where he'd fallen asleep leaning against the car window. 'Cheese and flippin' rice, has everybody been struck dumb?'

Amy thought she might faint, but knew she wouldn't. She wasn't a fainter, she hadn't been brought up to be one. Nor would she shed a tear when anyone was looking. Gladys had taught her well.

'Wesley has gone away for a spell,' Amy told them. 'He's been having a bad time with his nerves. He's gone somewhere quiet to find himself. He left a note.'

'He'll have a job,' Gladys said right out. 'If he doesn't know where he is at forty-one there's no point in starting looking now.'

No one else spoke or moved. Phyllis shot Gladys a look that would have split an oak tree, and Edgar sat down, closed his eyes and clutched at a spot beneath his ribs.

'It's delayed shell shock.' Gladys couldn't have kept quiet if she'd been paid to do so. 'I know a man who lives down Inkerman Street – he's still got it after twenty years. Men who fought in that terrible war are never the same. This man gets through a bottle of Phospherine a week. To steady his nerves. And on Bonfire Night he has to be tied down or else he'd be . . .'

'You silly woman!' Phyllis could stand no more.

Gladys accepted the rebuke. Her feelings weren't hurt. She knew she was silly and said stupid things sometimes, and that people often got irritated by her, but she didn't like Wesley's mother saying it.

'I'm not as silly as some,' she muttered at the kitchen sink, clattering the pots about.

Amy sat down on the piano stool. The copy of 'One Alone' was propped on the music stand. Wesley had sung it for them, unwillingly, she remembered, only at his mother's insistence.

'I think we should call the police,' Phyllis said. 'Give them a description. Tell them our boy is wandering about in the rain with his memory gone, knocking on doors, asking people who he is.'

'He'd packed a suitcase and taken his white riding mac,' Amy said. 'He must have hidden them round the back.' She hesitated. 'He was seen walking quickly down Balaclava Street. There's nothing wrong with his memory. He's probably gone to the Preston shop to sleep in the upstairs flat.'

14

'Did he say that in the note?' Phyllis narrowed her eyes. 'Don't you think that under the circumstances you should let us see it?'

'Clara is my life. Without her I am nothing . . .' Amy shivered. The flat above the Preston tobacconist's shop, furnished during the last railway strike with a second-hand sofa and chairs, a rickety bed covered by a faded candlewick spread . . . Wesley lying in it with his love, bending over her, kissing her eyes, her lips, her throat . . . 'At last,' he was saying in his beautifully modulated voice. 'Oh, my love, my own sweet love . . .'

'The letter is private,' Amy said. 'I'm sorry, Mrs Battersby.'

She willed them to go. They looked shaky, pathetically puzzled, much older, as though a veil of senility had suddenly descended on them. She prayed they would go.

Without another word Phyllis tied a lilac chiffon scarf over her grey waves and allowed herself to be helped into her musquash fur coat.

'You've been drinking, Father,' Amy heard her say as they went down the lobby. 'I can smell it on your breath.'

'Only a little snifter, Mother. For medicinal purposes.'

The car doors slammed, the engine coughed, spluttered, roared into life.

Gladys came through from the kitchen, still red in the face. She started brushing crumbs from the table into a cupped hand, needing something to do, unwilling to look at her daughter crouched in misery on the piano stool, her face all naked with despair as she rocked herself backwards and forwards. As if she had the stomach ache.

It wasn't true that Wesley had gone away on account of his nerves. Gladys had always known that one day he would lose his respect for her daughter. It always happened when a marriage was a shotgun affair. Even after twenty years she'd never forget seeing Amy standing there in the chapel wearing a grey costume and a hat like a boiler shovel, crying her way all through her vows. With half the Ladies' Class from Sunday school filling the back rows and gloating. Wesley in his khaki uniform, his mother in navy crêpe-de-Chine with a cross-over bodice, and his father wearing a dark suit and an expression that said he'd been determined that his son did the right thing by this schoolgirl he'd got into trouble. Seventeen years and one month old. Dear Lord, it had been more like a funeral than a wedding.

Gladys suspected that Wesley had gone off with another woman. He'd be spoilt for choice with all those stupid beggars at the Dramatics queueing up for half a chance. Amy would tell her when she felt like it, and not before. Secretive, that was Amy, clamming up tight if you asked her a question she didn't want to answer.

'I'll stop the night if you want,' Gladys said, out of her depth faced with all this misery, not knowing what to say or what to do for the best.

Amy went over to kneel down on the rug and add a couple of cobs of coal to the fire from the scuttle. 'I might not go to bed.'

The back of her neck reminded Gladys of when Amy was a baby, all soft and vulnerable, with a few tendrils of hair curling down. What a fidget she'd been, forever twitching, even in her sleep.

'Best have a hot drink then if you don't want me to stop the night, and put plenty of sugar in it. You've had a nasty shock.'

Amy took no notice.

They had said all they could say to each other, mother and daughter. Amy had no way of knowing that behind her back her mother could hardly bear it all. That seeing Amy so beat, so downcast was almost more than she could stomach. Gladys was buttoning herself up into her tweed coat, ramming a felt hat shaped like a chamber pot down over her pepper-and-salt hair, blinking tears to the backs of her eyes.

And equally, if there was a hurt child inside Amy crying out for loving arms around her, then that child had learned a long time ago to keep her sorrows to herself.

'I'll walk round the corner with you, Mam,' she said. 'It's late.'

'It's tomorrow,' Gladys agreed, 'but it's only a spit away, there's no need to bother. Best wet your face and give it a good rub with the towel. You don't want Wesley coming back and seeing you looking like a corpse.'

They left the house together, Gladys holding on to her hat

because a cold wind had sprung up. 'Straight from Siberia,' she said.

'Wesley won't be coming back,' Amy said.

'You talk as if he was dead.'

'I wish he was after what he's done to me tonight.'

Gladys waited, but it was obvious there weren't to be any more revelations, not yet.

'Don't you think Mr Battersby's aged?' she said as they turned the corner. 'I don't think he'll make old bones. I think he might have what your dad had wrong with him. He's a terrible colour.'

There was no goodbye at the door, not even a peck on the cheek. Amy was used to her mother coming and going without either a hail or farewell. There was merely a grating of the big key in its lock, a nod of the ugly hat, a closing of the door, leaving Amy standing forlorn on the flags.

Back in her own house she went through into the kitchen, saw the dishcloth looped over the tap and the tea-towel spread on the draining-board to dry.

'Your mother has a pinny mentality,' Wesley had once said. 'Look for Gladys and she's either down on her knees with a scrubbing brush or standing at a sink scouring away at something.'

Amy could remember exactly how he'd looked when he said it. She could recall the expression on his face. Teasing? Sarcastic? Derisory? Affectionate? It was hard to tell with Wesley. He could have her near to tears one minute and helpless with laughter the next. He could mimic her mother's flat vowels with a wicked accuracy, and the way she moved her lips in an exaggerated way as she spoke. A legacy from her days as a weaver in Hornby's cotton mill.

'It was to make themselves understood over the noise of the looms,' Amy had reminded him. 'My mother was working in a weaving shed when she was twelve years old, and before that she had no schooling to speak of, being the eldest of a big family. She used to be kept at home to look after her younger sisters and brothers. No wonder she's at home with a scrubbing brush in her hands and a pinny tied round her waist. No wonder she can barely read or write.'

17

Wesley had tucked an imaginary violin beneath his chin, played a few bars of an imaginary lament. Amy frowned. Why had the memory of that popped into her mind, just as if it had happened yesterday? She carried a chair through into the hardly used front parlour, wrinkling her nose at the smell of damp soot and wax polish.

'Shall I light a fire in here as well?' she'd asked him that morning before he left the house in time to catch the twenty minutes past seven train to Preston.

'Suit yourself,' he'd said, shrugging his shoulders almost up to his ears, a sure sign that he was preoccupied, not prepared to listen to trivia.

Was he planning it all, right at that moment? Wondering if he could pack a case later on while she was busy in the kitchen making the sandwiches and whipping the cream for the trifle? As she stood stock-still on the front-room hearthrug, pegged in mauve and grey to match the curtains, Amy felt sick.

Wesley must have been seeing Clara Marsden for months. The woolly piece of knitting that was Amy's head was beginning to unravel. Without conscious volition, she moved back into the living room. He must have been seeing her every time he said there was a rehearsal for the Dramatics. Every time he'd said he was stopping on at the shop for stocktaking. Every time he'd said he was going round to his mother's house. Amy leaned against the door, slumped against it in a gesture as theatrical as any Wesley could have made.

Had he made love to Clara Marsden? She moved her head from side to side. Well, of course he'd flippin' made love to her. She wouldn't put it past Clara Marsden catching the train to Preston and climbing the narrow staircase to the upstairs flat on some of Wesley's stocktaking nights. For a moment her mind was numbed, giving the storm inside her time to gather.

The thought of Wesley touching Clara Marsden with his long fingers, his pianist's fingers, surgeon's fingers, touching her, kissing her, undressing her . . . An expression of disgust twisted Amy's face. Didn't Wesley know that Charlie Marsden's wife was anybody's? Easy meat. That it was rumoured she had men in the house while her husband was at work?

Didn't Wesley know that Clara Marsden dyed her hair, bleached it at the front? Kept her house like a pigsty, let her daughter Lottie stay out till all hours? Bought shop cakes, never mopped her doorstep, lay all day on the settee reading magazines? Painted her nails purple, wore bras like ice-cream cones to show off her bust, and dresses cut low for the same reason?

Amy went to look at herself in the big mirror-back of the mahogany sideboard. Her hair had dried now, but it was flattened to her head as if stuck on with glue. The Crème Simone on her cheeks and nose had rubbed off so that she shone like a polished apple. She covered her face with her hands. Would Wesley have liked her better if she'd tarted herself up a bit more? Spit on a block of mascara and stabbed it on her eyelashes? Used Tangee lipstick to turn her lips orange? Used Pond's cream with its skin vitamins on her face every night? Kept her eyebrows neatly brushed into line with Vaseline? Had a voice as low and resonant as Claudette Colbert's? Worn a rosier powder? Taken Bile Beans to enhance her personal attractiveness? Padded her bra with cotton wool to make her bosoms look bigger?

Oh yes, she knew the score all right. But long, long ago, in the days of their loving, Wesley had told her that it had been her natural beauty which had drawn him to her.

'I don't want to go to bed with a wife with curlers in her hair and goo on her face,' he'd said. 'Your skin smells and tastes of honey,' he'd said. A long, long time ago.

The memory was a knife twisting beneath her ribs, a grinding ache low down in her stomach; it was an anger so suddenly all-consuming she saw the piano through a mist. The dog-eared copy of 'One Alone' was on the music stand. 'To be my own . . .' he had sung, thinking of that other one, the one who made his life complete.

Amy snatched the copy off the stand, tore it in two, then again, glorying in the sound of the paper tearing. Beside herself now, she lifted the lid of the stool, took out sheet after sheet of music, ripped them apart, scattered them over the blue and red carpet like pieces of overgrown confetti.

'She is my life. Without her I am nothing . . .'

Wesley with Clara Marsden, lying in bed with her, covering her body with his own.

There was a noise going on in the room, a harsh sobbing, a dreadful uncontrolled sound which surely wasn't her? Why hadn't she guessed? How had she and Wesley lived together, slept together, without her knowing?

'I hate you, Clara Marsden, hate you, hate you! I spit on you!' she shouted, kneeling down to get the better of a hardbacked edition of *Songs from the Shows*.

When it was all done and there was nothing left in the stool but fluff and an old and forgotten buttonhook, she started to cry, and once she began couldn't stop.

So that in her abject misery she failed to hear the almost apologetic rap of the iron knocker on the front door, or the sound of footsteps walking slowly away.

Lying in bed next door, Dora Ellis heard and wondered what was going on. First the Battersby car had jerked her awake with the slamming of its doors sounding like pistol shots, then half dozing she'd heard someone knocking on Amy's door. She half raised herself on an elbow, then lay down again. All sorts of peculiar things happened on New Year's Eve, especially after a few beers.

'You're not serving ginger wine again this year?' she'd asked Amy earlier. 'You don't really believe Wesley's mother thinks that never a drop passes her son's lips?'

'Wesley likes it that way. He likes people to see him not as he is, but as they would like him to be.'

Dora laughed. 'Remember I never won a scholarship to the High School like you. That's a bit too clever for me. Surely old Ma Battersby knows her husband lifts his elbow more often than now and again? And she's quite fond of a drop of sherry.'

'Mr Battersby drinks whisky for medicinal reasons. For his digestion,' Amy said. 'Wesley told me.'

Dora turned on her side and pulled the blankets over her face. 'Wesley told me. Wesley said. Wesley thinks . . .' Did Amy not realize that having walked in her husband's shadow for so long she'd become his echo? There were times when Dora wanted to shake her, to ask her what *she* thought, what *her* feelings were.

Dora grunted into her pillow. If she wrote down on a piece of silk what she thought about Wesley Battersby, there wouldn't be enough to make a butterfly a pair of knickers! With his Robert Taylor looks and come-to-bed eyes, Wesley Battersby was the answer to a maiden's prayer.

Thumping the flocks in her pillow into a more comfortable shape, Dora made a sound like a Victorian pshaw. She wouldn't have him if he came gift wrapped. She wouldn't have him if he came with a ribbon tied on his whatsit.

Edgar Battersby didn't believe his son had gone away to search for his soul. He'd seen the way women looked at Wesley, and the way he would give them a sly wink in return. He hoped all this funny business wasn't tied up with the Preston shop and its disappointing profits. It had a splendid frontage with double windows and couldn't be better situated, near to both station and the expanding shopping parade.

Could it be that some of the exotic cigars Wesley had brought into an already heavy stock had tipped the scales? In the Blackburn shop the Santago cigar, small but composed entirely of Havana leaf, had practically walked off the shelves. There was nothing more hidebound than a man's taste in cigars, though round about Christmas time it was the heavyweight Mexicans that were the most popular.

Edgar rinsed his empty whisky glass and put it back in the cupboard before going to bed. It was no good voicing his worries to his wife. Phyllis wasn't interested in the shops at all. He hoped that she was asleep, but no such luck. She lay on her back in her single bed, hands clad in white cotton gloves, her hair neatly netted in peach to match her nightdress and the bed jacket she slept in to stave off the chill in the big room with its tall windows and high ceilings. Her already sharp nose looked peaky with anxiety, and Edgar wanted to go to her and kiss her cheek, but she'd smell the whisky on his breath again and know he'd been having more than a last smoke of his pipe downstairs.

'That girl's driven Wesley away,' she said, averting her eyes as usual as he undressed. 'I've seen this coming.'

'In what way has Amy driven him away?' The exertion of climbing the stairs had set his heart beating so fast he could swear it was making his pyjama jacket move up and down as he fastened the buttons, and the pain beneath his ribs was starting again.

'From the beginning,' Phyllis said, 'she failed him.'

Edgar grunted. If he got into bed, lay down and tried to breathe deeply, then the thudding might slow down.

'She's had no ambition. I mean, what is she doing now? I ask you? Working afternoons as a fitter of corsets. Down on her knees with a tape measure. Granted her customers wear their long vests, so it's all done decently, but how could she possibly meet them socially when she knows their most intimate secrets? How do you think I felt when the Enrolling Member of the Mothers' Union told me that my daughter-in-law had told her that an all-in-one corselette would disguise her spare tyre better than a bust bodice and a corset finishing at the waist? Granted she laughed, but then Madeleine Cronshaw has always had a warped sense of humour. I don't think she graces her position at all.'

Edgar closed the bathroom door and sat down on a cork-topped stool. He wasn't in a fit state to argue with his wife, but he had wanted to remind her of so many things . . . so many things . . .

Phyllis knew as well as he did just why Amy hadn't qualified for a better job. How could she when Wesley had seduced her in her gym slip? How could she when over the years of their marriage she had lost two babies stillborn and miscarried at least three others? Until he had put Wesley in his Preston shop, what stability had the lass had with a husband losing or giving up one job after another? Good God in heaven, couldn't Phyllis see the truth about her precious son?

But he was Edgar's son too. He rocked himself backwards and

forwards, in a disappointment he thought had ceased to plague him years ago – a slightly drunk, overweight elderly man in striped pyjamas, knowing he would have to get back to bed before his wife came looking for him.

2

At five o'clock, as a filter of grey light seeped through the curtains, Amy turned on her side, pulled the blankets over her head and for the next two hours slept the sleep of the dead.

At seven o'clock she put a coat over her nightdress and went downstairs. The living room was as cold as a tomb, the all-night-burning fire a heap of grey ashes, choked to extinction by Wesley's sheet music. Amy wished she hadn't done it now. Suppose he came back today, changing his mind when he found out that Clara Marsden didn't get up with him to make his breakfast, that all she wanted a man for was a meal ticket? Amy used her mother's turn of speech without even noticing.

As she opened the back door on her way to empty the ashes in the dustbin at the bottom of the sloping yard, the powdery ash blew into her face, clinging to her lips, stinging her eyes.

Too miserable even to glance in the sideboard mirror – what did it matter how she looked? – Amy knelt down on the rug and relaid the fire, criss-crossing the sticks of firewood, cheating by using half a firelighter, arranging the coal in a pyramid. Wesley had liked to come down to the sight of leaping flames and the smell of bacon sizzling in the frying pan, half a tomato, a couple of sausages and an egg with the white nice and lacy. He was full of chat, even first thing in the morning. Sometimes, when the temperature was below freezing, she would warm his shoes before he put them on, and the inside of his woollen gloves.

'You do spoil me,' he would say, and grin. 'But I'm worth it.'

To help the fire draw, Amy put the blower up and held a sheet of newspaper across it; in her mind's eye was a picture of the flat over the Preston shop, with its tiny iron-canopied fireplace, its card table over by the window, and a carpet so thin the nicks of the floorboards were clearly visible through it. And a picture of Clara Marsden lying in Wesley's arms in the rickety bed, her black-rooted hair spread on the pillow.

The newspaper flared up and Amy pushed it quickly into the fire, burning a finger. It wasn't much, hardly enough to redden the tip, but enough to rush the tears to her eyes and make her moan in an exaggerated way.

If she could she would have rung the Preston shop, told Wesley that if he didn't come home she would put her head in the gas oven. She saw herself opening the door, taking out the roasting tin and the shelves, laying a settee cushion inside, turning on the gas, and making herself as comfortable as she could. She saw Wesley by her graveside in the cemetery on a windswept rainy afternoon, watching as they lowered her coffin into the earth, a broken man destined to live the rest of his life in the shadow of inconsolable regret.

She was dying for a cup of tea. The thought popped into her head even as she was imagining Wesley being led away, tears streaming down his face. Killing herself wouldn't do anybody any good. Telephoning Wesley would only humiliate her even more. But making herself a cup of tea made sense.

Moving like a sleepwalker, she swayed her way down the lobby to take the milk in, bent down to the step, straightened herself up to stare into the face of Mr Dale, smart as a funeral director in his dark overcoat, on his way to work in the Education Office down town.

'Good morning, Mrs Battersby.'

He was for stopping, but she was too quick for him. Before he could take one breath she had the door closed, leaving him standing there blinking.

Amy was so ashamed she went straight to the sideboard mirror to verify the worst, and what she saw made her step back in horror. Now Mr Dale would know why her husband had left her. Right this minute he'd be walking along the street wondering why it had taken Wesley so long!

Black soot striped one cheek. Her hair looked as if it had been combed with a rake and powered with blown ash. Mr Dale would think that she didn't possess a dressing gown, not knowing that she had spilled tea down it and put it in the wash.

'You look like something the cat's brought in and spit out,' her mother said, turning up before Amy had a chance to get dressed. 'I'm going down to the fish market. I'll bring you a herring if you like.'

'One, not two,' Amy said, wild-eyed with misery. 'From now on it's one chop, one rasher, one sausage.'

'One alone,' Gladys said, straight off. 'Who would have thought that all the time he was singing last night he was planning to run off?' She waited, but her daughter still wasn't for telling, so she placed a paper bag on the table. 'I've brought two pieces of fatty cake to have with our cups of tea. I don't suppose you've fancied any breakfast?'

'He hasn't run off with his nerves,' Amy said.

'No?'

'He's run off with Charlie Marsden's wife. You know Charlie Marsden. One of Wesley's friends.'

'Amos Marsden's lad? Master Plumbers, Ember Street? I remember Amos starting off with a handcart, zigzagging to get it up Shear Brow, and when he died, leaving a nice little business. Took the lad next door on as an apprentice last back end.'

Amy waited impatiently, knowing that until her mother had sorted out the Marsdens there was no point in continuing.

'Clara Marsden? Father unknown, and a mother who ended up in Queen's Park Hospital believing she was a brazil nut. Or was it an acorn? Something in that line. A rough lot if I remember rightly.'

'You've seen Clara Marsden at the Dramatics, Mam.' Amy sat down at the table and began to cry. 'She's smart. She has a new outfit every Easter, then another for winter. Coats and toning hats. And hair like Jean Harlow's.'

'Fur coat and no knickers, I wouldn't be surprised,' Gladys said.

There was a grey hair or two sprouting from her daughter's parting, and Amy not yet forty. Clara Marsden! Gladys's expression was murderous. She wasn't even pretty. Nowhere near as pretty as Amy, but there was no getting away from the fact that she could look like a mannequin when she tried. Gladys had heard it said many a time that half of Charlie Marsden's money went on his wife's back.

'Best go upstairs and get dressed while I put the kettle on,' she said briskly. 'And I'll give the kitchen floor a wipe over while I'm at it.'

When Amy came down wearing a black dress with white collar, ready to go to work that afternoon, Gladys said, 'When his passion's slaked he'll come back to you. He's a Battersby when all's said and done, with their good name to think about. The Battersbys would never stand for a divorce. It would kill his mother. She'd never lift her head up again.'

'Oh, Mam . . .' Amy's voice was raw with the hurt of it all. 'What am I going to do?'

Gladys felt a sharp stab through her heart. Amy had never asked her mother what she should do, not even during that awful time when Wesley had come on leave from France and taken her virginity before she was seventeen. The puppy-like pleading on her daughter's face was more than she could bear.

'Well, sitting crying won't get you nowhere, will it?' she said, going through to put the pieces of fatty cake on a plate.

Gladys had only just gone when the doorbell rang.

'Oh, it's you,' Amy told the square-built man standing outside, gazing at her with stricken eyes. 'You'd better come in.'

'If it's not convenient I'll go away,' he said, following her down the lobby, taking off a fawn trilby hat with a small green feather growing from the band.

'What are we going to do, Amy?' he asked, sitting down and bursting into tears, letting them trickle down his cheeks, making no attempt to wipe them away. 'What is our Lottie going to do? I've sent her to stop with her Auntie Maude for a day or two – till she's back at school anyroad.'

Amy was stunned. She couldn't look at him, so she stared down at the orange sunrise pegged into the half-moon rug in front of the fireplace. Charlie Marsden was crying so hard she could see the old forceps marks on his forehead turning purple. Funny she'd never noticed them before. Charlie was the joker in the pack of Wesley's friends, with a non-stoppable fund of jokes.

'Charlie told us a good one tonight,' Wesley would say, repeating

27

it with all the accents and the right emphasis on the punch line. 'Where he gets them from I don't know.'

'Clara's not a bad woman,' Charlie was saying now, after a trumpeting blow into his handkerchief. 'It's not the first time she's strayed from the straight and narrow, but they've been no more than passing fancies. She's never left home before.' He buried his big face in his hands. 'She's wanted for nothing.' His voice broke with emotion. 'It seems they can't live without each other. I fear it's the real thing this time.'

'But *this* is the real thing,' Amy cried, flinging both arms wide. 'This house, this room. Me! An' you, Charlie.'

'I know,' he said. 'I know.'

'Do twenty years of marriage count as nothing?'

'Seventeen for us.'

'Then how can you sit there and talk about the real thing?'

'Because I'm a realist. Because I saw them together not long ago without them seeing me, and it took just one glance at their faces to know.'

'Know what?' Amy thought she might be going to hit him, but worse was to come.

'That they were besotted. Oblivious to the world around them. Gazing into each other's eyes.'

'Where?' Amy demanded. 'Where?'

'On the Boulevard.'

'What day? What time?'

'Holding hands,' Charlie said, ignoring her. 'What does it matter what bloody day it was? I was in the van with one of the lads driving, or I'd have got out and thumped their heads together.' He balled his hands into fists. 'By heck, but I'd've liked to do that. As it was we were on our way to rescue a woman up to her waist in water in her back scullery. Half the bloody town's frozen solid. I'll be run off my feet when a thaw sets in.' He was talking at random, hardly knowing what he was saying, and Amy Battersby was standing there white as a sheet in a dark dress with a white collar that made her look like a Sister on a men's surgical ward. He groaned. 'She told me that Wesley wants to marry her,' he said.

28

Amy saw him through a red, hazy mist. Did he know what he'd just said?

'I hope you know a good solicitor.' He got up to go, then sat down again as Amy clutched at his sleeve.

'How can they get married when Clara's married to you and Wesley's married to me? Yesterday, at this time, she was your wife and Wesley was my husband. *Is* my husband.'

'Not in the true sense of the word she isn't my wife. We haven't had relations for months. I've been sleeping in the spare room.'

Amy felt her face flame. Surely Charlie wasn't expecting her to discuss her relations with Wesley? He seemed to be waiting. 'What about Lottie?' she asked, changing the subject. 'Doesn't she come into all this?'

Charlie shook his head. 'Clara never really took to her. Always found her difficult.'

'Not took to her? Her own child? How can you say that?'

'She got off to a bad start with her, Amy. Nearly died having her. Two days in labour then having to suffer with milk fever as well as white leg. She rejected her in the hospital, and can you wonder at it? She never fed her. Bound her breasts up to send her milk back.' He got up to stand by the sideboard, a kindly squat little man with eyes puffy with weeping. 'Anyway, Lottie's a big girl now, coming up to sixteen. She's started her monthlies.'

He set off down the lobby without a trace of his usual bouncy tread. At the door he turned to face her.

'I forgot to tell you. I came round last night – well, early on this morning really, but I only knocked once. You must have gone to bed.' He put his hat on and pushed it to the back of his head with a finger. 'I'll be in touch, though God knows where we go from here.' He nodded at the black saloon car drawing up at the kerb. 'Looks like you've got company.'

'Wasn't that Amos Marsden's lad?'

Edgar sat down in Wesley's chair, holding out both hands to the fire. 'Marsden and Sons, Ember Street? I thought that was one of his vans parked lower down the street. You haven't had a burst pipe, have you?'

'No, it's his wife Wesley's gone off with.'

Amy wished she hadn't blurted it out like that, the moment she said it. Mr Battersby looked so grey, so ill, sitting by the fire in his heavy overcoat with the velvet collar.

'Aye,' he said slowly. 'Aye . . .'

When she began to apologize for giving him a shock like that she put up a hand.

'Nay, lovey. You don't think I was born yesterday? I telephoned him at the shop early on, and they're stopping there for the time being. Seems Mrs Marsden has been moving things in on a regular basis for quite some time.'

Amy put a hand to her mouth in a small gesture of comfort. 'I didn't even suspect anything, Mr Battersby. I had no idea.' Her head drooped. 'You must think me very foolish not to have known.'

'No, not foolish, love. Too trusting mebbe, but not foolish.'

'Would you like to take your coat off? So you'll feel the benefit when you go. It won't take me a minute to make a pot of tea.'

She busied herself in the kitchen with the familiar routine of warming the pot, taking down the tea canister, setting out the cups and saucers. It was a funny thing, but in all the years of marriage to Wesley she didn't remember once being on her own like this with his father. She'd always liked him, but felt shy in his company, almost in awe of him. Now, here for the first time without his wife, he even looked different, more relaxed, younger, with the colour coming back into his face now he'd warmed up a bit.

'Mind if I put a drop of what the doctor ordered in my tea?' Edgar held up the silver flask and winked at her. 'Not a word to the missus,' he said, deadpan.

'You sound just like Wesley!' Amy shook her head in disbelief. 'I've never seen that likeness before, but when you winked just then . . .'

'Oh, I was a bit of a lad when I was young. That's why I've always been able to read Wesley like an open book.' He took a satisfying sip. 'You know, love, it will be a bad business if you let this sorry mess make you think you've failed in some way. Not been good enough, or anything daft like that. Our Wesley's a damn fool not to recognize pure gold when he's got it.' He winked again. 'I'll tell you something. If I was ten years younger – well, twenty or thirty, I could fall for you myself.' He tapped the side of his nose. 'Again, not a word to the missus.'

'Mr Battersby!' Amy laughed out loud at the surprise of it. 'That's the stuff you've put in your tea talking, not you.'

'Don't you believe it. And couldn't you call me Father, or Dad? That's what you used to call your own father, isn't it?'

Amy nodded.

'I liked him a lot.' Edgar held out his cup for a refill. 'He was one of the best, your dad. Used to see him sometimes by the bowling greens in the park. Used to take him for a pint in the pub off Revidge.'

'But my dad didn't drink! Mam has a nose on her like a ferret. She'd smell it on his breath before he'd turned the corner of the street!'

'Used to set the country to rights, me and your dad. He had some sound ideas for a Labour man. He'd have made a damn good Conservative, as a matter of fact.' Edgar chuckled. 'He called me a bloated capitalist more than once.'

'He would have died rather than vote Tory.'

'Aye, I grant you that. But given a fairer system where he could have benefited from the privileges of a decent education; given parents with a bit of brass, and he'd have seen things differently. I still say that at heart he was a true blue Tory. The main thing was that we listened to each other's point of view. I taught him a lot and by the left, he certainly opened my eyes to a few things.' He shifted in his chair. 'I've not said any of the things I came to say, but I want you to know that if Wesley doesn't see you right for money, you know where I am.'

To Amy's acute embarrassment he reached inside his jacket pocket.

'No. Honestly, no thank you! Wesley won't . . . he won't neglect that side of things . . .' The shame of it was almost choking her. 'I get paid this afternoon, so I'm all right . . . really . . . honestly . . .'

'Did he come for anything special?'

Gladys had bumped into Edgar on the doorstep. 'I could smell drink on his breath,' she said. 'It's a sure sign of alcoholism when they're at it in the mornings.'

When she'd gone, Amy unwrapped the small damp parcel left on the table. The pig's trotter, well boiled at the tripe works, its cleaves torn away, was a glutinous transparent yellowed jelly. Amy wrinkled her nose in distaste, yet Wesley had always enjoyed one sprinkled with salt and vinegar, eaten with a tomato and bread and butter for his tea.

Had liked. Already she was thinking about him in the past tense. Scooping up the trotter and its newspaper wrappings, she carried it down the backyard, lifted the dustbin lid and dropped it inside. If she didn't get out of the house right that minute, before anybody else called, she would scream.

It was only when she was almost at the East Park Road side entrance to the park that it dawned on her that Wesley could come back, realizing he'd made a terrible mistake. For a moment she hesitated, half turned on her heel, before walking on past the duck pond, as cold and unruffled as a frozen sheet of glass. She walked with her hands dug deep into the pockets of her grey coat, her head down, shrunk into herself as if she willed invisibility.

When she was up by the tennis courts, she was only a short distance away from the Battersby house, but in all the days of her marriage to Wesley she had never called uninvited, not since the one occasion when she had turned up unheralded and caught Phyllis wearing a mud pack in preparation for a Masonic Ladies' Night.

'I thought I'd just pop in,' Amy had faltered, blushing, only to be told that 'popping in' wasn't done round there, in the big houses up by the park. Not the way it is in your area, her expression had said. Remembering without a doubt the time she had accepted an invitation to tea with Amy, only to be confronted by Gladys yoohooing herself in without knocking, bearing a small basin of home-pressed potted meat. The look on Phyllis's face had stayed with Amy for a long, long time.

Amy trudged on, averting her eyes from a couple sitting close together on a bench, purple with cold but blissfully entwined.

It was very cold in the Battersby bedroom with its pale peppermint walls and dark mahogany furniture, where Dora Ellis was flat on her stomach with a long brush sweeping up every vestige of grey fluff from the linoleum underneath a bed.

Something was going on, she was sure of it. First Mrs Battersby had opened the back door with a face on her like a wet weekend, then *he* had driven off somewhere and come back within the hour. Now they were downstairs in the drawing room with the door shut, having words. She couldn't catch a single sentence, but she knew that feathers were flying all right.

Dora got up from the floor, picked the fluff from the brush and put it on a piece of newspaper for Mrs Battersby to see. The old bat liked proof that Dora had bottomed a room thoroughly. Dora pulled a face and walked over to the dressing table for a dab of Pond's face powder. Rachel-rose, used by Lady Rosamunde Berkeley, as it said in the adverts. Given a choice, Dora would have preferred the Sun Tan, but at half a crown a box, chance would have been a fine thing.

She felt sure her ears were flapping, she was straining so hard to hear, but it was no use, the doors in this big old house were too thick – not like at home where if next door turned over too quickly it was you who fell out of bed.

'I'm not surprised at what's happened,' Phyllis was saying for the fifth time. 'Marry out of your class and this is what happens.' Her face looked pinched and old. 'This girl he's gone with. I hope she comes from a good family, and it's not just someone who's got her claws into him.' She went to stare through the window. 'We should never have forced Wesley to marry, especially the way things turned out.'

'Amy couldn't help her baby being stillborn.' Edgar was still treasuring, still holding to himself the moment when, on the mention of her father, Amy's whole expression had softened, grown calm. To have been loved like that by a daughter . . . He pulled his pipe from his pocket, took out a soft leather tobacco pouch. 'As I remember it, the lass was lucky to pull through.'

'That terrible mother of hers!' Phyllis twitched a lace curtain into place. 'When I think how she described to me in detail on more than one occasion exactly what had "come away", as she put it.'

Edgar winced. His grandson. The pain inside him was a sudden twist of a red-hot knife. How could she say such things without knowing that it nigh on killed him? Did she never stop to think that the lad would have been a Battersby, the only one to carry on the line? Did she not realize that by now he could have been at Oxford University, where Wesley could have gone if he hadn't been so pigheaded, so adamant on wanting to leave school? He'd had the brains all right, but he wouldn't listen, not Wesley.

'That's another thing about Amy's mother,' his wife was saying. 'Her sort just love to go into detail about their insides. If they're not having miscarriages, they're having hot flushes, or hysterectomies. Having "all taken away", as they say.' She inclined her head towards the ceiling. 'Like Dora up there. I remarked that she looked at bit harassed this morning and she says she thinks she could be having an early change – and she can't be a day over forty.'

'Have you ever stopped to consider how hard Dora works?' Edgar could feel his heart begin to race. 'You know damned well she's up at five most mornings to clean the offices in Peel Street mill, then when she's finished she goes straight on to cleaning for folks like us. Do you ever look at her? Really look at her? Because if you did you'd see she's as thin as a picked sparrow, with a cough on her like the death rattle. She looks as if a puff of wind would blow her away.'

Phyllis always knew how to deal with her husband when he got on his Bolshie soapbox. She changed the subject. 'You're not putting Wesley in the wrong, are you? The only thing he did wrong was to marry that girl.'

34

'Because he got her into trouble. Because for once in his life he stood up to his responsibilities.'

'She's kept him down.'

'In what way has she kept him down?' Inside his head Edgar's heartbeat was a tom-tom banging, thudding, hurting his skull, and the pain in his side was beginning again.

'Well, up to you putting him in charge of the Preston shop he was doing very well as a railway officer. He would have got promotion eventually. How could he have taken her to meet anyone of importance?'

'Such as?' Edgar's voice rose. 'The boss of the LMS Railway Company? The Branch Secretary of the NUR? The Minister of Transport? The ruddy Mayor? Good God, woman, he was a railway clerk, dishing out tickets through a window, and how long did it last anyway? Two years? Three?'

'She talked him out of trying for RADA. He's wasted on an amateur society. He has a God-given voice.'

'He wouldn't even do his piano practice, or take any exams. You know that he's never stuck to anything requiring any effort.' Edgar was finding it hard to catch hold of his breath. His face was puffy, his eyes bleak. He looked in a state of collapse, but his wife wasn't seeing him, or hearing him. Listening only to herself.

'We never begrudged him anything.'

'More's the pity, woman! Can't you see that?' Edgar clenched both hands on the arms of his chair. 'I'm hoping that by walking out on his responsibilities he'll come to his senses. Realize what a jewel that lass he married is. Stop looking for something he thinks is greener. Stop always wanting different.'

Phyllis left the room at that, straight-backed, shaking with an anger held under tight control.

Upstairs in the bedroom she ran a finger across a polished tallboy, held it out to Dora Ellis. 'I won't have skimped work,' she said.

Edgar thought a breath of fresh air might revive him, but when he stood up the carpet rose, undulating before his eyes, like the waves of a turbulent sea.

It was too cold anyway, he told himself, and when Dora came down he would ask her to make him a cup of coffee, three-quarters milk, the way he liked it. Somehow he felt cold right through to his soul.

It was lovely and warm inside the Conservatory up by the tennis courts. Amy breathed in the damp, mildewed smell and stood for a long moment staring up at the array of colourful Prince of Wales plumes with their feathery fronds.

It was another world in here, a soft gentle world with no harsh wind to sting her face, a shut-away world of steamy humidity, a foreign world with foreign flowers cascading down the edges of a man-made waterfall. A trellis of passion fruit crawled across a high archway like a flight of humming birds. There were banana trees, pineapple plants, and a Chinese Funeral Cypress, dignified in its oriental beauty. Amy didn't need to look at the small aluminium tags to know the names of the tropical plants.

Her shoes made ringing noises on the iron grids. She knew it was pointless to keep asking herself the same questions over and over again, but her mind was a mouse on a treadmill trapped in a cage. Going round and round, round and round.

Why? Why had Wesley chosen such a cruel way to leave her? A humiliating way, with the family there to witness her reaction. Was it because he needed an audience response? Because he thrived on it just as he did on the stage? Would his imagination have been fired at the way it would be, with them all out looking for him as the bells rang in the New Year, and people thought of fresh beginnings? Was that why he'd chosen such a time? To embark on his own fresh beginnings? Striding off down Balaclava Street in his long white riding mac, carrying a case, throwing his head back and muttering to himself: 'This is a far better thing I do than I have ever done before – a far, far better place . . .'

Amy pulled herself up sharp by a towering date palm, folded both arms across her chest in a gesture of self-comfort, rocking backwards and forwards. Wesley could do Ronald Colman's voice to perfection, though Wesley would never sacrifice his life for a friend as the film actor had done in *A Tale of Two Cities*.

How did she suddenly know that for the truth? Amy stretched out a hand to a wanton display of Love Lies Bleeding – read it aloud with a curl of her lips. Wesley hated this place. Said it gave him the willies looking at plants that threatened to shoot out a long green tentacle and throttle you where you stood.

But her father had loved it. Amy remembered him pointing to a poisonous plant, explaining that if you chewed it your tongue went numb.

'How about taking a leaf home and putting it in Mam's tea?' he'd teased, and she'd leaned against him, feeling his laughter through the sleeve of his tweed jacket.

He would have known what to say, how to comfort her best. Amy lifted her head to blink tears from her eyes and saw Lottie Marsden trudging down the path from the tennis courts, head down, walking pigeon-toed as if her shoes were too tight for her. Lottie, with a mother who had never 'taken to her', a mother who had spent the night in Wesley's arms.

She caught up with Lottie by the duck pond. The girl was leaning over the railings, dirtying the front of her coat. Amy spoke to her quietly, not wanting to startle.

'Hallo, love. You remember me, don't you? At the last Dramatics. You were selling programmes.'

'It wasn't me.'

Amy blinked, remembered that Wesley had said Charlie's daughter could tell lies to music. She tried again.

'I think you do know me, so why don't we go back to my house and we'll make toast by the fire?'

Lottie turned then, and Amy saw the little white rivulets where the tears had rolled down her none too clean cheeks. She guessed they'd been wiped away with her navy-blue leather gauntlet gloves.

'Well?' she asked.

Lottie fixed her with a hostile stare. 'I've never seen you before in my life,' she said coldly. 'And my parents have told me not to talk to strangers, especially in the park. They worry about me all the time.'

'I'm sure they do,' Amy said carefully. 'If I had a pretty daughter like you I'd never know a moment's peace.'

For the mere blink of a moment the dark eyes were less hostile, then the shutters were down again. 'My mother's the worst. She thinks I'm still a child.' Lottie gave a silly trill of a laugh. 'I must go now. They had to bring the doctor to her one day last week when I stayed out late, she was so upset.'

She ran off, giving a little skip now and again as if to show how happy she was.

Amy watched her go. Charlie had said she was fifteen going on sixteen, but in her navy-blue gaberdine raincoat, with a red beret pulled low over her forehead, with her tear-stained cheeks, she could have passed for twelve.

Amy worried all the way back to the east side gate, and was halfway down Shear Brow when a flying figure caught up with her.

'What's going on?' Dora Ellis wanted to know. 'Your ma-in-law's on the warpath. She'd shoot you dead as soon as look at you this morning.'

'Wesley's left me,' Amy said straight out. 'He went outside to bring the New Year in and didn't come back.'

'Get away! You're having me on!'

Amy shook her head. 'I tell you. He left a note. He's fallen in love with someone else.'

'Who?'

'Nobody you know,' Amy said, as they turned into London Road. 'She's married and they have a little girl – well, quite a big girl. I've just seen her, and she's obviously not ready yet to accept what's happened, the poor kid.'

'No wonder you look awful,' Dora said kindly. 'And no wonder Ma Battersby looked like she'd lost half a crown and found a sixpence. You're not going to work this afternoon, are you?'

'Wesley's not dead,' Amy said sharply, 'just left home. He's moved her in with him over the Preston shop.'

'To live in sin?'

38

'What else?'

They walked along in silence. Dora seemed to have taken it very well. Amy glanced at her suspiciously.

'You didn't know anything about this, did you?'

'What did you say her name was?'

'I didn't, but it's Clara Marsden. She's in the Dramatics.'

'Hair bleached to straw with all the nature taken out of it?'

Amy's bad mood evaporated. 'The same.' She felt a glow of affection for Dora bustling along in her scuffed shoes, a brown coat and a halo hat worn by the Minister's wife for at least three years before Dora had come by it for fourpence in a jumble sale. 'That's her all right.'

'He'll be back, there's nothing more sure. Your Wesley knows which side his bread's buttered on. He's just playing at being the Red Shadow, spiriting his lady love off to his flamin' tent in the desert.'

'I thought you liked Wesley?'

'Look,' Dora said, 'I'll pop in tonight after tea. Unless you've something planned?'

'Well, I do have a date with Robert Taylor. He was going to fly me to Paris for me tea in his private plane, but I'm sure he'll understand if I put him off. 'Bye then, see you later, Dora.'

Dora had exactly twenty minutes in the house that day to make herself a pot of tea and eat a slice of bread and jam, just something to put her on until she came home again at half-past five.

That afternoon she was working for a Mrs Green, the wife of one of the mill bosses, a pernickety woman who had told Dora that she wanted every surface in her house so clean that you could eat your dinner off it.

'Including the lavatory seat?' Dora had said in her head, but not aloud, of course, Mrs Green being so top drawer that the word lavatory spoken aloud would have brought her out in a rash.

That afternoon one of Dora's jobs was to wipe over the new white tiles in the bathroom with a cloth dipped in milk, then polish them till they shone like mirrors. And it being a Friday the silver would have to have its weekly cleaning. Dora had been shown how to push a small brush down the spout of the Georgian teapot till it was as clean as the outside.

'She'd have me wiping the coal over before I brought it in from the yard,' Dora had told Amy once. 'She'd had the fireback whitewashed to look nice in the front room.'

'Really?' Amy had said, not knowing whether to believe it or not.

Dora banked up her own fire with slack and put the fireguard back in place. Poor Amy. Sweet, kind, trusting Amy. Eternally grateful that Wesley had married her, rescuing her from a life of shame. Kow-towing to him from ever on to show that gratitude. When Dora's husband, Greg, had been alive he'd had a soft spot for Amy. He would lie in bed in the front downstairs room and follow her around with his eyes. He would lie there listening as she read to him when he became too weak even to hold a book in his hands. He'd liked Wesley too – in his own way.

Dora gave her face a quick splash at the cold tap in the kitchen. Greg had been dead for over four years, but he still walked into her mind, taking her unawares, catching her off guard.

Ramming the halo hat back on to her head, buttoning the brown coat up to her neck, she rushed out of the house, walking so fast she almost fell over, leaning forward into the freezing wind.

In the upstairs fitting room of the shop where Amy worked afternoons, she had only one fitting, with a Mrs Moffat, which was as well, as downstairs they were getting ready for the January sales.

'I would like you,' the stout little woman told her, 'to machine-stitch a tuck along the cups of my brassière when it arrives, to take in the shape.'

Amy wrote down the measurements carefully in her little notebook. 'But won't that flatten your front?'

'Exactly.' Mrs Moffat nodded all her chins. 'Showing the shape of *two* bosoms is very vulgar. And remember I want steel bones in my corsets, not the other kind. And I'd like the ends well padded. I'm not one of those who fillet their corsets the minute they get home. Oh, and remember to order two extra suspenders – they make all the difference to the fit of silk stockings.'

40

Compared to some Amy could mention, Mrs Moffat wasn't really a difficult customer, and if she wanted to look like a lagged cistern then that was her choice. Amy showed her to the door, promising she would have the corsets and brassière ready for fitting within three weeks at the most.

'I saw that nice husband of yours twice last week when I was meeting Mr Moffat off the Manchester train. He was talking to a young lady with fair hair.' She tapped Amy playfully on her arm. 'It's a good job you can trust him, isn't it? She was quite a bobbydazzler.'

'Nice woman,' one of the assistants remarked. 'Fussy, I grant you, but she always knows exactly what she wants.'

'She's evil,' Amy said, rushing round the counter and back up the stairs. 'Didn't you see the horns poking through the sides of her stupid hat?'

3

Dora gave three sharp raps on Amy's vestibule door, called out 'It's only me,' and walked straight in. Mrs Green had had her down on her knees in the spare room picking bits of fluff out of the nicks in the floorboards with a crochet hook, and she wanted to tell Amy about it and make her laugh. But Amy looked awful – almost in a state of collapse.

'Everybody knows about it!' she cried as soon as Dora showed her face. 'They must have been talking about me behind my back for ages. Laughing at me!'

'They say the wife is always the last to know.'

Amy looked at her sharply. If Dora was trying to be jokey then she'd come to the wrong place. 'I'm not laughing,' she said. 'I'm so angry, so humiliated, I could burst.'

'Do you want Wesley back? Could you forgive him if he does come back?'

Amy looked down at the carpet then up at the ceiling, trying hard to blink back the tears. Dora was her friend, but she wasn't going to cry in front of her. Dora wouldn't know where to look. Instead, she sat down, pulled herself together and handed Dora a cigarette.

'You don't smoke, Amy!'

'I do now.' They were long, slim black cigarettes. Russian, Dora guessed, from Wesley's shop. 'There's more where these come from,' Amy said. 'I found them at the back of his top drawer. I've been having a good snoop. Would you like a drink?'

'I've just had me tea, thank you.'

Amy raised her eyebrows as if searching for patience. 'I mean a proper drink. Whisky.'

'Wesley's?'

Amy nodded.

'Then I'll have a double.'

It seemed rather a lot when Amy poured it out, and it didn't look right in cups somehow, but after the first sip you got used to it. The cigarette made her cough and feel sick, but Dora was managing both with aplomb.

Dora sat there in Wesley's chair, still wearing her flowered pinny, with her stockings wrinkled like a concertina, and three kirby grips fastening her hair back when one would have been quite enough. She took deep drags of the exotic cigarette, then flicked the ash on to the tiled hearth, ignoring the ashtray fastened down on the chair arm by a leather thong.

'You remind me of Bette Davis,' Amy told her, 'sitting there smoking and flicking the ash like that.'

'And you remind me of Janet Gaynor,' Dora said after a while. 'You look all wrong puffing away like that. And you shouldn't drink whisky as if it was dandelion and burdock, you know.'

'Charles Farrell,' Amy simpered, screwing her eyes up. 'Janet Gaynor and Charlie Farrell.' She topped up her drink, passing the bottle over to Dora.

'Wesley is my life,' Amy said suddenly in a broken voice. 'I was only sixteen when we met. He was the first boy I'd ever looked at. The first boy who'd ever looked at me.' She was talking with the cigarette stuck to her bottom lip, so that it wobbled as she spoke. 'I was at school, coming up to sitting for my School Certificate.' Amy removed the cigarette, stared at it in distaste and threw it in the fire. 'I was going to be a teacher, Dora.'

'You'd have made a good teacher, Amy.'

'My dad badly wanted me to go to college. He'd worked out they could just about manage for money . . . this whisky is making me feel sick.'

'Don't drink it, Amy.'

'No, I don't think I will, Dora. He wanted me to have all the advantages he never had, you see.'

'I never knew my dad.'

'It was all planned. I was going to stop on at school and take my

Higher School Certificate when I was eighteen, then I was going to college.'

'I left school when I was thirteen.' Dora felt a wodge of self-pity rise up in her throat.

They stared sadly at each other, then into the fire. Fell silent for a while.

'I met Wesley one day in the park on my way home from school. The park beds were full of tulips. Darwin tulips,' Amy explained. 'The sun was shining.'

'I used to go with my mother to help her clean the trams at the depot, but she wouldn't let me go in the mill. Not good enough for me.' Dora gave a hard short laugh, startling Amy for a moment.

'Wesley was on leave from France. He was wearing a checked sports jacket, grey flannels and a blue spotted cra . . . cra . . . ?'

'Cravat?'

Amy nodded a thank you. 'He looked so handsome. I can see him now.' A simpering smile spread across her face. 'He stood with his fists on his hips, barring my path – and that was that.'

'You'd have him back, wouldn't you?'

Amy stood up, clasping her hands together. 'Not loving someone else I wouldn't. Not still loving Clara Marsden.'

'The peroxided slut.'

'The painted prostitute,' said Amy, reaching for another slim black cigarette. 'The cheap whore.'

'I wouldn't have thought you knew that word, Amy.'

Amy sniggered. 'I know a lot more.' She lit her cigarette, inhaled, and blew smoke down her nose. 'My dad used to say that if you couldn't express yourself without swearing, then you should . . . ?' She frowned, obviously having difficulty in remembering.

'Shut your gob?' Dora suggested.

'Keep your mouth shut,' Amy contradicted at once. 'My father was a little gentleman.'

'Mine might have been of royal blood for all I know.'

Dora had never, in all her wildest dreams, imagined that Amy Battersby could or would behave like this. Greg had always said that little Amy from next door had hidden depths, was a dark horse, a two-headed woman. It was the whisky of course, but the change in her was startling. The drink had flushed her cheeks, made her eyes sparkle and deepen to a brilliant blue. Her hair, mussed out of its usual neat cap of finger waves, tumbled over her forehead. Amy was halfway to being beautiful, and from the bottom of her heart Dora just wished that Wesley would walk in and see her looking the way she did, smoking his cigarettes, drinking his whisky.

'Wesley was my life,' Amy said suddenly, taking another swig.

Dora nodded. 'That was always your problem,' she said. 'There is no man alive worth that kind of devotion. There's none of them worth a tuppenny button.'

They talked and dozed, then drank endless cups of tea, till at ten o'clock Dora said it was well past her bedtime, left abruptly and went straight home to bed. Between them they had sorted out the rest of Amy's life without Wesley as best they could. Amy would need to earn more money than the corset job paid, so Dora had offered to put a word in with one of her ladies. Mrs Green's daughter was getting married and needed a woman for the rough, and the woman who did the outside steps of the big offices in Richmond Terrace was bad with consumption and expecting to be forced to leave any day now. Also, there was the big factory opening soon for making gas masks in readiness for another war, though Dora for one didn't believe there would be one. Memories weren't as short as that, surely? Greg had taken a long time to die from the effects of gas poisoning, and he was one of the lucky ones. How could anyone in their right senses even think there might be going to be another war? Over seven million men had been killed, and many many more had died of the terrible effects since then, so who could seriously think that it was all going to start over again?

Dora wished her mind would stop going round and round so she could get some sleep. She pulled the blankets over her head and snuggled her stone hot-water bottle uncomfortably to her chest.

She'd seen Adolf Hitler on the Pathetone News at the pictures the Saturday before Christmas, and wondered who had told him he suited that awful stub of a moustache. His fight was for the peace of the world, he'd said, stabbing a finger in the air. Look how all the

Germans kow-towed to him – they wouldn't do that if they thought he was dead set on another war. No, she could forget that kind of silly talk. There would never be another war – folks weren't as daft as that.

When she slept at last it was to dream of her mother taking the tiny Dora with her to work, both of them snuggled into one shawl because they didn't own a coat between them. It was to dream about her mother standing in the kitchen of a big house scraping a piece of bread round the bacon fat left in the frying pan and handing it to Dora to eat. It was remembering how good it had tasted to a child who had left her house with nothing more than a drink of cold water to line her stomach.

Dora fell asleep smacking her lips.

At around half-past three, after no more than an hour's restless sleep, Edgar Battersby made up his mind to drive over to the Preston shop as soon as it came light and have a straight talk to Wesley. He was bound to be there. It had long been an unspoken agreement that Edgar would keep away, leaving the business entirely in his son's hands, but when wholesalers started sending bills to him, Wesley's bills, Final Demands to be blunt, there was a deal needing sorting out.

If only he could feel better – if only he didn't feel so under the weather most of the time. If only Phyllis would stop this constant everlasting championing of her son. Edgar tried to subdue a cough, failed and reached out to his bedside table for a Victory V lozenge.

By his side Phyllis feigned sleep. It was a long time since she had said a personal prayer, not having felt the need, she supposed. She closed her eyes in church naturally, folded her hands and joined in the prayers for the sick, the dying and the soldiers fighting in the Spanish Civil War. And for those less fortunate than herself, of course. Now, at this moment, she asked God to send Wesley to see her soon, so that she could reassure him that she understood. That whatever he did or did not do she would always understand.

He wouldn't have done what he did if he hadn't been driven to it.

It was all right Edgar sticking up for Amy, but he was a man and couldn't or wouldn't see that it had been a wrong marriage from the beginning. Wesley needed someone to back him up more, be more of a conversationalist, dress up more. Encourage him. Do more entertaining of her husband's business contacts, instead of always having her nose stuck in a book. How did Edgar think she'd felt during the war when week after week in the local newspaper there were photographs of soldiers home on leave from France marrying into good families? Directors' daughters in wreaths and veils, with four bridesmaids, even though there was a war on. With detailed descriptions of the dresses. 'The bride wore a dress of white slipper-satin with a train, and her mother's veil of Brussels lace with an orange blossom headdress.'

Why was it Amy's clothes always seemed to resemble uniforms? She'd been a lady tram conductor to the life at her wedding to Wesley, in that awful square chapel with not even the Minister dressed properly. And what about one of her uncles at the reception tapping cigarette ash into the turn-ups of his trousers when he thought nobody was looking? No one could forget a thing like that.

'Please, God, let Wesley come tomorrow,' she prayed. 'Let all this be for the best.'

She slept and woke at six o'clock to find Edgar by her side burning with a fever through his winceyette pyjamas, breathing with puffing rasping noises, mumbling to himself. Fit to go nowhere, not even well enough to get out of bed.

'Mother sent for me,' Wesley told Amy, walking in on the Sunday morning, looking sheepish and defiant at one and the same time. 'Father has influenza and the doctor says he'll be in bed for at least a week.' The front door key, on its ring, dangled from his fingers. 'So I thought I'd come round and collect a few of my things.'

'Kill two birds with one stone?' Amy suggested. 'Thinking I would be in chapel?' She had always thought that anger was hot, searing like a flame, but the crawling sensation down her spine was the drip of water from an icicle. 'You can put that key down on the table, Wesley. I don't think you have the right to be able to walk in

47

just when you feel like it.' She was trembling now, standing there on legs that seemed to be disintegrating. She banged the flat of her hand down hard on the table. 'The key, Wesley!'

Immediately he dropped it into the pocket of the camelhair coat swathed round him like a dressing gown.

'Don't be unreasonable, now,' he said, turning to go up the stairs, taking them two at a time.

'I'll have the locks changed!' she shouted after him, then gnawed at a fist as she heard a drawer jerked open followed by the creak of the wardrobe door.

She didn't know what to do. The sight of him, when he had been the last person on earth she had expected to see, had shocked her into all the wrong reactions. One minute she had been sitting there regretting her cowardice in not going to the morning service, telling herself that she would have to meet people some day, when there he was, come in from the cold, tall and broad-shouldered, with his handsome face, the features bold and well-defined, a face you could trust to the ends of the earth.

Another drawer banged upstairs, snapping her out of her trancelike state.

She didn't remember climbing the stairs, but there she was snatching a shirt out of his hand, screwing it up into a ball, hurling it to the far corner of the bedroom.

'What do you think you're doing? Who do you think you are?' Was that alien raucous voice her own? 'Coming here as though nothing had happened. Sure I wouldn't be in. What would you have done? Left another flamin' letter?' Her eyes blazed. 'Bringing your suitcase back to fill it again?' She clapped a hand to her forehead. 'Oh, I saw it all right. I saw you leave it at the bottom of the stairs.' Before he could stop her she grabbed the case from the bed, swirled it round, scattering its contents across the carpet. 'Do you think . . .' she shouted, 'do you think you can do this to me? Do you . . . ?'

He caught her wrists as she drummed her fists against his chest, held her so tightly she could only pant and struggle till pain held her still. His face was so close she could see the green flecks in his brown eyes, the faint bags beneath them, the bags he'd anguished over in the mirror, till she'd told him they made him look more handsome than ever, swearing that no one would ever guess he was forty-one.

'Pull yourself together, love,' he said softly. When she opened her mouth and screamed, he let go of one of her wrists to slap her so hard her head rocked back on her shoulders. Her eyes flew wide and when she began to cry with hard shuddering sobs he led her over to the bed and sat down beside her.

'I'm not enjoying this,' he told her in his caress of a voice. 'Seeing you upset like this distresses me too, Amy.' He turned his profile towards her. 'I am ready to admit that I should have discussed the situation with you a long time ago, but every time I tried you did or said something so sweet, so caring I just couldn't find the words. Any other woman but you would have guessed I was going through hell. Wounding people I am fond of doesn't come easy to me, you know.' He put out a hand to touch her hair, but she jerked away as if his touch would burn her.

'Keep your hands off me,' she said through clenched teeth. 'If you touch me I'll be sick.'

He stood up looking honestly bewildered. 'I thought you had more respect for yourself than to behave like this, Amy.' He sounded deeply wounded, badly done to. 'Can't you see that in the end there was only one way to leave and that was quickly with no harsh words between us, no quarrelling, no explaining.'

'Respect?' She picked on the only word she'd managed to take in. 'I lost that when I married you. Or rather when you were good enough to marry me! You've held it over me ever since. Especially when it turned out not to have been necessary after all.' The words had been stored up inside her for a long time. 'You were forced to marry me, because your father convinced you it was the only honourable thing to do.'

'I married you because I loved you.'

'But you don't love me now.'

'Of course I love you. There'll always be a corner of my heart just kept for you, but not in the way I love . . . Oh God, Amy, I can't help myself.' Apparently overcome, he buried his face in his hands and sat down beside her again.

All at once she was reminded of Charlie Marsden sitting in exactly the same attitude, the tears trickling down between his fingers. But there were no tears this time. She knew that for sure.

'The way you love her,' she finished for him.

He nodded into his hands.

She had always loved his thick dark hair, the way it sprang from the parting in deep waves. There were tiny threads of silver in it; it smelled of bay rum and cigarettes, a manly Wesley kind of smell. She moved closer to him and, all the control ebbing away again, put her arms around him, forced his head up and began to kiss his cheeks, his eyes, his mouth, and yes, she had been right, there were no tears.

This time he held her gently but firmly away from him, searched her face with sad reproachful eyes. 'Oh, Amy. Dear, sweet Amy, what are we doing to each other?'

'What did I do wrong?' she wanted to know. 'You can see how low you've brought me when I can ask a thing like that.'

'You did nothing wrong, nothing at all.'

Thinking she was calmer, he put her aside and began to sort out a clutch of ties, wrapping the chosen ones round a hand, tucking them neatly into the sides of the case retrieved from the floor.

'In fact, I don't think there is a better, more generous person in the length and breadth of England. I can't fault you in any way.'

'That's nice.'

Busily rolling up a Chilprufe vest, he missed the sarcasm entirely, reached across her for a pair of underpants.

'Clara is no home-breaker, you know. She and Charlie had been drifting apart for a long time, and she knew that we lived together as brother and sister – more or less.'

'Oh, my God!' Amy uttered the blasphemy without even noticing. 'So you must have committed incest at least once a month?'

'That's no word for a woman to use.' He betrayed his agitation by the way he grabbed a heap of socks from a drawer, shoving them into the case any old how.

50

'I know worse ones than that!' Amy was on her feet again. 'Like whore,' she shouted. 'Clara Marsden's middle name.'

'Jealousy doesn't become you either.'

'Bugger jealousy,' said Amy, advancing on him, trying to snatch at the handle of the case.

'I've never heard you swear before.' He sounded genuinely aggrieved. 'And I don't like it at all. I think I'd better go,' he said, sidestepping round her. 'I came full of good intentions, to try and sort a few things out.'

'So I see,' Amy said, glaring at the case.

'To arrange some kind of weekly payment.'

'Stuff your weekly payments!'

He was going and she couldn't bear it. This time he might not come back. She had said all the wrong things, showed herself up, let herself down, in a rage that trembled her into a terrible uncontrollable fury.

'I wish you'd listen to me,' he said from the door.

'Shut your gob!'

He was killing her. Couldn't he see? He was all that she had and he was walking away. It wasn't *her* swearing and saying all those mean and petty vulgar things, it was someone she didn't know. It was a woman she glimpsed now in the dressing-table mirror, wild of eye, flushed of face.

'I hate you!' she called after him, watching him go down the narrow staircase with the case banging against the wall.

The face he turned up to her was full of hurt disbelief. 'I'll come back when you're more in control of yourself. I don't know you today.'

'Don't you patronize me! As if I'm the one in the wrong!' Without conscious volition she rushed back into the bedroom, threw up the sash window and flung down a fair-isle pullover left on the bed. 'You forgot this!' she bellowed at the top of her voice, hurling it as far as she could.

Drawing back in shame as it landed on the head of Mr Dale, innocently coming back from the newsagent's with the *Sunday Times* tucked underneath his arm.

At once the fire went out of her. She closed the window and went slowly back down the stairs, the bile of shame sour in her throat.

4

The fair-isle pullover came back that afternoon.

Amy heard the doorbell ping just once and found a brown paper parcel lying on the mat.

'I believe you dropped this,' the note pinned to the V-neck of the pullover said in neat clerical writing, with the initials B.D. underneath.

'I heard you yelling your head off at Wesley,' Dora said, letting herself in without knocking, 'so I thought I'd give you a chance to cool down before I came in. What's all this about?' She picked up the pullover and read the note.

'I threw it through the window after Wesley, but it landed on Mr Dale's head,' Amy explained. 'What he thinks about me I daren't imagine.'

'He wouldn't think anything. He just lets people be. Never condemns. He's a nice man.'

Dora was so tired that even her eyeballs ached. As an extra favour to Mrs Green and because she had been offered double pay, she had cleaned through the empty house waiting for Mrs Green's daughter to settle down in after her marriage. The previous owners hadn't wiped the paintwork down for years, and when they'd taken the carpets up had left the tacks in the floorboards. Dora had nearly knocked an eye out struggling to remove them with a pair of pliers.

'I saw Wesley coming in as I turned the corner,' she said. 'He didn't stop long, did he?'

Dora wasn't being inquisitive, just friendly and nosey. Amy accepted that, but all at once she felt hemmed in, suffocated, as though the walls were closing in on her.

'I'll have to get out,' she said.

'What, right this minute?'

'Or I won't be responsible, Dora.'

'I'll go and get me coat on . . .'

Dora wanted nothing more than to have a nice lie-down on the bed, but Amy didn't look fit to be let out alone. Screaming and yelling like that must have taken a lot out of her.

Amy wanted nothing more than to be left on her own, to walk as fast and as far as she could. To forget the terrible things she had said to Wesley, the way she had sworn at him, his disgust of her. Every single nerve in her body was still alive and jangling; if anyone had touched her she was sure she would have twanged like a ukulele.

'Why do you say Mr Dale's a nice man?' she wanted to know, before they had turned up the hill towards the park. 'Wesley always said he was a jessie.'

Dora was at the stage of exhaustion akin to intoxication. She had left the brown halo hat at home and tied a woollen scarf round her head, fastening it beneath her chin with a bow. With her prematurely wrinkled face and her habit of walking leaning forward as if battling against a force-ten gale, she looked at least ten years older than Amy.

'He's not a jessie.' Dora looked smug all of a sudden. 'The town looks quite nice when you see it from up here on a fine day like this, when there's no smoke from the mill chimneys and the hills are covered in snow.' Dora stopped and narrowed her eyes as if she intended drawing what she could see. She turned to Amy. 'I know that he's not a jessie because once, years ago, we were lovers,' she said. 'I'll tell you about it some time.'

Not another word would she say, though they skirted the duck pond in the park and started off at a brisk pace down the Broad Walk. Amy was so flabbergasted that she saw nothing of the people going for their Sunday walks, husbands and wives, arms linked, grumbling children trailing on behind, two stray dogs fighting, a tramp rooting in a wire bin, a couple out of Hodder Street who had a stall on the market on a Wednesday and Saturday, walking along having a good old row.

Dora must be having her on – she could say the most outrageous things when she wanted to. Deep, too. Amy glanced at her now, swinging her arms, walking like a soldier, as if her revelation had put fresh heart into her. The park was beautiful with the trees etched boldly against an ochre-pale sky heavy with the promise of snow, but Amy was oblivious to it all. Until Dora enlarged on the preposterous statement she had just made Amy could think of nothing else. Not even at that moment of Wesley.

Amy hadn't been to chapel that morning and she wasn't at the afternoon Sunday school, either. Gladys sat at the back of the big room with the Ladies' Class, and after Miss Barton at the piano had played the opening chords of the first hymn, gave up watching the door.

'Stand up! Stand up for Jesus,' she sang. One thing was certain. Wesley would never dare to show his face in here again; wouldn't have the cheek. Not that he'd attended Sunday school regularly. Gladys stared at the Men's Class on her left, singing away at the tops of their voices. Like a miners' choir without the tin hats and lamps. Wesley would have been a credit to them, but his parents were church, not chapel, and church-goers didn't seem to sing as loud as Methodists somehow.

'From victory unto victory. His army He shall lead.' More than half the men singing their heads off had been in the last war. Gladys had always thought old soldiers had a stamp about them. Those terrible trenches, that terrible mud. Three of the women in the Ladies' Class had been widowed, left to struggle on a pittance, to bring children up without fathers, deny them scholarships, because their wages were needed. Now they were talking about another war.

'Forth to the mighty conflict,' Gladys sang. She'd pop round to see Amy on her way home and take her a barm cake spread with a bit of rum butter left over from Christmas.

After the hymn, the various classes dispersed to the vestries for their own individual lessons and prayers. Mrs Rakestraw, who lived opposite to Amy, caught Gladys up in the passage.

'A right old bust-up this morning,' she whispered. 'Your Amy was leaning out of the upstairs window chucking all her husband's clothes down into the street. Has he gone back to his mother? I believe they're very close.'

In the small vestry the women arranged themselves on the little hard chairs set round the walls.

'Let us pray,' the Minister's wife said, and Gladys buried her face in her hands. 'For the peace of the world, and that men may learn to love one another. That all violence and thoughts of violence may cease.'

Gladys was certain of one thing. If she'd had a gun on her at that moment, Mrs Rakestraw would be a gonner.

'If you don't tell me about you and Mr Dale I shall burst,' Amy said the minute they got back to the house. They had actually met him on their way home and Amy had thought she would die of embarrassment if he stopped to talk to them, but he had merely raised his hat and walked on.

Dora suggested that they had a cup of tea first and perhaps a couple of biscuits as she hadn't had time for any dinner, and anyway what was the hurry when it was a secret she had kept for years.

In the kitchen Amy willed the kettle to come to the boil. 'Why haven't you told me before?'

'Because when Wesley was here you would have been shocked.'

'And I'm not shocked now?'

'Well, are you?'

Amy handed Dora a cup of tea. 'Fascinated, but no, not all that shocked.'

'He saved my life.' Dora settled back in Wesley's chair. 'If he hadn't made me feel I could go on living, I don't know what would have happened. But I still put Greg away eventually.'

'You didn't put Greg away! You had no choice but let him go into hospital when he became incapable. He needed specialized care.'

'An institution,' Dora said, 'with a lot of broken men from the war, men who were taking too long to die. Men rejected by their families.'

'You didn't have any family, Dora. There was only you.'

'There was a man in the next bed to him with hardly any face.'

56

Amy put her cup down on the tiled hearth. 'Don't tell me about Mr Dale and you today. It's bringing bad memories back and besides, you must know you've nothing to reproach yourself for. Wesley said Mr Dale was a conscientious objector during the war.'

Dora immediately snapped out of herself. 'And so he was. At the very beginning, but they sent him off to the front line in the thick of the fighting and tied him to a post with all the killing and the dying going on around him. You can imagine what that did to a man like him who wouldn't step on an ant if he could walk round it.' She drew in her breath. 'Anyway he joined up right away after that, and they sent him as a stretcher bearer. At the end of the war he had spent over eighteen months in the trenches. He got a medal, too.' Her voice was fierce. 'You and Wesley don't know the first thing about him, do you?'

'He's always struck me as wanting to keep himself to himself, and anyway . . . with . . .'

'With Wesley not liking him you decided not to like him either!'

'That's unfair.'

'It's the truth.'

Amy suddenly saw that it was. Mr Dale had certainly been very kind to her. If you hadn't known differently you might have thought he was a real medical man. He had knelt by her side and held her hands in his; he had calmed her down . . .

'He calmed me down,' Dora was saying. 'At that time I was working all day, then running to catch the tram to Queen's Park Hospital. I was sitting with Greg every evening by his bed, though for the last few months he didn't know me most of the time. He would tell me I never went to see him, forgetting I'd been just a day before, and worst of all, towards the end he turned against me. His voice went deep and rough and he looked at me as if he hated me.' She sighed. 'So because of what had been between us, I was able to tell Mr Dale all that, and he understood. He explained that Greg, the real Greg, had gone away from me a long time ago, leaving this drug-filled weary man who lashed out at the person he instinctively felt he could hurt the most. Me. He said that men who had been in the thick of it, like Greg, still paid a terrible price of suffering. Greg was lying in a water-filled shell hole for two days before they found him. His leg was rotted, Amy, and the rats had got to him . . .'

'Don't talk any more if you don't want to.' Amy was worried at the sudden pallor of Dora's face. 'Would you like another cup of tea with a slosh of Wesley's whisky in it?'

'Yes, please, but without the tea if you don't mind.' She held out her cup. 'I was working for Mr Dale,' she said, after a short nap she didn't know she'd had. 'He didn't really need me, but I used to pop in and do his ironing, things like that. Light dusting he called it.' She smiled. 'He was lonely, not being long up here, and not knowing many people. He'd had a wicked few years himself down south after the war. We needed each other, like . . . well, like grass needs rain. But now we never speak of it.'

'But you still love each other?'

Dora couldn't help but smile. Amy Battersby was staring at her with eyes and mouth wide open, determined not to be shocked. There was a sweetness and innocence about her that was hard to credit when she'd been married to such as Wesley Battersby for all these years. There she sat sipping whisky out of a bright yellow cup, hardly able to believe what she was hearing, yet ready to accept and fall over herself trying to understand because Dora was her friend.

'Amy Battersby, with the unclouded eyes, always looking for something better round the next corner.' Now why did she suddenly remember Mr Dale saying that?

'I'm trying to make sense of it for you,' she said. 'Mr Dale was kind to me at a time when kindness meant more than food or the money to make ends meet. He paid me well over the rate, and one day he came home early from work as I was dusting round the living room. I'd been crying, and he noticed, and I found myself telling him about the way it was with Greg and me, that since the war Greg had never been a husband to me, not in that sense.' She lowered her eyes. 'He took the duster from my hand and led me upstairs.'

The silence was so acute that a pin dropping onto the thick pegged rug would have been heard a mile away. Amy was sure of it.

'It happened round about half-past five every Thursday afternoon for about three months. Then I got more work, Mr Dale admitted he could manage to look after himself, and the times got further and further apart. He began to call in at the hospital to read and talk to Greg, and once that happened it couldn't go on.'

'Oh no, of course not.' Amy hesitated. 'But don't you feel sort of embarrassed when you see him now? Flustered? Uncomfortable?'

Dora shook her head. 'No, not in the slightest. Not with Mr Dale. I told you. He just lets people be, the way they are. The way they need to be.'

Amy thought that was beautiful. In fact, she thought the whole story was beautiful, but it should have had a happy ending. Dora and Mr Dale should have walked off together, hand in hand into the sunset, meant for each other, except that by no stretch of the imagination could anybody think they were meant for each other. Even the most romantic person couldn't see them as a modern Romeo and Juliet. They were as different as chalk and cheese.

'I see you're getting thick with Dora Ellis,' Gladys said, coming in unannounced and catching them together four times running. 'She's rough, you know. Born the wrong side of the blanket. Her mother was that poor she used to go down on the market late on a Saturday night for the oranges they used to cut open to display at the front of the stalls. Cut oranges, bruised apples and squashed tomatoes. Scratting about for them between the stalls. No shame.'

'Did that make her any less of a person? I never knew poverty was a sin.'

Gladys looked sharply at her daughter, not quite knowing what to make of her. In the first two weeks after Wesley left, Amy had cried a lot, then she had seemed to come to some sort of terms. She was getting thick with Wesley's father too. Twice that Gladys knew of, since he'd had the flu, he'd come down in his car and sat round the fire smoking his pipe. Gladys couldn't make any of it out. The pattern was wrong. Everybody was stepping out of line since Wesley had gone away. 'Mam?' Amy had gone red, though her mother couldn't think why. 'I've been thinking about things a lot lately – about Wesley and me – and, well, wondering if I failed him in any way. You know, let him down.'

'In what way let him down?' Gladys's voice was already taut with indignation. 'You waited on him hand and foot! I've seen you have his dinner out of the oven and on the table before he's had time to take his hat and coat off.'

'I don't mean food, Mam. What I mean is . . .' Amy let the words out with a rush. 'Did you and Dad have a satisfactory relationship?'

Gladys's eyebrows shot up almost to her hairline. She knew what Amy meant, but never ever had she thought the day would come when her own daughter asked her a question like that. It was beyond belief.

'I've put it badly.' Amy looked distressed, forlorn. 'I didn't mean to be personal. No. What I wondered was . . . is that side of marriage all-important?'

'I made your dad sign the pledge in that respect long before he was forty, if that's what you mean.' Gladys fidgeted with her belt. 'There are some women who like that sort of thing, of course, but usually they're the sort who charge for it.' She didn't know where to look. Any minute now and Amy was going to come out with something she'd rather not hear. Like that woman in the paper who got a divorce on the grounds of her husband's unnatural practices. Whatever they might be. Surely Amy wasn't hinting at something like that?

'I thought,' Amy whispered, 'that because *I* wasn't keen on that side of marriage then Wesley wasn't either. You'd always said that side of things was best left to the man. So I've been wondering . . .' she swallowed hard '. . . if I let him down.'

Gladys's indignation was getting the better of her. 'If you had shown him you were keen he would have lost all respect for you. A wife's role is just to put up with it as her duty, though some men are never satisfied. I once heard tell of a poor woman out of Altom Street whose husband used to be at it during his dinner hour. He should have been castigated.'

'You don't like men, do you?'

'I think they're the cause of most of the trouble in the world.'

'I think you were only pretending to like Wesley.'

'What a thing to say!'

'Mam?' Amy almost stretched out a hand to touch her mother's cheek, then drew it back. 'Let's start talking properly to each other. Like we are now. Telling the truth. Saying what we really mean.' She took a deep breath. 'Did . . . do you like Wesley?'

Gladys was getting totally out of her depth again. This was the way Amy and her father used to talk to each other. Asking questions about feelings, probing for the truth. Making her feel left out. Thinking they didn't consider her clever enough to join in.

'I was proud of the fact that Wesley didn't wear overalls to work,' she said at last. 'That he never came home in his dirt, always finding himself a white-collar job. I used to like to see you together, and I used to like telling people he was my son-in-law when he was up on the stage singing.'

'But do you like him, Mam? Really like him?'

It was too much. For the hurt he'd caused Amy, Gladys could cheerfully have knifed him.

'Of course I like him,' she said. 'What a thing to ask. You know better than to talk like that.'

Amy took a long time getting off to sleep that night. She no longer listened with bated breath for every creak in the house, every rattle of the windows, every sigh of the wind outside. No longer did she imagine a footstep on the stairs. She left the door unbolted in case Wesley decided to return in the middle of the night. The bed felt too big for her, perhaps because she still kept to her own side of it. Wesley had been a fidgety sleeper, kicking out with his feet, snoring at times when he lay on his back. She stared up into the darkness, crossed her hands on her chest and hoped that at that very moment he was snoring his head off, with Clara Marsden livid and sleepless by his side. Never having envisaged a Red Shadow who snored.

Amy laughed, then immediately sat up, the small sound frightening her to death. Maybe she had laughed too much? Sex – she even *thought* such a word with difficulty – hadn't impressed her all that much. A paragraph in a library book had been a real eye-opener when it said that as the hero made love to his young bride on their honeymoon, she had 'screamed her ecstasy to the stars'.

She lay down again. Had she disappointed Wesley because never the slightest scream had passed her lips during his lovemaking? Was she cold? Frigid even? Was that why he had turned to someone more . . . more rousable? Hotter? Charlie had said this wasn't the first time his wife had strayed, so was that the reason Wesley had fallen madly in love with her? Because Clara was more of an expert?

When Wesley came again she would ask him straight out had she been unsatisfactory in that connection. She would stay calm and unruffled, and she would put it to him, and if he told her that yes, she had been a great disappointment to him, then she would know that his leaving had been her fault.

Yet, in spite of all this reasoning, if she really was lacking in that respect, why was it that she couldn't rid herself of the image of the quiet Mr Dale coming into the house in his dark suit, taking the duster from Dora and leading her gently upstairs? Whispering to her in his Robert Donat husky voice as they made love. And why was the very thought of it making her knees wobble? Even in bed.

Dora's Mrs Green brought her younger daughter into the fitting room the next afternoon.

'Winifred is to be bridesmaid at her sister's wedding.' Mrs Green spoke at Amy, not to her. 'I'd like her fitted with a brassière.' She turned to the cringing stoop-shouldered girl. 'Take your coat off, dear.'

Though Amy did no more than advance smiling with the tape measure, the girl backed away with a look of horror. 'I don't want a brassière, Mother. I don't need one.' She crossed both arms over a blossoming chest. 'Please. Don't make me.'

Mrs Green tapped an impatient foot. 'You are not being bridesmaid wearing a liberty-bodice underneath a twenty-five pounds Kendal Milne frock, with shoes dyed to tone.' She addressed a point to the side of Amy's head. 'She's afraid that a brassière will reveal her secret to the world.' She lowered her voice slightly. 'They're no bigger than a couple of walnuts anyway.'

The girl's blush brought actual tears to her eyes. Amy smiled at her. 'No one will be able to tell you're wearing one, love. I promise.'

62

Gently she slid the navy-blue gaberdine raincoat from the girl's arms. 'I'll measure you on top of your gymslip. See? That wasn't too bad, was it?' She took the measurements as unobtrusively as she could.

'Lottie Marsden's mother makes her wear one like two ice-cream cornets stuck on her chest. It won't be like that, will it?'

'Are you in the same form as Lottie?' Amy wrote the figures down in her little black-bound notebook. 'Is she your friend?'

Winifred sniffed. 'Lottie Marsden? She's nobody's friend. She tells lies. And goes with boys. And her father drinks. Who would want to be her friend, for goodness' sake?'

Immediately Amy's sympathy for the peaky-faced girl evaporated.

'The brassière will be ready within the week, Mrs Green,' she said in her professional voice.

By one of those coincidences, as though there was something in telepathy after all, just as Amy was thinking about Lottie Marsden that evening and what the girl in the shop had said, Charlie rang the doorbell.

'I've come about Lottie,' he said, without preamble, so obviously worried he forgot to take off his hat. 'She's knocking about with some boy, and I know for a fact he comes in the house. I smell him.'

'Smell him?'

'He works in the fish market. His father's got a stall. They go off to Fleetwood every morning for the fish. He skives off work and Lottie skives off school, and they meet in the house.' He sat down without being asked to, forgetting his good manners for once. 'God knows what they get up to.'

'How old is he, Charlie?'

'She says he's eighteen, but he could be anything from twelve to forty. Lottie makes things up to suit herself.'

'Where is she now?'

'At her Auntie Maude's. At least she's supposed to be at her Auntie Maude's, but she could be anywhere. She took her mother's black leather coat from the wardrobe.'

'It never suited her,' Amy said quickly, then could have bitten her tongue out.

But Charlie didn't notice. 'I was wondering if you could have a word with Lottie? Her mother was no good at that sort of thing, said she would have to find out for herself soon enough.' He coughed. 'I can't say anything, can I? It's not a father's job.'

'You mean you want me to talk to Lottie about things her own mother should have told her long ago?'

Charlie looked as if he was wishing a hole would suddenly appear for him to drop into. 'You know. The things your mother told you.'

'She told me nothing. I got into trouble when I was sixteen, remember? It wasn't because I didn't know where babies come from, or how they're made. Girls at school go pretty deep into those subjects, you know. It was because she never explained to me how an innocent kiss can become something else – how when a young girl falls in love, helplessly in love, she wants to give, not to hold back. That's what my mother should have told me, Charlie. And that's what Clara should have told your Lottie. Don't you see?'

He didn't know where to look. She was saying things she'd no right to, without Wesley there. What he'd always liked about Amy was the way she could always see the funny side of things, the way a man could feel unchallenged in any way when she was around. Not that she wasn't pretty; come to think of it she was more than pretty in her own way. Usually her hair was tamed back with a slide, but now she had it falling to the side across her forehead, giving her a totally different look. She was flushed too, and no wonder with the conversation taking such a turn. She looked as if she'd just come out of a hot bath. Kissable . . . Charlie took his hat off. It was a funny thing, but right till this moment he had never considered Wesley's wife to be anything out of the ordinary. He ran a finger round his collar.

'I saw Lottie once, a while ago, and she pretended she didn't know me,' Amy said.

He tried to bring his mind back to matters in hand. 'She's like that. Awkward. Embroiders the truth.'

64

'Her mind's disturbed, Charlie.'

'You will talk to her?'

He was going to cry again. Amy was sure of it. He was such a harmless little man, kind to the point of idiocy. Wesley had often said that Charlie Marsden would give his last penny to any beggar who stretched out a hand, even if final demands littered his mantelpiece.

'Come to your dinner one Sunday,' she said impulsively. 'I'll do roast beef and Yorkshire pudding and I'll see if I can find a way to talk to Lottie then. In a little while, when we're both less emotional about things, more reconciled.'

For a startled moment she thought he was about to kiss her. He took a step forward, seemed to think better of it and stepped back.

'You're a good woman, Amy.'

She laughed. 'Don't insult me! I'd much rather you told me I filled you with uncontrollable desire.'

He couldn't believe the things she was saying. Wesley would have been shocked to the marrow to hear his wife say such things. Was she teasing him? Flirting with him? Egging him on? He'd always known that Amy Battersby had plenty up top. Once, when he and Lottie were having a proper conversation, she had told him that Amy's name was up in the assembly hall at school, picked out in letters of gold:

'Amy Renshawe. English Literature Prize 1915.'

'We'll be glad to come to dinner in a few weeks' time, whenever you say,' he said. 'Just thinking of a roast dinner makes my mouth water. Clara wasn't one for cooking. We usually had sausages and mash on a Sunday.'

Amy tried her hardest not to look too pleased.

'Sausage and mash can be very tasty,' she said with deep insincerity. 'You'll have to excuse me, Charlie, but my friend from next door will be in any minute. We're going to the pictures to see Deanna Durbin in *Three Smart Girls*, and I've to bank the fire up yet.'

Charlie bumped into Dora on the doorstep, snatched his hat off and said something about *two* smart girls and if they couldn't be good then to be careful.

'What a lovely man he is,' Dora said. 'And good-looking with it.'

'Charlie good-looking?' Amy put the fireguard in place. 'How long is it since you had your eyes tested, Dora? I can't see Charlie as being anything to write home about at all. Nothing about him to turn the milk sour, I grant you, but no Tarzan neither.'

'Do you know how much a nice piece of topside will cost you?' Gladys dropped in on her way back from the market. 'You'll get a large tin of corned beef for eightpence from the Co-op, with divi to take into account. It all adds up.' She put a small parcel down on the table. 'I bought a quarter of ham sliced from the bone, and got him to wrap it twice. There's two ounces here. Give me twopence and we'll call it straight. What are you going to give them for pudding? If this dinner comes off.'

'Apple sponge and custard. I think Lottie will like that better than rice pudding.'

'What are you doing for money? I know it's none of my business, but you've never said and your wages won't get you far, unless you've a bit put by.'

'I'm all right, Mam. Wesley will be calling again soon for us to talk over the situation. He's never been mean with money.'

'Generous to a fault,' Gladys agreed. 'Just as long as he's not for forgetting his obligations.'

'Mam! I don't look on him as a meal ticket.'

Gladys could barely conceal her irritation. Amy was standing there smiling with her hair needing brushing back, wearing too much lipstick and smelling of scent first thing in the morning. She knew what it was all in aid of. Amy was waiting and hoping that Wesley would walk in. She was trying to snare him back by tarting herself up like they advised in magazines. Gladys quite forgot that only a very short while ago she was wishing that her daughter would make more of herself.

'That Dora Ellis is leading you into bad ways,' she said. 'Going to the second house pictures together. You'll be sitting in pubs with her next. Drinking.'

Off she went, worried stiff, not liking the way things were shaping

66

at all. Disappointed that Amy hadn't got her husband back long before this.

The minute her mother had gone Amy went upstairs into the back bedroom. The hope that it would one day hold a treasure cot draped in pink organdie had faded a long time ago. Now it was filled with clutter.

A doll's house, made for the young Amy by her father and stored against the day when her own little girl would play with it. The brick patterned wallpaper peeling, the lace curtains at the cellophane windows hanging in tattered strips. Wesley's old tennis racket, still screwed into its heavy press, lolled against a wall. There was an ice-cream making contraption that had proved to be more trouble than it was worth, a book on forensic medicine with rude explicit drawings, a bedding chest with a cracked glass top, and a few strips of left-over carpet.

The wellingtons were in the cupboard housing the hot water cistern. They fitted neatly into the space below the wooden slats used for airing sheets and towels. Amy hadn't worn them in years, preferring to wear her rubber overshoes when it snowed. Wesley had said the wellingtons would perish in the warmth of the cupboard, but they hadn't.

She got down on her knees, took one out and pushed her hand all the way down to the toe. Nothing. Disbelieving, she took out the other one and searched deep inside. Still nothing. The linings were slightly torn and she ripped them partly away, pushing fingers well down in case the money had somehow slipped inside. She upended both boots, shook them as hard as she could. Scrabbled on the floor of the cupboard. Nothing.

It hadn't exactly been a fortune, and Christmas had accounted for some of it, but it was her nest egg, her rainy-day money, her one and only claim to financial independence.

The money had been saved week by week. It represented the only cash of her own she had ever possessed. Not just in her marriage, but in her life. It wasn't much, only twenty pounds five shillings at the last count.

She sat back on her heels, feeling sick.

'Why on earth don't you give it to me to put in the bank?' Wesley had asked, more than once. 'That way you'll earn interest on it.'

'I like to have it near me.'

'Well, why not put it inside a sock underneath the bed? I bet that's where Gladys keeps hers, isn't it? I don't expect she trusts banks, either.'

'She's never had enough money to save to open a bank account, for goodness' sake! Every last farthing has to be accounted for. She'd pretend she wasn't hungry when there wasn't enough food to go round. She wore cardboard insoles in her shoes when she couldn't afford to have them mended.'

Wesley had tucked an imaginary violin beneath his chin and played an imaginary soulful tune. He had looked so funny that, God forgive her, she had laughed.

Amy stood up and shivered, as if a door had opened, letting in a sudden draught. Standing there in the bitterly cold room, filled with things of no use to anybody, she felt drained of feeling, numbed.

When exactly had Wesley taken it? Before he went away, or when he came back briefly? Had there been time for him to cross the little landing to the spare room while she was downstairs?

Maybe she herself had moved it, hidden it somewhere else? Her mind had been playing strange tricks on her lately. Only yesterday she couldn't for the life of her remember whether one of her customers wanted a bust bodice and corset in pink brocade or a full corselette, an all-in-one much favoured at the moment by the town's matrons. Even now she wasn't sure. She couldn't concentrate these days, couldn't think of anything else but Wesley – what he'd said and what he'd done those last weeks before he left. It was a going over and over in her mind, a desperate knowing that he no longer needed her.

Amy tried to pull herself together. Wesley might have let her down, deceived her, betrayed her, but he wasn't a thief. Not a mean and petty thief, stealing from his wife. She refused to believe it.

Slowly at first she began to search. She looked in drawers, felt in pockets, upended vases, even pulled all her books from the glass-fronted bookcase. She reminded herself that Wesley had come to sort things out; he had intimated that, and what had she done but fly at him, yelling and screaming swear-words and chucking his pullover through the window. Becoming more frantic by the minute, she began her search again.

Why, oh why had she relied so much on Wesley? Accepting that he was paying the bills, even handing over her wages as he said it made more sense to have just the one kitty. Why had she never questioned where the money was coming from for all his many little extravagances? The special hair-trims always followed by a bayrum massage, the chromium cigarette case with matching lighter which he had said was damaged stock. The coat made of real camelhair, his gold-plated wristwatch, cuff links and tiepin. Wesley hadn't stinted himself for anything. Why had it never angered her before? Why had she never even realized the unfairness of it before?

She lifted the velvet settee cushions and probed down the sides of the upholstery. It was time to bank the fire up and get ready for work, though it might not be all that long before she was sitting by an empty grate, clutching a shawl to her chin, the mantelpiece bare of its Westminster chime clock, candlesticks and the hear no evil, speak no evil, see no evil brass monkeys. The house bare of any ornaments at all.

Edgar Battersby was full of worries he could do nothing about with this hacking cough hanging on him weeks after his flu was finished. The doctor had told him that if he left the house he would be dead before he got his car out of the garage.

Wesley was conspicuous by his absence, though he sent the usual returns through with a note saying they would understand if he lay low for the time being. Lay low! What game was he playing now? Talking like George Raft in a gangster film. Couldn't he try to imagine what he was putting his mother through? Phyllis had taken to hovering by the front-room window in the afternoons when she wasn't out playing whist with her cronies, or going to the Inner Wheel wearing a Robin Hood hat to hear talks about foreign holidays other folks had been on. Amy hadn't been round, either, though he couldn't blame her. Dora had told him Amy was perfectly all right, thank you very much, and would he mind lifting his feet so she could get the Ewbank round his chair.

He felt helpless, frustrated, old as Pendle Hill. Once, long ago, he had walked to Preston and back, over twenty miles all together; another time he had cycled to Blackpool, left his bike tied to some railings and had a swim in the sea before riding back. Now he was puffed just sitting in his chair, and the pain beneath his right ribs was with him nearly all the time. Some days it almost creased him up.

Dora didn't like the look of him at all, but she wasn't going to burden Amy with more worry. She met Mr Dale in the street and told him she was sure something bad was happening next door. Amy had started looking for a full-time job which paid more, but as he didn't need telling, B.Sc.s were sweeping the roads, so what chance was there for a woman of Amy's age with the ability to read a tape measure the only qualification to her name?

'How do you mean, something bad?' Mr Dale had wanted to know.

'Well, I think she's stopped eating,' Dora had told him, 'apart from the scraps her mother brings in now and again, but she'd rather die than let on, she's that proud.'

Amy got wet through walking home from work to save the bus fare from town, so she decided to have a bath then let the fire go out. The coal in the shed outside was dwindling rapidly, and for the last two nights she'd gone to bed at eight o'clock to keep warm. That was one of the advantages, she supposed, of living alone. Going to bed when you liked, bathing when you felt like it – every day if you didn't know it would take all the oils from your skin and wrinkle you like a prune by the time you were fifty.

The bathroom was as narrow as a shoe box with a skylight window let into the roof. Amy sprinkled the last of a bottle of shocking-pink bath crystals into the water, sat down and lay back, just as the doorbell shrilled out.

Wesley! She had put the catch on the vestibule door without

thinking, soaked through and miserable as she came in. The bell shrilled again, just as if someone had left their finger on it. Wesley! She knew it was him.

As she flung the door wide, the towel slipped from one shoulder to reveal a rounded breast. Snatching it up in frantic haste, Amy knew a moment of blind panic as she looked down and saw she was showing the unmentionable.

'I see I've come at an awkward time,' Mr Dale said, raising his trilby politely. 'I'll call again, if I may.'

5

The following week, at the time Wesley would, under happier circumstances, have been coming home from work, he walked into the house and counted a pile of pound notes out on the table, adding two half crowns with a flourish.

'Hell's bells,' he said, seeing her face, 'don't tell me you'd missed it? I relied on you not finding out. I wouldn't have dreamed of borrowing it if the need hadn't been dire.' He seemed genuinely upset.

Amy could hardly bear to look at him. His thick black hair was beaded with rain; a lock of it fell in a neglected wave over his forehead. For years she had seen him neglecting it every time he stared into the mirror. He was standing so close to her she could smell his last cigarette. How could she have forgotten how beautiful he was, how easy-going and relaxed, how strong his features, how mobile his mouth.

He was wary of her – she could read his expression, sense his embarrassment. He was unsure of her reaction since that last awful time, standing there just waiting for the ranting and raving to begin. All at once she wanted to cry.

'I feel awful.' He sat down on the piano stool, put a hand to his forehead. 'You didn't really think I'd stolen it, did you?'

'Yes, that's exactly what I thought,' Amy said quietly.

He winced, annoyed with her because she had misjudged him, she could see. Waiting for her to apologize – she could see that too.

Amy felt in full control of herself this time. Shouting and screaming would never bring Wesley back to her. He couldn't stand rows, never had been able to. He'd told her once that he could count on one hand the number of times his mother had raised her voice to him. Rows upset him, gave him headaches.

'Well, I did go through the house with a fine-tooth comb,' she admitted. 'And I did imagine myself trekking to a pawn shop carrying my best coat over one arm and the clock off the mantelpiece under the other.'

He seemed to notice for the first time that she was wearing a coat and scarf, and that the fire was banked up with slack without a flicker of a flame. 'You're going out,' he accused. 'Where to? It's coming on to rain.' He sighed. 'I've got such a bad head. I've had it all day.'

'I'll get you a Cephos powder.'

Amy's reaction was instinctive and immediate, and even as she spoke she saw the way Wesley's shoulders relaxed. He had always loved being made a fuss of, so that over the long years she had trickled cough medicine into his mouth, stood over him to make sure he swallowed aspirins, peeled his oranges, stripped the stringy bits from the celery he enjoyed so much, hand-knitted his socks because he preferred them to shop bought, and even on occasions cleaned his shoes.

Carefully now she opened the small paper of powder, folded it neatly so she could slide the powder into a tablespoon of milk, and guided it into his mouth.

'All gone?'

Had his mother always done that for him? Asked that? Amy was suddenly quite sure she had, just as his mother had conditioned him into believing that a man never cooked a meal, never lifted a cup from the table except to drink from it, never turned on the kitchen tap except to wash his hands or add a drop of water to his whisky.

'I saw Charlie and he tells me you and Clara want to get married.' She kept her voice nice and casual. 'Is that so?'

'You've seen Charlie?'

'Oh yes. As a matter of fact I'm making him a meal one of these days. Soon, maybe.' She glanced at the money on the table. 'A nice piece of topside with crispy potatoes and Yorkshire pudding, with apple sponge and custard to follow.'

He swallowed hard. Because his mouth was watering, she hoped.

The truth was he couldn't make head nor tail of her. She even looked different, thinner in the face, taller surely, which was ridiculous. He felt rattled, illogically disappointed in her.

'I've been waiting for you to throw something at me.' He produced his chromium case, took out a cigarette, tapped it three times as he always did before flicking his lighter into action. She tried not to stare too hard at him. It would never do for him to realize how she felt watching his surgeon's hands, his concert pianist's hands, busy with the familiar ritual.

She wanted to go down on her knees and plead with him to stay, to forget what had happened and walk back into her life just as easily as he had walked out of it. To live with someone for twenty years must mean something to him. She could feel the hurt, the bewilderment, the pain of his rejection tightening her throat, welling up so that any minute now she would be shouting her frustration and fury aloud. If she did that he would look reproachfully at her, get up and leave. Once again he had managed to make her feel as if all this was her fault – that what had happened was none of his doing. She saw the injustice of it, but at that moment was prepared to accept it.

'There's no point in fighting,' she said.

'I can allow you a pound a week.'

She stared down at the carpet, clenching her hands, the humiliation a deep hurt inside her. 'All right then, but only till I get a better job,' she mumbled. 'One that pays more.'

He got up, moved the piano stool, frowned for a moment then walked to the door.

'Well, Amy . . .'

'Wesley?'

There was a hint of a catch in his voice. 'I still care about you. I still need to know that you're all right. There's still a corner of my heart kept specially for you.'

'Don't I look all right?' Amy sat down and crossed her legs prettily. 'Thank you for coming, Wesley.'

He was waiting for her to accompany him down the lobby to the door, to show him out, to stand on the step and watch him walk down the street, just as she had never failed to do in all the years of their marriage.

'I'll say goodbye then, Amy.'

'Goodbye, Wesley,' she said. Firmly, but nicely.

He hadn't left her the pound he had promised. She gathered her savings together, the pound notes and the two half crowns, stood with them in her hand. He had forgotten, that was it, purely and simply. Or had he thought that by bringing her savings back to her he had absolved himself from any further obligations for the time being?

All at once she began to laugh, standing there in the chilly room in her coat and scarf, clutching the money to her chest. It was a laugh that held more than a touch of hysteria in it, a laugh that stopped as suddenly as it had begun.

She asked at work if she could possibly be taken on full time, but it was out of the question they said. Surely she realized how lucky she was as a married woman to have a job at all? Most of the shops roundabout were taking on school-leavers for two years, training them for low pay then sacking them and starting again, but not this establishment. Mr Mott's jowls worked as convulsively as if Amy had accused him of such depravity.

She knew just how invaluable she was. Not one of her regulars would be willing to stand in the upstairs room in their rayon knickers and long vests while a school-leaver ran round them with a tape measure. They trusted quiet little Mrs Battersby, who spoke nicely, sounded her aitches, and never caught their eyes as she trundled her tape measure round their D-cup bosoms or well-cushioned hips. When Mr Mott himself bowed them out through the front door he never, by even a flicker of the eyelid, betrayed the fact that he knew what had been going on upstairs.

'A rise?' Amy suggested in desperation, reminding him that it was two years since . . . Her voice tailed away in embarrassment.

Mr Mott's righteous indignation increased. Didn't she know that the town was in the middle of a slump, with mills closing down every week. Why, one up Bolton Road way was already changed over to a raincoat factory, with all the looms ripped out and rows of sewing machines in their places.

She would work longer hours, Amy said, trembling now. She would come back in the evenings, come early in the mornings, anything . . .

Mr Mott couldn't believe what he was hearing. One of the reasons he had taken young Mrs Battersby on was because of her connections. Her father-in-law had been put forward as a potential mayor at one time, and wasn't her mother-in-law on the Board of Governors of the High School?

The pleading look on Amy's face was beginning to get on his nerves. He pulled at his full lower lip. Hadn't his wife once told him, a long time ago, that Mrs Battersby Senior had snubbed her in the Market House, stalking past with her nose in the air because she considered no doubt that tobacco came very high in the scale of things compared to corsets and fancy goods.

Now his wife was dead, and Mrs Battersby Senior was still lording it around the town with her fox furs slung round her shoulders, having tea in Booth's Cafe practically every afternoon. And buying her own foundation garments no doubt from one of the big shops in Manchester or even from an Ambrose Wilson catalogue, where he believed you could get an all-in-one corselette for eight shillings and elevenpence, postage paid. No, not once had Mrs high-and-mighty Battersby put a foot inside his shop.

Almost bursting out of his waistcoat buttons with self-induced fury, he gave Amy a week's cash in lieu of notice, telling her to pick up the money at the desk on her way out.

For a startled moment he thought she was going to go over – faint dead away. The blood drained from her face, then she swayed, clutching her throat.

'You can't sack me! You mustn't sack me!' White to the lips, she stood her ground. Through a window, slightly open at the top, came the familiar market-day sounds: the clatter of trams, rumbling of lorries, hooting of horns, footsteps on the pavements, a child's loud wail.

Mr Mott looked trapped. Never in the whole of his natural would he have dreamt that quiet polite little Mrs Battersby could display such behaviour. It couldn't be the money, oh dear me no. The

Battersbys wouldn't be going short, not them! He would actually be easing his social conscience by giving his corset fitter's job to a younger girl, or an unmarried woman. As a matter of fact, his niece would jump at the chance of working here, mixing and talking with nice people all day. Since her husband had died things hadn't been easy for his sister.

'My mind is made up,' he said, with as much dignity as he could muster. Just as, like a gift from God, the downstairs assistant came in to say the traveller in belts and scarves was waiting for his order.

Amy's legs trembled so much she didn't know how she found herself outside the shop, breathless and bewildered by the confrontation which seemed to have erupted from nothing. What had got into Mr Mott? And what was wrong with her? There they'd been, the two of them, overwhelmed by emotion, saying little, but meaning a lot more. At one point Mr Mott's pleasant features had been contorted with a rage so immense she had thought he would have a stroke. What had brought all that on?

The gnawing pain in her stomach reminded her that all she'd had that morning was a cup of tea at breakfast time and now, as she turned into King William Street, the smell of ground coffee, of hams and cheeses, brought bile up into her throat, sour tasting. It was the kind of day that whispered spring might not be too far away, and to go to work that afternoon she had decided to wear her best coat, a fawn knock-about with matching hat, and her best fleecy-lined gauntlet gloves. For the first time in weeks it was neither windy nor raining, and the soot-blackened buildings were washed to a warmth by the pale sunshine. On a day like this, if you sniffed hard enough you could almost smell the salt in the air, wafted over thirty miles of fields and woods from Blackpool.

Amy caught sight of herself in a shop's long mirror and immediately perked up. Wesley had always liked her in that outfit, said that fawn was always classy, and that the little hat with its piping of scarlet suited the shape of her face.

'Pansy-face,' he'd called her long, long ago.

Knowing she looked good, she felt decidedly more cheerful –

wasn't losing her job a sign that something better was around the corner? Might it not, in the long run, have been all for the best?

Amy turned and retraced her steps.

'Wasn't that your daughter-in-law?' The woman in the squirrel coat, walking down Church Street to the arcade, turned to Phyllis. 'I thought she worked at Mott's Emporium in the afternoons? Fitting corsets.'

'She does.' Phyllis stopped at the hand-made chocolate shop, determined to change the subject. 'If I go home without a quarter of coffee creams for Edgar he'll never forgive me. I forgot last week and he actually sulked.'

'Men!' said the squirrel coat. 'Is he any better?'

'He has his off days,' said Phyllis.

'Don't we all?' said the squirrel coat.

At the Labour Exchange Amy went straight through the door marked Women. There was a long queue but she didn't mind. She was already glad to her very soul that her days of touching soft billowy flesh as she measured and fitted pink brocade on middle-aged matrons was finished. There would be something far more suited to her personality. Things were often meant to be.

'You are wasted in that shop,' Wesley had often said, but he had never suggested she leave. Amy looked round quickly as if she had spoken such disloyalty aloud and smiled at a girl with bright red hair.

'Your first time?' the girl asked.

Amy nodded.

'Well, a good tip is to say you are experienced at anything they come up with.'

'Such as lion taming?'

'Even that. I've come prepared to accept a job in a brothel if the pay's good. I've got a degree in Philosophy but as far as they're concerned that qualifies me for exactly nothing.'

'Wesley often said that there are plenty of B.Sc.s sweeping the streets. Bits of paper, he called qualifications.'

'Wesley?'

'My husband.' Amy blushed and turned round again.

She was given a form to fill in, and by the time it was her turn to move into the interviewing room her mood of optimism had evaporated. The clerk had a dark fringe of pit-black hair and an incipient moustache, and looked as if she was expecting it to rain.

'Your age is against you, of course.' She glanced at the form. 'I see you're married. Hubby out of work?'

'No.'

'Children?'

'No.'

The clerk bent her head over a pile of cards, riffled through them. She had the widest parting Amy had ever seen. It ran like a white arterial road across her scalp.

'Typing?' she asked, without looking up. 'Shorthand? Book-keeping? Filing? Adding machines? Duplicating? Calligraphy?'

Amy said she was good with people.

The clerk spoiled the set of her thick fringe by poking it with a pencil. Here was yet another of them. A bored housewife looking for a little job that wouldn't chip her nail varnish. One that gave her a nice little bit of pin money for crêpe-de-Chine camiknickers, pure silk stockings, Elizabeth Arden face powder at twelve shillings and sixpence a box. She stared belligerently at Amy's coat and matching hat with the thin band of scarlet petersham ribbon round the brim. She took in the gauntlet gloves, and the way Amy's hair waved softly beneath the stylish hat. Shiny, toffee-coloured hair, like a Devon cream caramel. She herself was going home after work to old parents who got on each other's nerves. She had never once in the whole of her fifty-four years strayed from the straight and narrow for the sad reason that no one had ever asked her to. And here was this well-dressed woman thinking she could just walk in here and waste her time!

Amy wished she had worn her old raincoat, and tied her hair back with string. She wished she could open her mouth and explain that she was a deserted wife, that after her nest egg was spent there would be no money coming in unless her faithless husband came to her rescue.

She stood up, bringing the interview to an end herself.

Deeply upset, filled with a renewed sense of outrage, she set off for home, ignoring the smells of food from the market stalls, averting her eyes from the shrimp ladies sitting in their poke bonnets at their little tables. Wesley had loved potted shrimps with their yellow lids of butter, expecially with brown bread cut thin. If Wesley hadn't gone away she would already be rehearsing in her mind how she was going to tell him the story of her double-edged rejection, first by Mr Mott, then by the witch-like clerk at the Labour Exchange.

By the time she had acted out both scenes – 'Typing, Mrs Battersby? Shorthand? Book-keeping? Filing? Adding machines? Duplicating? Calligraphy?' – each word fired like a pistol shot from beneath the heavy fringe of hair – Wesley would be laughing, enjoying her being in this mood, taking none of it seriously. Except himself, she thought bleakly, crossing the road by the Majestic Cinema, turning into Town Hall Street.

But Wesley wasn't at home, was he? And what had happened that afternoon wasn't funny at all. She stopped outside the library. Oh, dear God, if she couldn't find a job soon she didn't know what she would do. Waves of totally unexpected panic beat at her brain. She looked up at the sky and her legs went to blancmange. She forced herself to cross the road, taking deep breaths, putting one foot in front of the other. Seeing a terrible picture of herself collapsing on the pavement with a crowd gathering round; seeing herself wrapped in a red blanket being whipped into an ambulance; seeing herself in the end bed of a ward in the infirmary, her name in the paper: 'Woman collapses in street, malnutrition suspected.' Somebody help me please . . . Was that in her mind, or had she said it aloud?

A fat woman with two library books in her shopping basket stared at Amy strangely. 'Are you all right, love? Are you lost?'

The voice was kind, the woman's expression full of concern, but Amy backed away from her touch.

'I'm going in here,' she said. 'Thank you. I'm perfectly all right.'

The Education Office had a window on the right of the entrance hall with 'Inquiries' written above it. Amy pressed the bell.

'I'd like to see Mr Dale,' she told the girl who appeared. 'Could you tell me the way to his office, please?'

Bernard was dictating a letter to the secretary he shared with the Assistant Director of Education when Amy was shown in. His eyes widened slightly but, showing no sign of the astonishment he was feeling, he motioned to the girl to close her notebook and go away.

'Later,' he said. 'We'll finish off later.' As she was about to close the door he said, still in the same quiet unhurried way, 'Bring two cups of tea, please, Marjorie, and biscuits if there are any left.'

Amy stood rooted to the spot. What on earth was she going to say? What had possessed her to do this? Mr Dale looked so different behind the big leather-topped desk, so prosperous, so important, so apprehensive of what she was going to do or say. Who could blame him? Not once had they had what could be termed a normal conversation. He was a virtual stranger, and yet he had seen her at her very worst – dazed with shock on the night Wesley left her, straight out of bed when there hadn't been a comb near her hair, opening the door in her birthday suit, throwing Wesley's pullover through the window. If he had any opinion of her at all, which she doubted, it must be that she was . . . that she was . . . She swayed as the faintness came over her again.

'Steady on, lassie.' He came round the desk, pushed her gently down on to the chair his secretary had left placed at right angles to the desk. 'Now . . . take your time. There's no hurry. Just take your time . . .' As if sensing her embarrassment, he went back round his desk to sit with his hands clasped on the blotter in front of him.

Amy lifted her head, blinked hard to stop tears from filling her eyes, let out a deep sigh. 'I . . . I was just passing,' she said, then had to stop as the distress deep inside her welled up into her throat. 'Just passing.' She choked back a sob.

'I'm so glad you came to see me,' he was saying, recognizing deep despair when he saw it. 'It isn't very often that a friend drops in to see me during a working day. We are friends, aren't we? I'd like to think so.'

81

Amy nodded, staring down at her hands, twisting them together. 'You must think I'm a very foolish, silly woman.'

'No, just an unhappy one. With something on her mind that would be better for the telling. Am I right?'

She nodded again. 'I don't know what to do,' she whispered. 'I've lost my job this afternoon because I asked for a rise. I didn't say the right things, you see. I gave in too easily. My blood was up because he, my boss, looked at me as if he couldn't bear the sight of me.' She frowned. 'An' that's not all. I went to the Labour Exchange and when the woman there looked at me in the same way, I got up and walked out.' Her voice rose. 'Like I said, I don't know what to do.'

She was crying inside now, gulping back the sobs, determined not to make a fool of herself again, staring hard at the floor as the girl came in with two cups of tea and four marie biscuits on a thick white plate.

He waited until the door closed behind her. 'Did the way they looked at you make you feel rejected?'

She inclined her head.

'Unloved? Unwanted?'

'Hated,' she said firmly.

'So one more rejection was too much to bear?'

Her eyes, wet with tears, widened. She knew exactly what he was getting at. 'You mean that coming on top of Wesley walking out on me . . . ? That I'm too touchy because of it?'

'Understandably so.' He passed the plate of biscuits. 'I can't guarantee that they won't be soft.'

He saw the way she nibbled round the edges, trying not to cram it into her mouth. To make her feel better he took one himself, bit into it vigorously. What was it Dora had said? 'I think she's stopped eating.'

'Would you mind if I called you by your first name, Amy?' He didn't wait for an answer. 'Here, have another biscuit. How do you see yourself, Amy? Do you like yourself?'

'Like myself?'

Bernard was all at once very sorry for her, but he persisted. 'You see, if we don't like ourselves, we make it very hard for other people to like us. Drink up your tea before it gets cold. Have you ever evaluated your good points? Considered what makes you the person you are?'

Stung by the suspicion that he was patronizing her, Amy told him that she too had once read a book on psychology.

'There you are!' he said at once, laughing. 'There's one asset you have that's a gift from the Gods.'

'Surprise me.'

'A ready wit, a way of flashing out with funny remarks. A sense of humour.'

'As well as all that, I can see straight through people who are trying to patronize me.'

'And your blood's coming to the boil again?'

'On the simmer.'

He saw the way she visibly relaxed. The tea had brought the colour back to her cheeks and the sparkle to her eyes.

'I'm sorry,' she said. 'Now I'm fighting with you. These days I don't know whether I'm coming or going.' She stood up.

'And right at this moment you're going.'

They smiled at each other, and she thought how much younger he looked when he smiled, how quite good-looking really, not in the least handsome like Wesley but a lot more than passable with his twinkly grey eyes.

'Yes, I'm going,' she said, and held out her hand. 'Thank you for giving me so much of your time.' She felt comforted, as if she had passed some of her mixed-up feelings over to him, as if he had taken the burden of them from her. She knew in that moment that he cared what happened to her, not about her, of course, but what became of her.

His eyes never left her face. 'I would like to help you,' he said quietly. 'I think I can . . .'

At once Amy snatched her hand from his, her face flaming. She remembered Dora sitting there describing how it had been between them – 'Then he took the duster from my hand and led me upstairs'. Amy could still hear her saying it.

'I'd like to talk to you more privately.' The door opened an inch and he called out for someone hovering outside to come in. 'Yes, that would be much better.'

As she walked towards the door she could feel his eyes on her back, on her legs. She walked stiffly, trying not to wiggle her bottom.

On the way home she called in at her mother's to tell her about losing her job and the unsatisfactory visit to the Labour Exchange.

'Did she have a ring on her finger?' Gladys wanted to know. 'Civil servants are all like that. Frustrated crab apples. Run a mile if a man winked at them. Cracking on they have a sweetheart lying in a foreign grave somewhere in France. I know civil servants all right.'

'She thought I was a pampered wife looking for a nice little job because playing whist every afternoon was beginning to bore me.'

'How do you mean, playing whist? You don't play whist! We could have gone to many a whist drive together.'

'But you don't play whist either, Mam.'

'What has that got to do with it?' Gladys had never seen her daughter look so beat, so defeated. That fawn coat and hat didn't suit her neither. Drained her. Made her look as if she was sickening for something. Not that she would tell her mother if she was. Look at the times in her marriage when she was in the family way but not letting on till she'd miscarried. Look at that time she'd gone to work and bled all over the floor. Never once had she run to her mam and said, 'Mam, I need you. Mam, help me.'

'You can stop to your tea if you want.'

'I'd like that,' Amy said, and took her hat and coat off.

In the back kitchen Gladys stared at the two ounces of boiled ham pieces, the cheap off-cuts from the giant slicer in the Home and Colonial. Spread out on a plate and garnished with a few slices of the beetroot she'd boiled that morning, together with bread cut thin, followed by a couple of coconut macaroons . . .

'I'd just had my meal when you came,' she lied, 'but I'm always ready for a cup of tea.'

'You can see the pattern on the plate through this ham. What did he shave it with, Mam, a razor blade? If I sat on a slice of it my feet would still dangle.'

Gladys was well content. Amy wasn't going to open up any more, but then she never had. It was enough that she was sitting there coming out with wisecracks and getting some food down her.

'I never liked that Mr Mott neither,' she said, putting the top of the milk in Amy's tea. 'His eyes are too close together. Ee, but it's a long time since you came to your tea, like this.'

'Wesley liked me to be in when he came home,' Amy said.

'Mrs Battersby will have a pink fit if she comes back from town and finds you've gone out,' Dora said, looking up from polishing the silver spread out on newspapers on the kitchen table. 'You don't look fit enough to go further than the gate. I know you went out last week without telling anybody, but you won't get away with it every time.'

'I'm taking the car, Dora.' Edgar put a finger to his lips. 'I'll be back long before Mrs Battersby. You know what you ladies can be like when you get behind the silver teapots and buttered teacakes in Booth's cafe.'

Dora didn't know, but what she did know was that Mr Battersby Senior was a very, very sick man. In the past weeks the flesh had dropped from him, leaving him stringy-necked and hollow-cheeked. There was a yellow look about his skin, and sometimes when the pain was on him it was as much as Dora could do not to fetch the doctor herself. She didn't like to use the dreaded word for what she thought was wrong with him, but in her opinion her employer should be seeing a specialist from Manchester, not that doctor in the tweed plus-fours who seemed to spend most of his time on the golf course. And where was the wonderful Wesley when all this was going on?

Dora vented her feelings on an ornate silver tray, rubbing it up till she could see her face in it. Determined to speak her mind to Amy that evening, to tell her that if something wasn't done about her father-in-law, and soon, he'd be dropping off his perch.

Edgar crouched over the steering wheel to peer more closely through the windscreen. Twice since leaving the house he'd had to wipe the sweat from his forehead, which was ridiculous on a day like this. He'd never have thought that being confined to the house for such a comparatively short time could weaken him like this. He doubted if he'd have the strength to blow the skin off a plate of rice pudding.

The pain was there, underneath his ribs today, but he could ignore it if it didn't get any worse. The liver salts the doctor had advised him to take every day seemed to be helping a little. Old-fashioned remedies were often the best. Look how his mother had sworn by arrowroot for every ailment. He reckoned she'd have spread it on a plaster, or put it in his tea given the chance.

Amy should be back from work by now, and with any luck he would be back home before Phyllis came in. He blinked as the sweat and the heat coming from him steamed up his glasses, missed a woman crossing the road by jamming his foot down hard on the brake pedal. Why was she shaking her fist and mouthing something at him? Was he going too fast? He couldn't see the speedometer but it didn't feel like he was going very quickly. He drew up outside Amy's house with a screech of brakes.

The pain came on him as he lifted a hand to the iron knocker set high in Amy's front door, ignoring the bell. He knew she wasn't in; she'd told him herself she only closed the big door when she went up to bed at night. The disappointment was like a clout to his head, and he clutched the door post for support, unable to move for the stab of agony piercing his side. He gasped, tried to straighten up, and the effort almost killed him. He groped his way across the pavement to his car and forced himself to slide slowly into the driving seat.

'Aw God,' he prayed, laying his head on the steering wheel, 'if I'm going to die let it be now. Just take this pain away, it's crucifying me.'

The bright promise of the day had drifted into a damp clinging drizzle. Weavers climbed the narrow streets to their homes, shop-girls hurried along, wanting to get round the fires in their cosy back living rooms, to the teas their mothers would have all ready to go on the table. Because it was Wednesday and a market day, there would more than likely be something extra tasty, such as tripe and onions stewed in milk, polony sliced thin, or black puddings with their distinctive spicy taste.

Lottie Marsden walked slowly, going home the long way round because she liked the feel of the feather-soft drizzle on her face and the way it beaded her navy-blue coat. She had walked through the park where the dripping trees, the dark rocks looming up on either side of the paths and the sound of running water had frightened her halfway to death. She had been kept in by the Scripture Mistress for not handing in last week's homework and for talking her way through the lesson.

'I was only telling Mildred Howarth that my mother's consumption is bad at the moment,' she had explained. 'And that I had been up all night praying for her. She's in a sanatorium in Switzerland.'

The Scripture Mistress, who also taught needlework, had been warned to take everything Lottie Marsden said with a pinch of salt – but suppose it were true?

'You poor child,' she said. 'You poor child. You may go, dear. Just try and remember to do your homework next time,' the mistress said, looking at Lottie's oval face and silk-smooth hair, thinking what a beautiful Virgin Mary she would make at next year's nativity concert, which was to be on a lavish scale.

Coming out of the park gate Lottie could see the town stretched out before her. The houses up at this side of the town were hidden by tall privet hedges. Husbands drove home from their offices, turning their cars into gravelled drives. Some of the fee-paying girls lived up here. They had piano lessons as optional extras and went to private elocution classes, even though they knew quite well how and where to sound their aitches. They wore gymslips with pleats that kept in on account of the superior material, and white linings to their navy-blue knickers for the sake of hygiene. Lottie avoided them as much as she could, much preferring the company of the scholarship girls who wore their coats all the year round because their parents couldn't afford blazers, and who never had linings in their knickers.

The rain was coming down heavier now, bouncing off the flagstones, wetting her through. She hoped she got pneumonia and died before her mother could come to pay her last respects. She hoped her mother would be forced to live the rest of her life in terrible remorse. She hoped her mother got ringworm so that they had to shave her head, or that her teeth dropped out. So that staring at herself in a mirror all day would drive her crazy.

Lottie was disappointed to see that Mrs Battersby's house looked just like all the others in the long terrace. The front door was closed and there was no sign of a light anywhere, but there was a car outside with the dim figure of a man crouched over the steering wheel. His hat had fallen off and the bald part of his head gleamed white like a bar of shiny soap. Lottie averted her eyes and quickened her step.

'I saw a dead man on my way back from school,' she was to tell her father in a conversational tone much later that evening.

Charlie looked at her over the top of his newspaper. There were times, and this was one of them, when he wondered if she was quite right in the head. 'Oh, yes?' He turned to the sports page. 'That must have given you quite a turn.'

'It was right outside Mrs Battersby's house.'

Charlie felt his stomach lurch. 'Lottie,' he said through clenched teeth, 'are you quite, quite sure this man was dead?'

Lottie's dark eyes narrowed into calculating slits. 'Of course,' she said loftily.

'Because if he was, you had no right to come home without telling someone.'

'Oh, I told the police,' she said airily, blotting a line in her exercise book with exaggerated care.

'How did you tell the police?' Charlie knew he would have to shake her. 'Did you go all the way down to the police station? *Did* you? I want the truth! And if I don't get it, I'll find out for myself.' He got up from his chair. 'I'll phone them now.'

The telephone was in the hall, on a half-moon table with a chair by the side. There was an oval mirror hanging on the wall from a gold link chain. Clara used to sit for hours talking and watching herself in the mirror at the same time. Charlie lifted the receiver.

'He might have been drunk.' Lottie appeared in the doorway. 'It was hard to tell.'

'You saw nothing!' Charlie slammed the receiver back hard on the cradle, followed his daughter back into the living room. How small she was, how unkempt, untidy, pale, with dark shadows beneath her eyes. Suddenly the urge to shake her was gone. 'Why do you do it, Lottie? Nobody likes a liar, and that's what you are. A liar! A terrible thing to be. They're not fairy stories you're always telling – they're lies. Cruel untruths. Would you like to put your pen down and we'll talk about it? Perhaps you can explain to me why you do it and we can work something out together.' The sigh came from deep inside him. 'Put your pen down, lovey.'

'I have three more subjects to do,' Lottie lied. 'English, geography and algebra, and I've got the main part in the Easter play so I've two pages of that to learn.'

'And you didn't see a man crouched over a wheel in a car outside Mrs Battersby's house? You made it all up?'

'Yes, I made it up,' Lottie said, genuinely wanting to please him. Her father looked so bothered, so badly done to. 'As a matter of fact, I didn't come home that way at all.'

Charlie went back to his chair, tried to read the report of the Rovers' current form, found he couldn't concentrate so went to stand at the back door, staring out at the rain-sodden garden, thinking how awful and depressing everything was.

6

Phyllis was not in the habit of talking to her domestics about anything other than tins of polish or which vegetables to prepare for their evening meal, but when she arrived back from town an hour later than she had intended, saw the garage doors open and the car gone, she went straight to the kitchen.

'Has Mr Battersby taken the car out again, Dora?' She looked agitated, the schooner-sized sherry she'd drunk at her friend's house flushing her cheeks.

Dora looked up from the carrot she was scraping. 'He wouldn't listen, Mrs Battersby. I told him he wasn't fit, but would he listen? Might just as well have been talking to myself. He pleases himself, as well you know.'

'Did he say where he was going?'

It took Phyllis all her time to ask that. The question put her on the same footing as Dora, so to speak, but Edgar had been far from well that morning, certainly in no fit state to drive the car.

Dora slid the chopped carrots into a casserole dish. 'My guess is he's gone to see Amy. I can't tell you how I come to think that, but I have this feeling somehow. He must have forgotten she doesn't get home from work till gone six o'clock. His memory's not what it was.' Both pairs of eyes swivelled towards the clock on the wall. 'He'll be back any minute, I expect,' Dora said.

'Couldn't you have stopped him?' Phyllis felt worry settle like a poultice round her heart. 'No. I don't suppose you could.'

'There's no shifting him when his mind's made up, Mrs Battersby. Sets like concrete, his mind does. He had that stubborn face on him.'

Enough was enough. Phyllis shrank back into herself. Any minute now and Dora would be inviting her to sit down at her own kitchen table and share a pot of tea while they discussed Edgar's funny ways.

'You can go now, Dora,' she said.

Her face was smooth again, her head up as though there was a bad smell underneath her nose. Dora watched her march straight-backed across the hall and into the drawing room, heard the door click and knew she'd be on the phone to the wonderful Wesley before she took off her hat and coat.

She half considered bending her ear to the door and having a listen, but all she wanted was to get home, put the kettle on and make a sandwich from the slice of corned beef she'd filched from the casserole. She opened the oven door and slid the brown dish inside. Why, she wondered, was the same recipe called a beef casserole in the houses up by the park, when round where she lived it was called tater-ash?

Dora saw herself as more of a female Robin Hood than a thief. She knew she earned every brass farthing of the sixpence an hour Mrs Battersby paid her. With a bit of extra Bisto added to the casserole, who was going to miss a paltry slice of corned beef? She eyed the fruit dish and wondered if the old bat had counted the oranges, decided it wasn't worth the risk and took her coat and scarf from the cubbyhole by the back door.

Phyllis didn't hear the back door slam. She was listening to the sound of the telephone ringing in the Preston shop. They had never had an extension put in upstairs, so it would take a minute or so for Wesley to come down. She could actually 'see' him running down the uncarpeted stairs, picking up the receiver, modulating his voice to the one he kept specially for the telephone.

'Hallo? Who is it, please?'

This was a voice she had only heard once or twice, but recognized straight away. Arnold Porrit, the school-leaver Wesley had taken on for the Christmas rush, was still there, though Edgar had complained that he couldn't see why Wesley had got rid of old Mr Lewis who knew to keep the popular brands of cigarettes all together by the till, the cigars in boxes, even though he was quite prepared to sell them singly. Mr Lewis might be coming up to sixty-five, but he knew the tobacco business inside out. Shags, cut-cake, cut Cavendish – Mr Lewis could calculate a customer's order to the thousandth of an inch, hardly needing to use the weigh-scales to check, confident he would be accurate to the last flake.

'Arnold?' This wasn't the time to tell the boy he should always answer the telephone properly, giving the name. Wesley always did it so beautifully: 'Battersby's Tobacconist. Mr Battersby Junior speaking,' he would say. Phyllis sighed. 'Arnold, I would like to speak to Mr Battersby. Will you ask him to come to the telephone, please? This is his mother speaking.'

'Mrs Battersby?'

'Yes.'

'Old Mrs Battersby?'

'Yes.' Phyllis gritted his teeth.

'Only Mr Battersby doesn't wish to speak to the young Mrs Battersby, I have to say he's not in.'

'Well, he will certainly wish to speak to me!' Phyllis gripped the telephone hard. God grant me patience, her expression said.

'He's not in, Mrs Battersby.'

Phyllis felt she could weep with frustration. Edgar had been right. Taking on this untrained, stupid boy in the place of the ever courteous and knowledgeable Mr Lewis had been a bad mistake, even accounting for the saving in wages. She closed her eyes.

'This is an urgent message, Arnold. I wish to speak to Mr . . . to my son. Now. Without delay.'

'They've gone to Blackpool, Mrs Battersby. To the pictures. I was just going to lock up when the telephone rang. I'd best be going, or I'll miss me train. They don't all stop at Bamber Bridge, tha knows.'

Phyllis put the receiver down and stared at it in disbelief. Then she took her coat and hat upstairs, put them away, smoothed down an already smooth counterpane, shivered at the cold feel to the large high-ceilinged room, went back downstairs. And poured herself a drop of comforting sherry.

*

Amy came away from her mother's house carrying a covered basin filled with good marrow-bone stock gone to jelly. For nourishing broth, Gladys had said, noticing her daughter's pinched face and shadowed eyes.

'There's not a man alive worth making yourself ill over,' she'd said. 'The more I see of life the more I believe that the only good men are the dead ones. It's a man's world – always has been and always will be.'

Amy saw Edgar trying to walk from his car to her front door, and ran straight to him, spilling most of the marrow-bone jelly down her best coat.

When she got him in the warm she saw that he'd been sweating so much his high stiff collar was all stringy and crumpled. His eyes were glazed and expressionless, his skin a dingy grey colour, and for those first frightening moments she thought he was going to die.

'I'm all right, love.' He was trying to smile, which upset her so much she knelt down by his chair and gently stroked his face. 'Stop fretting,' he whispered. 'Just let me sit here for a while then I'll be getting back. Mother will be wondering where I've got to. It was the pain,' he went on, catching his breath at the memory of it. 'That stuff the doctor's giving me isn't doing any good. I'll have to get a bottle of something that hits the spot more.' He tried the wavery smile again. 'It's nice here,' he said, when Amy had poked the fire into life. 'This house and you go together. I've always liked coming here.'

'You have?' Amy was astonished. 'Shall I tell you something? I've always liked you coming here too!' They smiled at each other in a new warm way.

'But I'd better be getting back. I'll talk to you another time.'

He pushed himself up to a standing position, his eyes widening with the effort. Amy saw the jaundiced look about them, their slight protuberance. She spoke quickly.

'Sit down again. Please, Mr Battersby. You can't possibly drive the car.'

She stood before him, uncertain what to do, wishing that Wesley would walk in and take over. The single-decker bus was trundling past, rattling the ruby-red panes of glass in the vestibule door the way it always did. If only Wesley could be getting off it, walking quickly into the house.

'Yoo-hoo!'

Amy spun round and saw Dora, so thin and slight she could have been blown in on the wind. Gawping at the man huddled in the chair.

'Mr Battersby! You'll get what for when you go home. I thought I was seeing things when I spotted your car outside.' She went up to Edgar and laid a hand on his forehead. 'Your temperature's up again. Your forehead's that hot I could fry an egg on it – and just look at your coat! You've been sick again, haven't you?'

'It's marrow-bone jelly,' Amy whispered. 'I spilled it when I helped him inside.'

She motioned Dora through into the kitchen, though Edgar seemed to have dropped off to sleep with his mouth open, making a bubbly noise in his throat. They looked at each other.

'I found him staggering about outside the house.' Amy frowned. 'Why hadn't you told me how ill he was? Dyspepsia, you said it was. Dyspepsia! He's got more than that. He looks like my dad did when he was on his last.'

'It's only today he's had a fever on him,' Dora hissed. 'Don't you go thinking the worst. If the old bat had brought a decent doctor to him weeks ago things would never have got this far. The one she swears by is about as much good as a chocolate fireguard.' She peered round the door at Edgar. 'You stop with him and I'll go and telephone Mrs Battersby. The infirmary's the best place for him. I'll go and ask Mr Dale if I can use his phone. He'll be home by now.'

'C'mon, c'mon,' she muttered two minutes later, standing on the pavement outside the house four doors down. 'Don't say you're at a meeting or sat in the pictures, or round at a friend's house having your tea. Just answer the door!'

When Bernard saw who it was he looked surprised, but stood back at once for her to go in.

Phyllis answered the telephone at the second ring, her voice a bit slurred because she was on her third sherry, not counting the schooner she'd had at her friend's house. Not knowing where Edgar was or what to do for the best had made her feel quite ill. She would have rung the police if she could have been sure it wouldn't have got their name in the papers. She would have walked up the next-door drive and told them, if she hadn't imagined the look on their faces when she said she didn't know where her husband was. Besides, they would be having their meal. It was quite the wrong time to call. She had rung Wesley's number again, but the wretched Arnold must have told her the truth. There was no one there.

Now Dora, shouting as though she was speaking from Outer Mongolia, was telling her that Edgar was at Amy's house, feeling proper poorly, not fit to drive himself home. She was ringing, she said, from a house lower down the street.

'Hold the line!' she suddenly yelled, then after a moment or two came back at full blast. 'It's all right, Mrs Battersby. Mr Dale is going to bring Mr Battersby back. He can drive a car. Don't worry,' she added, before slamming down the receiver.

'You can get used to speaking on the telephone, can't you?' she told Bernard as they walked down the street together. 'Mrs Battersby isn't keen on me talking on hers, though God knows why. She'd been at the sherry again. I could nearly smell it through the telephone.'

She was very put out when she realized that her part in the drama was over and that Amy was going off with Mr Battersby in the car, sitting with him in the back seat, leaving Dora – as per usual – to see to things. But wasn't that the story of her life? Stopping behind seeing to things, while others went off and enjoyed the excitement. Years and bloomin' years of tending other folk's fires for them to sit round, preparing meals for others to eat, mopping floors for other feet to walk on and make mucky again.

Chunnering to herself, she placed Amy's fireguard in position, carried the basin containing what was left of the marrow-bone jelly through into the kitchen and decided to have a bit of a scout round.

The oven shelves could do with a good rub-up with panshine, and who would have thought Amy had nothing in her meat-safe but three eggs in a brown dish? Her cake tin was nicely filled, however.

Dora counted eight rock buns, decided seven would have to do Amy and took one to have after the slice of corned beef she'd pinched from old Ma Battersby.

On her way out through the living room the wonderful Wesley seemed to be leering at her from the large chromium-plated frame on the piano. Fancying himself as John Boles in *The Desert Song*. Dora had a good mind to spit at him. She held the frame at the right distance but controlled herself. The wonderful Wesley wasn't worth wasting good spit on.

It could easily have been a case of rape that time when he made a pass at her. For a moment Dora could feel his hands on her, his mouth wet and searching, his tongue probing. All at a time when Greg was hardly cold in his grave and when Amy was within earshot on the other side of their dividing wall, getting over her fourth – or was it her fifth? – miscarriage. Dora put the photograph face down and walked out of the house.

Suppose she told Amy? Somebody needed to pull the wool from her eyes. But since the Red Shadow had galloped off into the night, she and Amy had got to know and understand each other a lot better. In fact, they'd become really good friends now that Amy had stopped quoting Wesley every other sentence.

Dora tended the fire before taking off her coat. Since the embarrassing episode when she'd kneed Wesley where it hurt most to stop him slavering over her, she had avoided being in the same room with him if possible. He might look like Robert Taylor, but looks weren't everything. Anyway, he wasn't her type. She liked men a bit more cuddly, shorter, clean-shaven, who liked a bit of a laugh.

Chunnering to herself again, she brought the margarine through to the fire to warm, tilting the saucer towards the flames to speed things up.

Greg had been just like that before he went to France all those years ago. When he put his little short arms around her and squeezed the breath from her body, it was like being hugged by a plush teddy bear. Greg had never said smarmy things to her, or sang at her. Their lovemaking had been a joyous thing, with laughter a part of it, especially when it didn't come up to their expectations. A German bullet fired from a sniper's gun in no-man's-land had put paid to all that. For the left-over life Greg was forced to live there was precious little laughter and no lovemaking at all. Had she done the right thing in letting him go into hospital? Into an institution? Why not call a spade a spade and not a bloody shovel? Could she have managed if she'd tried harder, hadn't been so tired?

As tears blurred her eyes, Dora shook her head to blink them away. She saw the slab of yellow margarine slide from the saucer to be swallowed and hissed to a bubbling nothing by the flames.

It wasn't a nice word she uttered but it did her a power of good.

Phyllis took to Bernard straight away. He was so polite, so nicely spoken. She was sure he must be a friend of Wesley's. Soothed and comforted by his white shirt, discreet tie and his London accent, she listened gratefully when he told her that in his opinion her husband should see a doctor without delay.

'He's been seeing a doctor regularly for quite some time, Mr Dale.'

'I'm sure he's had the best attention, Mrs Battersby, but at the moment he has a fever, and there's a hardness underneath his right ribs that I don't like.'

They were talking together in the hall, leaving Amy to settle Edgar in his chair and help him off with his coat.

'Are you a medical man?'

Bernard shook his head. 'Red Cross trained, and even that a long time ago, but I know enough to see when genuine medical advice is necessary.'

'I've been trying to reach my son, but he's not available.' Phyllis fidgeted with her two-stranded pearl necklace. 'He'll be most upset when he hears.'

'The doctor's telephone number? I'll speak to him if you wish.'

Phyllis nodded. It was strange that Wesley had never mentioned this very personable friend of his. Perhaps he was something to do with the Light Operatic Society? Honorary Secretary or Musical Director? He had that authoritative look about him and in the tone of his voice. When he came off the phone and said the doctor was coming straight away, she wasn't surprised.

'It is so kind of you to help my daughter-in-law like this. You must know my charlady, Mrs Ellis, as she telephoned from your home?'

'Dora and I are old friends,' Bernard said, wondering why Amy shot him a startled look, then blushed bright red.

He stared at Phyllis. Was this woman real? She had done no more than give her husband a cursory glance, leaving Amy to kneel by her father-in-law's chair, holding his hand and whispering to him. It was obvious the woman was agitated, but where was her warmth, her distress? Her milk of human kindness?

'I'll just go upstairs on the extension and try to get Wesley again,' she was saying. 'He may be there now.'

Amy patted Edgar's hand. The pain was creeping back – she saw it in his eyes, felt it in the way his fingers dug into her wrist. He was frowning at his feet, biting his lips.

'We'll soon have you fixed up, sir. Hold on,' Bernard whispered.

Edgar felt he should have known this nice young chap, but for the life of him he couldn't bring him to mind. Looked all right though. Officer material, he wouldn't wonder. Oh, dear dear God, he wished he didn't feel so damned awful. Wished he wasn't such a trouble to everybody. Wished he was in his bed and fast asleep. He closed his eyes.

Bernard exchanged a look with Amy.

Upstairs Phyllis pressed the receiver against a pearl earring, hearing the ringing tone going on and on. At last she went back downstairs.

'Wesley's still out,' she told them. 'I'll get some things together. If hospital is called for I'll need to do that.'

Her sharp nose was coated with white face powder, patted into the wrinkles beneath her eyes. Her mouth, with not enough lip to it, had raspberry lipstick running down into the vertical creases. Amy felt suddenly achingly sorry for her.

'Can I come and help you?' she asked, standing up. 'I'd like to. Please.'

98

'No need for that.' Phyllis's voice was as brisk as her step. 'I can manage quite well, thank you.'

Bernard's eyes were telling Amy not to mind, so she smiled at him to show she didn't.

In the house next door to Amy's Dora was making chips to have with Phyllis's slice of corned beef. She still felt restless, uneasy in her mind, left out, slighted, badly done to. So she was making chips. Other people might scrub floors, tidy drawers, whistle, wash curtains, go for a walk when they felt miserable and frustrated. Dora made chips.

The important thing was to lift the wire basket clear of the bubbling fat when the chips were almost done, then plunge them back to make them crisp and brown. Dora shook them out on to a plate, feeling more cheerful already.

But even perfectly cooked chips couldn't take her mind off poor Mr Battersby. How did a lovely man like that have a son like the wonderful Wesley? Dora bet it was Wesley's antics that had brought on his father's illness. Mr Dale had once explained to her that the mind and worry could affect a person's health. Dora speared a chip on her fork, dipped it into a mound of tomato sauce and chewed thoughtfully. Suppose Mr Battersby died? She put down her fork.

She would be very sorry if he died. Mr Battersby had always been kind to her. Dora ate another chip. Somehow she had always thought how lonely he was, in spite of his businesses and his meetings in town. They had no fun, Mr and Mrs Battersby. Dora had never heard them laugh together, never seen the old man give his wife a playful slap on her bottom. But then, old Ma Battersby had no bottom to speak of, had she?

Suppose he did die? Dora pushed her plate away, her appetite quite gone. She would be sorry of course, and she'd miss him. But since Greg's death there was this thick lump where her heart should be, so that she could sympathize but not anguish. The hurt had been so bad that she knew that never again could she ache so much, cry so much. Not for anything or anybody.

Did that make her into some kind of monster?

Up at the infirmary they sat in a long corridor on chairs lined up against the wall. Nurses passed and re-passed, their crêpe-soled shoes making little sucking sounds on the polished floor.

Phyllis said that if only they'd had more time her husband could have been got into the Masonic Hospital, or at least into somewhere more in keeping. She explained to anyone who would listen that her son would be there if he'd any idea his father was so ill.

Then she fell silent, drooping her head down as if she might drop off to sleep.

'Mrs Battersby?' The doctor was very young, with horn-rimmed glasses slipping down an inadequate nose. 'You can see your husband for a couple of minutes now. He's very drowsy, but he'll know you're there.' He hesitated. 'It's a straightforward gall bladder problem, and normally we would operate as soon as possible.' He looked at Bernard. 'You're the patient's son?'

Phyllis bridled, sat up straight, looked on the young doctor with a kind of pity. 'My son is out of town. Unavoidably detained.' She looked stricken and her face was tense with anxiety. 'He would be here if he had any idea ...' She turned to Amy, actually pleading. 'He *would* be here, wouldn't he?'

'Like a shot,' said Amy, squeezing her hand. 'Wild horses wouldn't keep him away if he knew.'

'If you'd like to come with me ...' The young doctor spoke to Phyllis but smiled at Amy.

'Daughter-in-law,' Amy said, feeling she needed explaining, turning to Bernard as soon as they were out of sight. 'Why can't they operate as soon as possible?'

Bernard had planned a quiet evening, reading and listening to the wireless – *La Traviata* in its entirety. When Dora had called to use the telephone he was just about to cook his supper, which Amy Battersby would undoubtedly call his tea. He was willing to help out, of course, who wouldn't be? But he was being involved against his wishes; he wanted no part of all this. For two pins he'd make his excuses and leave.

Then he turned to the girl by his side, met her eyes and was at once so inexplicably moved, so filled with a total unexpected compassion that he had to look away.

'I'm sorry, Mr Dale,' she was saying in her soft voice. 'I shouldn't ask you questions like that.' She paused, as if making up her mind about something. 'It's not right you being here. That's twice today you've been put in an impossible position.' She sounded cross. 'I bet you haven't had your tea!'

'You're quite right, I haven't.' He glanced down the long corridor to where a stout nurse with large splayed-out feet was presiding over a bedtime drinks trolley. 'Stay right there, Amy.'

She blinked as he used her christian name for the first time. He was a bit of a dark horse all right, secretive almost, wrapped up in himself, but not in a conceited way. Serious, thoughtful, yet with an in-built twinkle in his eyes. She knew nothing about him really, yet he knew almost everything there was to know about her. Amy stared bleakly at the opposite wall, dark green at the bottom and a bilious yellow at the top.

He had read Wesley's farewell letter. She had forced him to read it against his wishes, just as he had been forced to come here tonight. Amy studied his back as he stood talking to the nurse at the end of the corridor. There was an incipient bald patch at the back of his head though his hair was thick and a pleasing shade of brown. Wesley would have gone mad if his glossy black hair had begun to thin – not that it stood much chance with its weekly bay rum massage and the daily application of a tiny bead of Brylcreme. Amy sighed deeply, causing a passing probationer nurse to look at her with concern.

As well as reading Wesley's farewell letter, the man accepting two cups of tea from the stout nurse had seen Wesley's wife in her nightie and also without her nightie. He had seen her tears that afternoon when she had walked into his office without an appointment, and now here he was again involved when she was sure that was the last thing he wanted to be.

He was bowing slightly to the nurse, thanking her politely. In his own way, Amy supposed, Mr Dale was just as charming as Wesley, though she could recognize his technique as being totally different.

Wesley would have flirted with the plain nurse, paid her outrageous compliments, lingered, conscious of the effect he was having on her, leaving her bemused, wondering whether she was coming or going.

'All done with a smile,' Bernard grinned, and passed Amy a thick white cup of reasonably hot tea.

'I don't suppose many women can resist your smile,' Amy said quick as a lick, all mixed up in her troubled mind because he wasn't Wesley when he should have been, and because she still couldn't understand why Mr Battersby was too ill for his operation. 'Sorry, I didn't mean to say that. I never seem to show myself up in a good light to you, do I? I always seem to be at my worst when you're around.'

'That's true,' Bernard said, his eyes twinkling at her. 'If you suddenly jumped up and went screaming down the corridor I don't suppose I'd turn a hair.'

'Wesley's mother's coming back.'

Amy stood up as Phyllis came towards them, an unreadable expression on her face. She held out a hand, but what Phyllis had to say she was obviously going to say to Bernard.

It had been a most unusual day for the time of year and when Wesley and Clara came out of the pictures it was pleasant enough for them to walk along the promenade without danger of being blown out to sea. Clara tied a scarf over her hair and clung to Wesley's arm.

'I like Blackpool out of season,' she said all at once.

Still filled with the sound of Richard Tauber's voice and the soaring music, Wesley was in one of his romantic moods. He stopped so that Clara had to stop too. 'The sea is half asleep,' he said. 'Just listen to it, whispering against the sea wall.' Reluctantly, urged on by Clara, he walked on.

'Why don't we stay the night?' Clara asked.

'What? You're joking!'

'No, I'm not.' Clara whipped the scarf from her head and laughed out loud. 'We can get up early in the morning and catch a train back in time to open up the shop.' She waved an arm. 'We can book a room with a window overlooking the sea. We can sleep with the curtains drawn back and lie and watch the moonlight shining on the sea.' She flung her arms round his neck. 'We can make love in a bed big enough to move around in instead of squashing together in that camp-bed over the shop.' She moved herself against him. 'Oh Wesley, why don't we? That awful little room is stifling me, with its gas fire going plop all the time, and cartons of cigars piled all over the place.'

'You once said that room was your idea of heaven.'

'And so it is.' She kissed him in a teasing way, butterfly kisses, just missing his mouth.

He felt his senses quicken. 'Kiss me properly,' he whispered, and when his mouth opened over her own she knew she had won. They would stay the night.

Charlie Marsden couldn't settle that night. He usually went down to the pub about half-past nine to have a couple of pints and meet Billy Warton, Tom Sowerbutts, Ernie Sutcliffe and Alf Hothersall. Usually he was the life and soul, thinking up harmless jokes about Irishmen or Jews or mean-minded Scots. But it hadn't been the same since Wesley went away. Say what you liked but Wesley Battersby had brought a touch of class with him. Charlie would be the first to admit that as far as money was concerned he could buy and sell Wesley and still have a few quid left over, but Wesley had done the unforgiveable when he had run off with a mate's wife. Spitting on his own doorstep, so to speak.

After that first shock which had reduced him to tears of disbelief, he'd realized that it wasn't so much Clara he was missing as her presence. He liked having a woman about the place, liked the smell of her scent in the bathroom, liked watching her dry her hair kneeling down on the rug by the fire, brushing it up from the nape of her neck.

That night Lottie had washed her hair before going up to bed. She had knelt between his knees while he rubbed it dry with a towel, the moment so intimate, so cosy he had tried to have a proper fatherly talk with her.

103

'We're managing all right, you and me, aren't we, chuck?'

'We managed before she went,' Lottie said, snatching the towel from him and finishing off herself. 'Mrs Tunstall looked after us then and she's looking after us now. I don't know why you don't marry her.'

Charlie kept his voice calm, gave a fatherly chuckle. 'Mrs Tunstall is fifty-four years old.' He gave Lottie's shoulder a playful shake. 'Besides, she's not my type.'

'She'd jump at the chance,' Lottie said, picking up her hairbrush. 'I've seen her kissing your pyjama jacket.'

Why had she said that about Mrs Tunstall? Lottie lay flat on her back in bed, determined not to go to sleep. If her father even thought of marrying Mrs Tunstall she would run away, catch a train to London and go on the streets. She'd smoke cigarettes in a long black holder, wear black fishnet stockings and tuck the money she earned into red garters. Once, during one of their shouting rows she had heard her father call her mother a whore, and though she'd looked it up in a dictionary under 'h' she hadn't been able to find it. Then she read a paperback book bought for twopence from a stall on the market, and all became clear. Mrs Tunstall had made her throw the book into the fire when she saw it, saying the picture on the front showing a woman in black stockings and red garters smoking a cigarette in a long black holder was enough to turn her stomach.

'I'm just going out for a while, chuck.' Lottie opened her eyes to see her father standing in the doorway wearing his raincoat and his little trilby hat. 'You'll be all right?'

She feigned drowsiness. 'Quite all right.'

Charlie hesitated, thought of going over to the bed and kissing her goodnight, then changed his mind. That revelation about Mrs Tunstall had unnerved him. The very thought of the big woman with the incipient moustache and hairy chin kissing his pyjama jacket was nauseating. It was more than nauseating – it was obscene.

'Goodnight, then. I'll leave the hall light on.'

'G'night.'

Lottie waited until she heard the front door slam, then got out of her bed, pulled her dressing gown round her and went downstairs to telephone her friend Olive who never went to bed before ten o'clock.

'Are they in?'

Olive said they were, but that they were playing bridge. As per usual.

'I saw a dead man sitting in a car on my way home from school.'

Olive's eyes grew round. 'Did you tell the police?'

'I might have been accused of doing it.'

'Was there any blood about?'

'I didn't wait to find out.'

'No, of course not. But I still think you should tell your father. I would tell mine about a thing like that. I really would, Lottie.'

'He's gone out drinking,' Lottie said at once. 'As per usual.'

Charlie drew up outside Amy's house, switched off the lights and sat in the van feeling rather foolish, almost wishing he had followed his intention of meeting up with his pals in the pub. He stared through the van window at Amy's front door. No sign of life anywhere, no light in the upstairs room, no glimmer coming from the back showing through the parlour window. Certainly no dead man slumped over the wheel of his car. He drummed with his fingers on the steering wheel.

Oh, Lottie, Lottie – what was to become of her? What was to become of any of them, come to that? Wesley hadn't exactly been a tower of strength, not even the hub of the wheel, but since he went away things seemed to have gone from bad to worse. Charlie pushed his hat back on his head and whistled through his teeth, a sure sign he was upset. Damn it, he needed to talk to Amy, to ask her advice about Lottie, maybe to have a bit of a laugh about Mrs Tunstall and his pyjama jacket. He groaned. Clara had used to say that he could laugh at nowt, that it was his everlasting laughing at nowt that had driven her nearly potty. Charlie leaned forward and switched on the ignition. Maybe he'd go and have a couple of pints with the lads after all.

He was actually on the point of drawing away from the kerb when a woman suddenly shot out of the house next door to Amy's and into the road, causing him to brake hard. Charlie wound down the window, ready with a mouthful, and instead heard Amy's next-door neighbour, Dora Ellis, politely inviting him to step inside her house as she had quite a lot to tell him.

'Amy's up at the infirmary,' she began, as he followed her down a darkened lobby. 'Wesley's father was taken ill right outside her front door this afternoon.'

Taking off his trilby, Charlie advanced towards the rocking chair by the fire, urged towards it by this pleasant little woman who was whipping off her pinny and fluffing up her hair.

So Lottie had been partly right all along and he hadn't believed her. Charlie said that yes, a hot drink would be welcome on such a cold evening, thank you very much. He glanced around him, touched to the quick by the threadbare shabbiness of everything.

And Lottie had been telling the truth about Mrs Tunstall, too. He'd stake his life on that.

7

Phyllis, speaking directly to Bernard, ignoring Amy, explained that the reason for delaying Edgar's operation was that he had developed septicaemia. She stretched out a hand for Bernard's cup. 'Tea. Lovely.'

'Sit down, Mrs Battersby,' he said gently.

Amy had gone very white. Septicaemia. Blood poisoning. Call it what you liked. Once that set in there was very little hope. She looked at her mother-in-law sipping Bernard's cup of tea, apparently totally unmoved. There was no point in reaching out to her in comfort. Amy was sure she would have winced away.

'He wants to see you, Amy,' she was saying now. 'They've sedated him but he's still awake. A minute, that's all.'

Amy left them together, Bernard standing awkwardly, waiting to take the cup from Phyllis when she'd finished. Marvelling, if Amy could have read his thoughts, at the tight control of this too thin woman with the sharp features that seemed to be carved out of granite, a woman with the vulnerability of a steamroller, the humanity of a marble statue, as far as he could make out. Could anything crack her composure?

'I think I'll try again to see if Wesley answers the phone,' she said abruptly, getting up and walking quickly down the corridor.

In the long ward a nurse at a table busily writing by the light from a shaded lamp, pointed out Edgar's bed. She smiled a professional soothing smile and went back to her records.

For a terrifying moment Amy thought her father-in-law had died without anyone knowing. He lay on his back, his arms stretched out on top of the white bedspread, his nose as peaked and bony as her own father's had been in his coffin. The strange bronze-yellow of his skin was accentuated by the white pillows and turned-down sheet. Amy felt awkward, surprised by her embarrassment, very conscious that the man in the next bed might be listening. He was awake; she had seen him raise his head from his pillow as she walked past.

'Mr Battersby?' She touched Edgar's hand and at once his eyelids lifted a fraction.

'Amy?'

'Yes. I'm here.'

'Good.' Edgar closed his eyes again. His feet seemed trapped in with the tight bed coverings. She wanted to unmitre the corners, pull out the sheets to make him more comfortable. 'Don't worry, love.'

Amy bent over him. 'I'm not worrying. And neither must you.'

She wanted to tell him that while they were waiting in the long corridor Bernard Dale had told her that gall bladders were very unimportant things, that horses and pigeons didn't even have one. 'Better out than in,' she would have said, making him smile.

She prayed, but the prayer didn't sound reverent enough for her liking. She was still acutely aware of the man in the next bed who was fixing her with an unblinking stare.

'Don't let him die, please,' she asked God underneath her breath. 'Not when I'm just getting to know him better. Not when I need him so much. Not when I've just found out I love him.'

'No need to worry about . . .' Edgar whispered again, and again Amy assured him that worry about him couldn't be further from her mind. He turned his head slowly from side to side. 'About the . . .' His voice tailed away. 'I've seen to . . .'

The nurse had left her table and was standing at the foot of the bed. 'He'll sleep now, dear. I've just advised your mother-in-law to go home.' She walked with Amy to the swing door at the end of the ward. 'She seems to be greatly upset at not being able to contact her son.'

'They're very close,' Amy told her. 'Him being the only one.'

They didn't talk much on the long walk back, after they'd seen

108

Phyllis safely home. Bernard offered Amy the warmth of his coat pocket. 'We can keep one hand warm anyway.'

'There wasn't the time for gloves.' She liked the dry safe feel of his hand. 'I bet Wesley's mother stays up all night. Till she gets through to him, anyway.'

A policeman on his beat shone his lamp at them. 'A bit parky tonight, sir.'

'It is indeed, officer. Not a bit like spring.'

'I'm surprised you know what "parky" means, coming from London,' Amy said.

He laughed. 'I even know what a chip butty is. I could murder one right now.'

Amy felt awful. It was all her fault that he was hungry. To be polite she ought to offer to make him a meal, even though it was the middle of the night. Food hadn't interested her all that much lately, but she knew there were eggs. Boiled? Poached? Fried with a few potato scallops? Scrambled in a pan with a drop of milk and grated cheese? An omelette? Mumbled? With bacon? Had she any bacon? She couldn't very well knock on Dora's door and wake her up to ask to borrow a rasher of bacon.

By the clenching and unclenching of her hand in his pocket Bernard guessed she was fretting herself about something, but he didn't ask. Instead, when they reached the house he took the key from her, turned it in the lock, and opened the door with the flat of his hand.

'If you'd like . . .' Amy began, but already he was backing away. 'Don't go,' she heard herself say too loudly. 'The least I can do is . . .'

So gently she could hardly believe what he was doing, he came back to her and held her face between his hands. 'It's been a long day, Amy, for both of us.' For the briefest of seconds he laid his mouth on hers. 'Pretty Amy,' he said softly, tucking her hair behind her ears and smiling. 'Pretty Amy.'

After she'd closed the door she leaned against it, clasping both hands to her breast. She ran a finger round the shape of her lips, hardly able to credit what had happened. She was thirty-seven years old, going on for forty, for heaven's sake. She had been married for more than twenty years, and in all that time Wesley had been the only one. No other man had touched her, nor had she wanted them to.

But Wesley had gone away. He had rejected her, left her in this awful state of numbness, feeling useless, fit for nothing but the knacker's yard. Ugly, unattractive, no glamour, nothing. Slowly she walked down the lobby into the living room, straight to the scalloped mirror hanging from its gilded chain.

'Pretty Amy.' What gentle eyes he had and his voice reminded her of someone – who? – slightly husky, melodious – who?

She was getting into bed when it came to her. Robert Donat in *The Thirty-Nine Steps*, that lovely film actor, that real English actor – till you remembered he was partly Polish. That was who Mr Dale – Bernard, as he had asked her to call him – reminded her of.

Amy wished she could tell Dora about the kiss, but even as she wished it knew she never would.

Next door, so slight she made no more than a mound in her bed, Dora Ellis had wakened with a start as Amy closed her front door. Since she'd put Greg away she had woken at the slightest sound, alert in the fraction of a second, ready to go to him if he needed her.

So Amy was back. If it wasn't the middle of the night she would get up and go next door to tell her the unbelievable news.

'Think about it,' Charlie Marsden had said, sitting by the fire and drinking her last bottle of milk stout. 'You'd be better off in more ways than one if you came to housekeep for me and our Lottie. Ten till six and a chance to put your feet up when you felt like it, and a proper wage. Not peanuts like you get at the mill and from old Ma Battersby. She wouldn't let you have the steam off her tea, that one.'

'But you've got a housekeeper,' Dora had pointed out. 'Amy once told me you've had her for a long time.'

That was when he had got up to go, putting on the too small trilby, pushing it to the back of his head with a finger.

'She's getting past it,' he'd said. 'Time she retired. It comes to us all in the end.'

110

He'd winked at her and gone away, asking her to think over what he'd suggested and let him know within the week.

Leaving Dora to float up to bed and fall asleep with a smile on her face.

Charlie had a look in at Lottie before he went to his own bed. She was lying on her back with her mouth slightly open, making little puffing noises. It was obvious she hadn't moved since he went out.

He wouldn't need any rocking himself, come to that. It had been an inspired notion to ask Dora Ellis to come and housekeep for them. He'd had no idea how hard her life was, how lacking in creature comforts that house of hers. Frayed carpet, chipped fireplace, threadbare curtains – that long illness of her husband's must have drained her mentally and physically. There'd be things she could have from here. Clara had thought nothing of buying new before the old was worn out.

He'd tell Mrs Tunstall the very next day. No need to wait for Dora Ellis's decision. When he'd mentioned the washing machine and the vacuum cleaner, the expression on her face had been like the sun coming up over Pendle Hill. They'd had a good laugh tonight. She was a bit of a caution all right. He got into bed still smiling.

In the room across the wide landing Lottie was having one of her nightmares. She was seven years old . . . she was coming home early from school because she'd been sick . . . her mother had known she was sick when she sent her that morning . . . she was coming in the house by the back door, whimpering a little because her stomach was still hurting . . . she was hearing something upstairs . . . her mother talking to someone in her bedroom . . . 'Mummy?' she was creeping up the thickly carpeted stairs, needing to tell how bad she felt, wanting to be comforted, reassured that being sick on the floor at school was nothing to worry about. That by tomorrow everyone would have forgotten about it.

She turned on her side, buried her face in the pillow.

She was opening the door of her mother's bedroom, seeing the man on the bed fighting her mother, jumping up and down on her

... she was hearing her mother making that terrible noise ... screaming? Shouting for help? 'I'm coming, Mummy,' she had yelled, bursting in on them.

She was awake now, suddenly, as if a light had been switched on in her head. She was struggling to get out of bed, beating back the waves of sleep.

'Lottie! Wake up, chuck. You're only dreaming. Come on now, lie down again. Go back to sleep.'

She opened her eyes and saw her father, clutching his pyjama trousers round him, hair tousled, blinking in the sudden glare of the electric light.

'I was only trying to stop him killing her,' she said from the pit of her dream.

'I know, chuck,' her father said. 'Hush up now. Go back to sleep.'

Twice during the night Wesley had got out of bed and, lifting the heavy lined curtains away from the window, had tried to peer out. The sea was there, he could hear its ebb and flow, but the trams had stopped running a couple of hours ago. He felt uneasy, disturbed in his mind, but couldn't think why.

From the bed Clara called his name. She was all softness, warm and inviting, crazy about him as he was about her. After they had made love she sat up and asked him for a cigarette. She switched on the lamp at her side of the bed and sat smoking, totally oblivious to the fact that she was naked.

Amy would have made some attempt to cover her breasts, but then Amy didn't smoke, or wrap her legs round him when they made love.

'When are we going to get out of that flat?' Clara asked him. 'I can't stand much more of it. You promised it was only a temporary thing. A house you said, Wesley. You promised me we would move to a house.' She pouted. 'You promised you'd climb up and get the moon down for me if only I'd leave Charlie and go away with you. Remember?'

When she lay down she snuggled her head on to his shoulder and slept almost at once. Wesley stared wide-eyed into the darkness.

Her hair tickled his chin; on her breath he could smell the wine she'd drunk. He moved his arm gingerly so as not to disturb her. Oh, dear dear God, a house ... the moon ... each one as unattainable as the other.

His father had long since developed cloth ears when money was mentioned. Wesley could see him now, bull-necked and intractable: 'I'm putting you in the Preston shop as manager,' he'd said. 'Manager and nowt else till you prove you can handle cash. Aye, and keep your fingers out of the till.'

The memory of that awful confrontation came back with such intensity that tears welled up in his eyes. They were the tears of self-pity, hurt pride, and wounded him as deeply as if all the hurtful things had been said only yesterday. The only decent thing his father had ever done above the bounds of duty was to buy their house when he married Amy. 'To make the best of a bad start,' he'd said at the time. 'To give you a chance to make something of yourself.'

Wesley buried his chin deep in the softness of Clara's hair, dozed for an hour, then woke again. He felt genuinely sorry for Amy. Hated upsetting her. She'd done nothing to deserve all this. Falling in love with Clara had nothing at all to do with Amy, who had somehow dissolved into a shadowy figure, no longer at all essential to his happiness.

No longer essential to his happiness – what a terrible ring of finality the words had to them. Life could be very cruel. And love. His eyes filled with tears again. He would call and see the old man this coming weekend, try and talk to him, make him see that everything wasn't just black and white, that sometimes people were victims of circumstances, that when you loved a woman beyond all understanding it was like being swept along on a relentless tide. That Clara possessed him body and soul.

That he was thinking in clichés never occurred to him. The words in his head sounded like poetry. He could almost convince himself that he had thought of them first.

Around half-past two that morning Phyllis stopped trying to ring the Preston shop and fell asleep on the chesterfield in the drawing room, wearing her fur coat like a blanket, her head lolling uncomfortably on a Sanderson patterned cushion bound with gold braid and edged with large tassels, which had left wavy red marks down one cheek when she woke up.

They were the first thing that Wesley noticed about her when he arrived breathless and penitent around ten o'clock, taking a taxi from the station, waving the change away, to rush into the house, long coat flying, black hair in need of a cut tumbling fetchingly over his forehead.

'Oh, my poor little mother. What have you done to your face?' He pulled her to him briefly then led her to a chair. 'I knew something was terribly wrong. I lay awake all night wondering why I couldn't sleep, feeling sad yet not being able to make any sense out of it.'

'I rang and rang.' In control of herself again, Phyllis shook her head from side to side. 'But you weren't to know.'

Wesley looked as if he might be going to cry.

'Of course you weren't to know,' she said again.

She told him about his father's illness, of the surgeon's predicament in not daring to operate until the septicaemia was cleared up. She said that his father had been behaving strangely lately and not just because of the pain, either. She said that Amy and he seemed to have become very friendly, and that Amy had been there at the infirmary the night before.

'We'll go now,' she said. 'But first you ought perhaps to go up to the bathroom and have a shave. Your father's razor blades are in the cabinet on the left-hand side. You don't mind me saying this, do you, son?'

'What do you think?' said Wesley, his mouth curving up into a tender smile, much too considerate to tell her that she didn't look too hot herself.

The nurse on Edgar's ward thought Wesley looked exactly like Robert Taylor, only twice as handsome. No resemblance to his father at all. In fact, it was almost impossible to believe they could be father and son. She was sure he was admiring her legs, but how

114

could that be when his father was so gravely ill? All the same, she was glad she was wearing her fully-fashioned black stockings that day and had washed her hair the night before.

And after all Edgar was asleep, hardly there, drifting in and out of consciousness. They were bringing in a Mr Jenkins from Manchester that afternoon, Sister told them – a brilliant man in his own field of haematology.

'Father . . .' Wesley said, bending over the still figure in the high white bed. 'Don't worry about a single thing. I'm here with Mother. We're both here.'

'He can't hear you,' Sister said, sounding nasty instead of kind and efficient, because the nice old man's son was already getting on her nerves. Too smarmy by half, too conscious of the effect he was having on all around him. *Thought* he was having, that was. Or was her instant dislike of Mr Battersby Junior merely due to the fact that she should have been off duty two hours ago?

'Father . . .' Wesley was saying again, laying a hand on the yellowed forehead. 'We'll come back again tonight. I'm taking good care of Mother.'

Dora was bursting to tell Amy the unbelievable news about Charlie Marsden and his offer of a job, but when she left the house at five o'clock that morning Amy's curtains were still drawn across both the upstairs and downstairs windows. For the fraction of a second she paused. Drawn curtains during the daytime meant only one thing. Death. Mr Battersby wasn't that ill. How could he be when he'd driven his car the day before? No, the old man wasn't ready for popping his clogs for a long time yet, she felt sure of it.

Down the steep street to the mill she ran, nimble as a mountain goat, wispy hair straggling from beneath the jumble sale hat, nose and cheeks shiny from their quick scrub with a worn-down bar of old Ma Battersby's Palmolive soap. Down to the mill before the streets were even aired, before even the knocker-up, with his umbrella spokes at the end of his long pole, came round to get the mill-workers from their beds. Into the mill to begin the familiar round of raking out grates in the offices, fetching coal, burnishing brass fire-irons, sweeping floors, polishing desks, emptying waste-paper baskets and kow-towing to everyone because there was no one lower down the scale than Dora Ellis.

She turned into the short street leading to the mill. To think that soon she could be stopping in bed till seven o'clock, beginning work at ten, wearing a black dress with a high collar and a fob-watch on her chest. Housekeeper to the Marsden Residence. Putting her feet up in the afternoons for forty winks and a read of the paper. She slipped through the small door let into the gate, already wishing the hours away till she could tell Amy her good fortune, maybe have a drink on it with the wonderful Wesley's whisky – if there was any left.

Wesley rang the bell once then walked in without knocking. After all, it was his house, wasn't it? Amy's mother was there, which didn't surprise him, wearing a hat made in the shape of Amy Johnson's flying helmet, green with earflaps, and with her everlasting flowered pinny showing at least three inches beneath her coat.

Nobody spoke for a moment. Amy's face paled, while Gladys as usual jumped in with both feet, gabbling because she was overcome at seeing him, saying something stupid simply because she was made that way.

'I boiled a small piece of silverside,' she told Wesley, pointing to a covered basin on the table. 'It potted nicely, set to a jelly, so I fetched it round for her to have with a boiled onion for her dinner.'

'Your father. . . ?' Amy looked as if she might faint.

'He's all right. I've just come from the infirmary. Mother and I went together.'

Sheer relief sharpened Amy's voice. 'She was trying for hours to get through to you on the phone. Your father might have died and you wouldn't have known.'

'I wasn't to know he was in hospital. I didn't even know he was ill enough to be in hospital.'

'He's not been well for a long time. You knew he was poorly at Christmas, but you've hardly kept in touch.' The colour had come back into Amy's cheeks. 'I thought when you walked in you'd come to tell me he'd died! He's been needing you, Wesley, and you've not been there.'

'Now, wait a minute . . .'

'And your mother . . .' Amy could feel control slipping from her, could do nothing to hold back the torrent of words. 'She was going crazy trying to contact you last night! Where were you, Wesley, or have I no right to ask that?'

'I'd best be going,' Gladys said, not wanting to be accused of interfering between husband and wife. 'I'll have the basin back when you've finished with it.'

'Don't go on my account, Mrs Renshawe,' Wesley said clearly. 'I'd almost forgotten you practically live here anyway.'

'Just go, Mam,' Amy said, without looking at her. 'I'll slip round and see you when Wesley's got what he's come for. What have you come for?' she asked when the front door slammed, shaking the house to its very foundations. 'I'm surprised you haven't brought an empty case with you this time, or maybe there's a furniture van outside?'

'I came to tell you about my father.' Wesley was all dignity and hurt feelings. 'But now you've said that, I might just as well take a few things with me.' He stretched out a hand and lifted the lid of the piano stool.

'It's not there,' Amy said quickly, because to say it quickly was the only way. 'I threw it all on the fire, the whole lot.' She swallowed. 'It took a long time to burn through. It almost put the fire out, clogging the grate up.' Amy couldn't forgive him for being so cruel to her mother. It wasn't even true!

Was she mad? Had she gone stark staring mad? Wesley narrowed his eyes as if the image of her standing there kept fading from his vision. She was wearing her hair different too, tucked behind her ears instead of drooping forward on to her cheeks. It altered the whole look of her, and the change in her appearance coupled with what she had done flared his temper.

'Do you know how many years it took me to collect that music?' He took two steps forward and grabbed her wrist. 'Some of those songs were as good as collector's pieces! They were my entire

117

repertoire! Part of me!' He twisted her wrist hard. 'That music meant more to me than you can ever hope to understand.'

'That's why I threw it on the fire,' Amy said into his face.

When he hit her it was as though her head had exploded. Her teeth caught her bottom lip, she tasted the saltiness of blood.

'I wanted to hurt you, just as you were hurting me,' she shouted, tears running down her cheeks and a trickle of blood running down her chin. 'If you'd been there and I'd had a knife I'd have stuck it in you!' Her voice broke on a sob. 'You let me down in front of everybody. You had to be centre stage – even to walk out on me!'

The second time he raised his hand to hit her, she jerked and backed away so quickly that her foot caught in the half-moon rug, making her lose her balance and fall, striking her forehead on the raised edge of the tiled hearth.

'Amy! Oh God, I'm sorry. God, I don't know what I'm doing.'

He helped her to her feet. She was alive, thank God. For a terrible heart-searing moment he had thought he might have killed her. She was holding a hand to her forehead, bringing it away and staring at the blood in disbelief.

'Amy? Let me get something . . . oh God, sit down here.'

He came back from the kitchen with a damp teacloth and held it to her forehead. She was going to have a lump like an egg, and there was a red bruise underneath her left eye. She looked awful, worse than awful, white and trembling, saying nothing. Driving him mad saying nothing.

'You fell,' he said. 'You tripped over the rug, twisted round and fell. Oh, God, Amy, speak to me! I wouldn't hurt you for all the world. You know that.'

She looked straight at him then, with an expression in her eyes he couldn't fathom. She was looking at him as if she was weighing him up and finding him wanting.

'Yes, you're right, I fell,' she said quietly. 'Now go, Wesley. Just go and leave me alone.'

How could he go with her sitting like that on the settee, with her face all out of flunter and her lower lip beginning to swell? His stomach churned. What would people say if they thought he'd done all that? They would think he was a monster, and he wasn't. They would think he was rough, like the men who came home drunk on a Friday night and knocked their wives about. It would get around, and people would believe Amy, not him, never dreaming she had provoked him beyond endurance, when he was worried sick about his father lying so ill in hospital. Never believing for one minute that she could be vindictive enough to burn all his music. The thought of what might be said about him, the light he would be seen in, trembled his legs, dried his throat so that he sat down in what used to be his chair when he lived there. He buried his face in his hands.

'I'm all right, Wesley.' Amy's voice was as calm now as if nothing had happened.

Which didn't surprise him. She was like that – always the one to reassure, to put things back on an even keel. She must have been of unsound mind the day she burned his music. He wished he didn't have such a vivid imagination, because with his eyes closed he could see her thrusting sheet after sheet of music into the fire, jabbing at them with the poker, glorying in the destruction of them. Was it any wonder he had lost control? Any man would have done the same – some men would have throttled her – some men had killed for less than that. No one would blame him if they knew the truth.

He lifted his head and saw her watching him, touching her forehead and wincing.

'I was going up to the infirmary to see your father this afternoon, but I'll wait until tomorrow, till this settles down.' She stood up, holding the tea-towel to her face. 'I'd like you to go now, Wesley.'

He stood up too, but how could he go until something was sorted out?

'I *fell*,' she said, reading his mind. 'I tripped over the rug and caught my head on the edge of the hearth. Thank you for coming to tell me your father is holding his own. I appreciate that.'

As he turned and walked away from her down the lobby to the front door he seemed to her to have shrunk, to have gone to nothing inside the beautiful camelhair coat, swathed round him like a dressing gown.

He closed the door quietly, with only the merest click.

She went upstairs, pulling herself up by the wall banister like an old, old woman. In the narrow bathroom, with grey light from the grey sky coming through the skylight, she bathed her face, trying to stem the blood from the small cut just lower than her hairline. She seemed to remember reading somewhere, or being told, that heads bled a lot, more than any other part of the body. A bit of blood went a long way, it was a well-known fact. But she didn't like the look of the cut on her forehead. It was like a small gaping mouth, obscene in its redness, still oozing blood.

She folded her face flannel into a square, pressed it against the place, rammed her hat over it, bringing the brim down almost to her eyebrows. Doctor Owen's surgery was a mere five minutes' walk away. Morning surgery was over, and he was on his way out to begin his calls, but when he saw Amy's face he turned back and led her through the dark and narrow passage beside his dispensary into his consulting room.

'I fell and bashed my head on the hearth, Doctor.' She sat down and removed her hat. 'It's me own fault for hitting the bottle before dinnertime. I was wondering if it needed an embroidery stitch in it?' She was laughing, as she always seemed to do when life hit her with a flat-handed slap.

The doctor's eyes were shrewd as he examined her face. 'You must have gone with an almighty wallop, lass.'

'Another step an' I'd have been up the chimney,' she said, quick as a flash.

How many miscarriages had she suffered? The good doctor didn't need to get down his boxes and take out her card to jog his memory. He'd been practising in Oldham when her first baby was born, perfect, but dead, a seven-pounds boy, but his predecessor had told him about it in grave detail.

'My guess is she'll never deliver a live child,' he had said, 'but she'll try and go on trying, if I'm not mistaken. She's not much more than a child herself and she's completely besotted by that husband of hers. He must have taken her straight from the classroom.'

Doctor Owen was touching the edges of the cut with expert fingers. 'I don't think there's any need for embroidery here.' He reached for the iodine bottle. 'A plaster maybe for a day or two. It's your lip that's come off the worst. You've nearly bitten through it, lass. Hubby all right?'

He knew. Amy was convinced of it. Were the marks of Wesley's fingers on her cheek? Had the bruises come up while she was walking to the surgery?

Her smile was agony, but she persevered with it. 'Wesley? He's fine. But his father's not well at all. He's got septicaemia. That's serious, isn't it?'

'Depends.' The doctor stood away from her to admire his handiwork. 'No special treatment for it as yet. No cure, but they'll come up with something one day.'

'People do recover from it, though?'

'Nothing the human spirit can do surprises me any more.'

'I like . . .' She hesitated. 'I love him very much, you see.'

She had shown herself up good and proper, she told herself, hurrying back up the hill, hoping not to bump into anyone she knew when she was looking like Greta Garbo hiding from her fans with her hat brim pulled low over her face. Fancy her telling the doctor that she loved Mr Battersby! Feeling the tears come into her eyes as she said it. It was funny, but since Wesley went away she was nowhere near as impassive – was that the word? – as she used to be. Every waking moment her heart was full of emotion so that she needed to tell those she was fond of that she cared for them. Was it in case they too went away and left her? She had a feeling Mr Dale – Bernard – would know the answer to that.

Turning the corner she bumped into Mrs Rakestraw from across the street on her way down to the Co-op.

'I fell,' she said quickly. 'But I'm expected to live.'

'You look like you've just gone three rounds with Joe Louis.' Mrs Rakestraw, clutching a big brown leather purse and a large shopping basket, barred her path. 'I saw your husband going in your house this morning.' She eyed Amy's swollen mouth. 'I hope you've patched things up and got together again. You've always been such a lovely couple.'

Amy tried to step round her, but the big woman hadn't quite finished.

'Did you know that Mrs Tunstall who works for Charlie Marsden happens to be a cousin of mine?' Amy was sure her lip was beginning to bleed again. 'She came round to see me first thing. Seems he's given her the sack, to set Dora Ellis on as his housekeeper. Don't tell me you don't know.'

'No, I didn't know.' Amy could only shake her head as she walked on.

'I always thought you were as thick as thieves.'

'So did I,' Amy muttered to herself, taking her key from her purse and letting herself thankfully into the house.

'I fell,' she told Dora, the first chance she got. 'Anyway, what are a few cuts and bruises here and there compared to your news? I've been sitting here all day waiting for you to come and tell me.'

Dora felt ill just looking at Amy's face. 'You look terrible,' she told her.

'Like I've just gone three rounds with Joe Louis?'

'I wouldn't say that exactly.'

'That's what Mrs Rakestraw said when she stopped me in the street to tell me that her cousin Mrs Tunstall had been round first thing sobbing on her chest because you're taking her job from her.'

Dora sat down with a thump on the empty piano stool. 'Charlie Marsden's jumped the gun! I haven't even given him my answer yet.' Her expression was filled with anxiety. 'He made me think Mrs Tunstall was past it and ready to retire – and all the time he was planning to cast her aside like a worn-out rag.'

'To replace her with someone younger and more beautiful,' Amy said, smiling – which was a mistake. The pain was no better and for the past hour she'd been wobbling a tooth with a finger, convinced it was coming loose.

'Wesley's there at the house with his mother.' Dora wasn't going to allow the suspicion that had just popped into her head to take root. Wesley Battersby might be a rotter, a villain of the deepest dye, but he would never strike a woman. He gave his seat up on the bus,

122

for goodness' sake, smoked Balkan Soubranie cigarettes, never missed sounding his aitches and never went without a tie except on his holidays.

'He came here to tell me about his father. To say he's holding his own.' Amy gave her tight wince of a smile. 'I'm glad he's supporting his mother.'

Dora's eyes narrowed. So he'd been here. Was that why he'd sat there all afternoon in the drawing room in his mother's house, smoking and telephoning Charlie Marsden's wife – arguing with her by the sound of it. Dora drew in her breath. What if Clara went back to Charlie? What price the housekeeper's job then? Suppose she chucked in her job at the mill, and the afternoon cleaning, only to find herself out of work?

'I wish Charlie Marsden hadn't jumped the gun,' she said, then immediately felt thoroughly ashamed of herself. Amy wasn't fit to be bothered with anybody else's problems just now. She looked so pale and so tired, and every time she pushed her hair behind her ears you could see her hands shaking. Dora frowned and chewed her bottom lip. How could you say to a person as proud and loyal as Amy: 'I think Wesley did that to you.'

'Are you sure I can't get you anything?' she asked again before she went. 'Promise me you'll go to bed right this minute.'

'I promise,' Amy said, sitting there just the same. As if she'd never move again.

There was no point in going back into her own house, not the way she felt. Dora knew she would never settle to anything. So after she'd closed Amy's front door behind her, she turned right instead of left.

If Bernard was surprised to see her, he didn't show it. 'To what do I owe this pleasure?' he teased, pulling a chair closer to the fire, lifting his jacket from the back of another one and putting it on.

'You don't need to do that,' Dora told him, though she knew that he would never sit talking to her in his shirt sleeves. This man wore politeness like a second skin. Like the wonderful Wesley? No, somehow not a bit like that. She sighed deeply.

123

'What's wrong, Dora?'

'Everything,' she answered. 'Life, I suppose.'

'Ah, life . . .' He sat down opposite to her, shook his head and smiled, ready to listen, she knew, willing to give her his undivided attention. She remembered him sitting like that with Greg in those last awful months, after she had him put away in an institution.

'Life is a bugger,' she said, leaned her head back and closed her eyes.

There was no embarrassment between them at all. Sometimes she would wonder if she had dreamed what had happened so long ago. She remembered watching this man lift Greg up on his pillows, and the way she would follow his hands, so gentle and yet strong. She would remember the way they had caressed her, soothed her, brought her back to life at a time when she was in total despair.

Bernard waited. Dora would talk when she was ready to, never using three words when two would do. He watched her carefully, realizing she was fighting sleep, knowing it was always like this for her if she stopped running, even for a moment.

No woman should have to work as hard as Dora Ellis. She was drooping with exhaustion, grey-faced, slack-eyed, her hands, idle for once, folded on her lap, red and raw-looking as potted meat, mottled, chapped, the nails stubbed and broken. The years caring for a semi-paralysed husband, going out to work, fighting her conscience, had broken her. Now, with only herself to care for, she was still running, forever telling herself that she must get back to the house where Greg still lay, a broken body lying in bed in that downstairs front room. Dora had told him quite recently that if she sat down for a minute she could still hear her husband's voice calling her, always needing, forever wanting.

'I've come about Amy,' she said at last. 'Not me.'

'So it's her life that's a bugger, not yours?' She was like a tiny cockney sparrow, he thought, the way she put her small head on one side and beaded her eyes at him.

'Nothing's troubling me, Mr Dale.'

'Bernard. Surely Bernard. Why can't you say it, Dora?'

She considered this for a moment. 'Because to me you're Mr

Dale. Always was and always will be. Sometimes I have to stop meself calling you Sir.'

'Dora! That's an insult!'

'No, it's not. It's a compliment if you set yourself to think about it.' She sat forward in her chair. 'Amy has to find a job. I mean that if she doesn't find one quick she'll starve. There's no money going into that house, Mr Dale, not a brass farthing. She worked part time for years and years and handed her wage packet over to the wonderful Wesley every Friday night.'

Bernard hid a smile. 'You don't like him much, do you?'

'I could stamp on his face and not bother to wipe the blood off me shoe. I could snatch the last drop of water from him when he was dying of thirst and pour it away.' She glared into space, savouring her dislike. 'Amy told me a long time ago that apart from a bit she had put by she had never had a penny piece to her name. Can you believe that?'

Bernard nodded. He could believe that all right. Down in London, not far from where he'd been born, women had chained themselves to railings for issues such as this. For the right to have at least a say in how the money they had earned was spent. Some of them had even died fighting for what they believed to be no more than a fundamental right, but up here in the north a woman like Amy Battersby still walked in her husband's shadow, echoing her husband's opinions, quoting him as if she had no mind of her own, handed over her wages as if she had no right to them. He wondered if this fiercely loyal friend of Amy's would have retained her independence if her own husband had been in a position to assert himself. He doubted it somehow.

'Has she any qualifications?'

'You mean certificates? Exams?' Dora gave a short laugh. 'Not a one. Amy is like me in that respect. Well, worse than me. I left school the day I was thirteen to go to work, but Amy was clever. She was going to try for college, go in for a big job like teaching, till you-know-who came along and kyboshed any hopes she'd ever had. His father frogmarched him to the altar from what I've heard, with Amy five months gone, and her future ma-in-law sobbing her socks off in the front pew.'

125

She was flushed now, certainly more animated. Sparring in this good-natured way had always been a bonus of their unusual friendship. Bernard could see she hadn't finished with him yet.

'And before you go on about night school, further education, adult training schemes, remember you tried that tack on me once. I told you then what I'm telling you now. As far as I was concerned it was a dead horse you were flogging. I'll go uneducated and ignorant to the grave, but Amy's got a better chance than me. She's got more up top than I'll ever have.'

'Oh, Dora, Dora . . .'

'It's true! She's always reading when she gets the chance. She's never away from the library.' She glanced at a book on the table. 'Ernest Hemingway. I bet she's read him, whoever he is when he's at home. None of your rubbish for her. Books about great lives, poetry even. And she does the crossword in the evening paper quicker than I could turn to the page. She's sharp is Amy.'

'You're fond of her, aren't you?'

The 'fond' was too much for Dora to cope with. 'What I admire about Amy is the way she's just carried on in spite of.'

'In spite of what?'

'Two babies born dead, and umpteen miscarriages, all because the Battersby line looks like ending with the wonderful Wesley.'

Bernard felt a physical jolt at her words. 'I knew about one baby but not that there were two.' He looked stricken. 'And certainly not about the other . . . the others . . . Oh, no wonder she has that defensive air about her. As though she's daring you to say anything kind to her.'

When he talked clever like this Dora lost the thread. 'So you see, she does deserve some help in the right direction. I don't want Amy to go down the same road as me. She deserves better.'

Anyone deserved better than Dora Ellis. Bernard wondered how long it had been since she'd had a cup of tea put into her hand, or eaten a meal she hadn't cooked, slept in sheets she hadn't washed. What was he supposed to do about Amy Battersby? What Dora had just told him about her was filling him with an illogical anger. He could see now why the two of them got on so well, had so much in common. On the surface nothing, but deep down everything.

126

'Last week,' he said quietly, 'there was a vacancy for a shorthand typist to work downstairs in General Office. We had ninety-nine applications, out of which we short-listed six. I had sorted through the applications myself, and found forty with School Certificates, most of them with credit passes, the vast majority able to type, some with diplomas from the Technical College. Ninety-nine hopefuls for the job of office girl whose main task would be to answer questions at the inquiry window.'

'So what chance is there for Amy? That's what you mean, isn't it?'

'I was thinking aloud.' He shrugged. 'The way things are going you'll need a First Class Honours Degree to work on the sweet counter at Woolworths, but I'll give the matter some thought. I don't suppose Amy can type?'

Dora relaxed. Now she had got Mr Dale working on Amy's problem there was bound to be a solution.

'She can learn,' she told him. 'Amy can learn anything she sets her mind to.'

Dora was just considering whether now was the right moment to tell him about her own incredible good fortune, when the telephone rang, almost jumping her out of her skin.

'Oh, no,' Bernard said when he answered it. 'Oh no. Oh, I'm so sorry.' He turned to Dora. 'Mr Battersby is dead,' he said. 'He died in his sleep at seven o'clock.'

8

Phyllis hoped that Amy's face would have healed up in time for the funeral. She knew that Amy would understand that the family must present a united front on such a sad occasion. There was a second cousin and his wife coming from Dorset, a first cousin in the shape of Ethel from St Helens and three Yorkshire relatives, all coming to pay their respects.

Amy said she understood perfectly, adding that by next week the plaster could be left off her forehead so that with a coating of Max Factor make-up no one would be the wiser. She wasn't being weak or lacking in spirit, she explained to Dora, just refusing to be difficult at a sad time like this.

'I can't think of anything more obscene than families quarrelling about funeral arrangements,' she said. 'So I'll go and stand with Wesley and his mother in the church and make everyone believe that there's no trouble between us.' Tears came into her eyes. 'For Mr Battersby's sake.'

'It's going to be a posh affair,' Dora said. 'No ham and tongue funeral spread – that wouldn't be grand enough. Old Ma Battersby's seeing her husband out with mushroom vol-au-vents. She's having all the food sent up from town. She's asking the Masonic lot and the Rotarians, not to mention her Inner Wheel friends and the staff from all three shops. I'm just waiting for her to ask me to wear a frilly pinny and cap, but since I told her I may be leaving to work for Charlie Marsden at the end of the month, I'm less than the dust.'

'I used pancake make-up once before and came out orange,' Amy said.

Dora knew she hadn't been listening, so there was no point in telling her that she was going round to Charlie Marsden's house that evening to square things up and get everything on a proper footing. Amy had taken it badly about losing her father-in-law. One thing on top of another, Dora supposed.

'I fell on the hearth. Tripped over the rug,' Amy had told Mr Dale, not taking the news in at first. 'I must go. I must go up to the house. Now!'

'The message was that you are not to do anything,' Bernard had told her gently. 'They're at the infirmary, anyway. It was just that they felt you ought to know.'

'I'll stop with you if you like,' Dora had offered, but Amy had refused and Mr Dale had agreed with her that there was really no need.

He had touched Amy's swollen lip with his finger and said that rugs were dangerous things, he'd always thought that. But Dora had suspected that he knew the truth.

Charlie Marsden apologized for his house being in such a mess. Apparently Mrs Tunstall had taken the huff and marched out with her pinnies and her slippers in a bag, refusing to work out her notice, saying that it would never have happened if Mrs Marsden had still been living there.

'I don't suppose it would,' Charlie had answered darkly, flummoxing poor Mrs Tunstall more than ever.

Lottie was doing her biology homework at one end of the dining-room table. 'This is Lottie,' Charlie said, just as the telephone rang. 'Excuse me,' he said, going into the hall and closing the door behind him.

Lottie blotted a line of spidery writing and gave Dora her full attention. 'Do you dye your hair?' she wanted to know. 'It's a funny colour.'

'Of course,' Dora said. 'I comb prune juice through it twice a week. It's a good job I like prunes, isn't it? They keep me regular as well, which is a bonus.'

Lottie rallied quickly. 'We're doing the chapter on reproduction. I'm writing about the placenta.' She narrowed her eyes. 'It's shed from the mother's body as part of the afterbirth.'

'Is that it?' Dora leaned over the table to study the diagram. 'Oh, look, there's the vagina. I've never seen a drawing of one of those before.' She glanced at the closed door, then nudged Lottie woman to woman. 'If I decide to come and work for your father, there's one thing I'd really like to know.' She lowered her voice to a whisper. 'What was it Mrs Tunstall did to get herself the sack? I'd like to know in case I make the same mistake.'

Lottie had already decided that she desperately wanted this funny little woman to take the job as housekeeper. Fancy her knowing about vaginas! Mrs Tunstall would have come over all indignant and walked away. Mrs Tunstall wouldn't even have known how to pronounce it. Let alone what it was for.

'She developed an uncontrolled passion for my father. Which embarrassed him. But don't let on I told you.'

'Did she tell him?'

'Not that I know of. She kept giving him burning glances, and the top off the milk.' Lottie picked up her pen as her father opened the door. 'I must get on.'

Dora studied Charlie in some depth as he showed her round the rest of the house. She knew Mrs Tunstall by sight, and the thought of the hatchet-faced elderly woman in the throes of unbridled passion for this fattish, red-faced little man, with receding hair and tiny blue watery eyes, was crazy. Why, he looked like he should be wearing violently checked baggy trousers and have a red ball stuck on his nose.

'This is the master bedroom,' he was saying, throwing a door open with a flourish. 'The sheets go to the laundry, but the other things . . .' He slapped his forehead with the flat of his hand. 'Mrs Tunstall should be telling you all this if she'd stayed to work her notice.'

Dora followed him out on to the landing. 'Perhaps she felt that you would understand her heart had its reasons.'

Charlie whipped round from showing her the inside of the large walk-in airing cupboard. 'What did you say, Dora?' He shook his head as if to show he must have imagined her remark. 'It's a big house as houses go. Mebbe some day . . . I don't know.' He led the way down the stairs and into the white-tiled kitchen with its magnificent Aga cooker. 'Only needs filling once and riddling twice,' Charlie told her proudly, turning round and pointing to the washing machine, with its round and gleaming stainless steel tub, and its rubber rollers clamped on top.

'There won't be any need for the laundry man to call here any more, I can tell you that,' Dora said. 'Not with this beauty there won't.'

'Does that mean you're going to take the job?' Charlie's little eyes lit up. 'Say you are and I'll go out and run the flag up.'

'Try and stop me,' Dora said, standing in the middle of the tiled floor, clasping her hands together with an ecstatic expression on her face.

She was quite a bonny woman, Charlie realized, from the depths of his sentimental heart. A nice little figure on her too.

Wesley told his mother that he thought The Cedars would be far too big for her now. He wasn't going to be so insensitive as to talk about sordid things like money, with his father lying in the Chapel of Rest down town, but he knew his father would have wanted him to take over the financial side of things.

'It's the ready that's going to be the problem,' he said. 'You know what Father was like about tying everything up to get the best dividends, and you know how secretive he was about his friendship with Harold Thomson. Solicitors shouldn't be personal friends with their clients, in my opinion.'

He sat beside Phyllis on the wide chesterfield and took her hand. 'What mustn't happen is you worrying about the paperwork. I bet Father never took the time to explain any of that side of the businesses to you?'

Phyllis's pointed chin wobbled. 'It wasn't that he didn't take the time, son. The shops were his side of our lives together. It was only natural that he didn't talk money to me. What man does?' Her eyes filled with tears. 'He kept any worries he might have had to himself. He didn't want me bothered.'

'And I'm here to see that you'll never be bothered.' Wesley

dropped a light kiss on her cheek. 'Now that I've got the car I can visit all three shops at least every other day.' He glanced at his watch. 'I must go, sweetheart, but I'll be back tomorrow. Try and have a little sleep.'

How good he was . . . Phyllis obediently closed her eyes. Edgar had always maintained that Wesley lacked moral fibre, but already the boy was proving him wrong. She sighed. What a pity he wasn't married to a girl of his own sort, with children at private schools, a dog, and a house in a better district.

She glanced at the telephone on its little round table. Amy would be ringing soon from a call-box asking for the umpteenth time was there anything she could do, anything at all that might help. Phyllis felt a teeny touch of guilt about refusing all Amy's offers, but surely the girl ought to realize that it would look far better if news of the trouble in the marriage didn't come out until after the funeral. She could cope with one, but not the other, not both together.

Anyway, Wesley had made it obvious he didn't want Amy round the house. He'd been most upset at bumping into her inside the Chapel of Rest where she'd apparently taken it upon herself to go and pay her last respects. Phyllis had seen the annoyance he tried in vain to hide. What did the girl look like with that red and bulging forehead and swollen mouth?

'I fell,' she'd said, which was obvious to anyone with eyes in their head. Besides which, she'd gone there in a fawn coat and hat trimmed with red, no decent black. It was a wonder the undertaker had let her in. But Amy had never had the slightest sense of occasion, always dressed as if she was going somewhere entirely different. God alone knew what she would turn up in for the funeral.

Looking up she saw an Inner Wheel friend coming up the path, bearing a huge sheaf of pink and white flowers and a suitably pious expression. Her car and chauffeur waited outside in the drive and as Phyllis let her in she knew for certain she had been right to keep Amy away.

Marriages in the Cresswell family didn't break up, they endured, they lasted through Silver and Ruby wedding celebrations, going on triumphantly to Gold. 'My son and his wife have split up . . .' Phyllis shuddered. How common it sounded. She'd read that two in every hundred marriages had failed last year. Just two, and her lovely Wesley had to be one of them.

Mrs Cresswell's son had married into Biscuits, and her daughter into Stainless Steel over in Yorkshire. A Paris-trained cordon bleu cook, the daughter gave dinner parties attended by the rich and famous. Phyllis was almost certain that J. B. Priestley had dined there a few years ago when he was in Yorkshire researching a book.

'Families are such a comfort at a time like this,' Mrs Cresswell was saying, looking round as if she expected to see a relative or two popping out of the wainscoting.

'My Cousin Ethel is coming to stay with me,' Phyllis said, making it up on the spot. 'Her parents were in Soap.'

Amy telephoned just before one o'clock. 'It's Amy. How are you, Mrs Battersby?'

She didn't really mean how are you; what she meant was you shouldn't be sitting up there in that big house all alone at a time like this. It wasn't natural. Amy's maternal grandmother had been a lapsed Catholic and she'd fascinated the young Amy with tales of family get-togethers that went on in Ireland from the moment of death to well after the funeral.

'There'd be cousins on every stair, babies asleep in the middle of the coats on the beds, and total strangers passing round the refreshments. Ater all, what is dying but the passing from one room into another?'

Amy wondered what her mother-in-law was making of death.

'Mr Battersby looked very peaceful,' she told her own mother. 'That awful jaundice seemed to have disappeared.'

'They touch them up,' Gladys said. 'I knew a woman with terrible acne, but in her coffin you could have taken her for Joan Crawford. Not a blemish!'

'If there's anything I can do . . .' Amy turned her back on a queue of one forming outside the call-box. 'I'm not working, you know. I could come at any time.'

'Dora's here this afternoon, and a friend called and brought me some lovely flowers. I was just arranging them when the telephone rang.' She sounded so cool, so composed. It was hard to believe what had happened. 'Wesley is being a tower of strength.' Phyllis's voice was tinged with pride. 'I always said his father didn't give him enough responsibility. Now he's proving his worth. I'm like any other woman who's been cherished all her married life. Now it's all left to me, I'm entirely at sea.'

'At least you would be if it wasn't for Wesley?'

'That's right, Amy. That's definitely right.'

What a strange conversation it was. The man outside the kiosk was glaring at Amy as if she'd been talking for at least an hour.

'Then I'll see you at the funeral, Mrs Battersby. Would you like me to go straight to the church?'

'Of course not. Wesley will come and pick you up around eleven and bring you here so that you can be in the first car following the hearse.'

Was her mother-in-law so bowed down with grief that she didn't know what she was saying? People often behaved strangely at times like this. Amy remembered her own mother busily unpicking and turning a blue skirt, pressing the seams with a thump thump of the iron, rushing to finish it even though she had no intention of ever wearing it. All that with her father lying in his coffin in the front parlour surrounded by flowers from practically every neighbour in the street. Had the truth not dawned on Mrs Battersby yet? Was she in shock?

'In shock?' Dora asked. 'She's in her element more like. She's already handed the car over to Wesley and yesterday I saw him loading the boot up with stuff.'

'What stuff?'

'Things from the house. I saw a small chair and a picture, and that little wine table that used to sit by Mr Battersby's chair, the one he kept his reading glasses and his smoking paraphernalia on. The one that was supposed to have belonged to Lord Derby at one time.'

'It did. Wesley told me once that The Cedars is stuffed with priceless antiques. The Battersby family goes right back.'

134

'So does mine. So does yours.'

'Who to, though? That's the question.'

'To Adam and Eve,' Dora said triumphantly. 'What I can't get over is the lack of modern equipment at your ma-in-law's. Did I tell you about Charlie Marsden's Aga cooker?'

'Only needs filling once and riddling twice.' Amy smiled. 'You have mentioned it once or twice.'

'And gas fires in every bedroom, and curtains with linings in, a brand new Hoover and a full set of tools. Best of all, a toilet upstairs. A white one with a polished mahogany seat.' She paused for breath. 'Did you know all that?'

'Wesley used to say the Marsdens were "jumped-up" because they've got rich quickly and all their possessions are new.'

'Therefore less posh?'

'Definitely less posh.'

Dora pondered on this. 'So a bedding chest that's all scratched and full of knot 'oles is of more value than a Lloyd Loom basket job with velvet padded seat?'

'Without a single doubt.'

'So the Battersby sideboard with woodworm scars at the back and drawers that won't open is supposed to be beautiful just because Oliver Cromwell once walked past it?'

'You're getting the idea, Dora.'

'Well, I'll be . . .'

Dora said a rude word, then in the very next breath asked Amy had she planned what to wear for the funeral?

'It all went off very well,' Dora remarked, after most of the mourners had gone. She filled a kettle and put it on the gas stove to boil. 'They didn't eat much, but I don't suppose they liked to tuck in, with it being a funeral.'

She thought that Amy looked as if she'd been carved out of a wooden plank, still and cold with no life in her eyes at all. In church earlier on, it had turned Dora's stomach to see her best friend standing there in the front pew on one side of Mrs Battersby, with the wonderful Wesley on the other. Just for the look of things; just

135

so the rest of the mourners could blink tears from their eyes and thank God for the never failing support and loyalty of families in their hour of need.

The black costume Amy had resurrected from the spare room wardrobe wasn't long enough in the skirt to be entirely in fashion, but the hat made up for it. Between them they had fashioned it from the top of a black woollen stocking, shaping it into a pirate's cap, pulling the top up into two points like small ears. Worn slightly on one side to cover the still visible mark on Amy's forehead, it suited her down to the ground. With her hair tucked behind her ears, turned under in a page-boy bob, her complexion glowing with Suntan powder and a touch of coral rouge, she looked Myrna Loyish, all sleek sophistication.

'It needs brightening up with something,' Dora had told her. 'A sparkly brooch or a link of coloured beads to fill in the neck.'

Amy said plain and simple were more her style, but she had accepted the loan of a pair of black silk stockings still in the cellophane wrapping, given to Dora as a token of gratitude when one of the boss men at the mill had moved to Manchester.

'Dora?' Wesley appeared in the doorway, smoking a cigarette. 'Mother says will you take the tea in now. I've just carried Cousin Ethel's luggage upstairs. She's in her element because she's staying on with Mother. I never knew they were all that friendly.'

In his dark suit, white shirt and black tie, with the brilliantine gleam of his thick hair catching the dying rays of the late afternoon sun, he looked handsome, strong. Twice the man he really was, Dora thought, only just managing to subdue an urge to bash him in the ribs with a corner of the heavy tray as she manoeuvred it past him.

As soon as she left the kitchen Wesley turned to Amy. 'Does it matter to you that I've hardly slept since . . .' He looked up at the ceiling as if unable to finish. 'You know that it wasn't me who did that?' He nodded at her swollen mouth.

'Who was it, then?'

'Amy . . . Amy . . . don't take that attitude. It doesn't become you.' He stubbed the cigarette out in an ashtray on the flat top of the old-fashioned wash boiler by the sink. 'What does become you is that costume and that very fetching hat. New, are they?'

Amy was sorely tempted to ask him where he thought the money would have come from to buy herself a new outfit, but she couldn't bring herself to say such a cheap remark at a time like this. For the past two hours the mourners in the drawing room had been carrying on as if it was a party, not a funeral. Wesley had chatted to everyone, the life and soul. If there'd been a piano in sight she wouldn't have put it past him to sit down and give them a turn. She had seen him topping up his mother's glass every time Phyllis put it down, and she had seen him sitting in his father's chair with his long grasshopper legs stretched out to the fire, smoking one cigarette after another.

'I'd like to say how much I appreciate the kindness you showed to the old man in the past few months. Mother told me you'd become good friends. He always had a soft spot for you.'

Amy could hardly bear to look at him. 'You don't need to thank me for being kind to your father. It wasn't exactly a trouble.' She swallowed. 'I liked him very much.' She bowed her head to hide the tears filling her eyes. 'I loved him, as a matter of fact.' Forgetting the tears she raised her head. 'What I can't help wondering is why I never really got to know him before . . .'

'Before what?' Wesley gave her a smile tinged with patience and gentle understanding.

'Before you went away.'

Wesley's smile became uneasy. 'Is that a stab in the back, love?' he stretched out a hand to flick the lapel of the black costume. 'You've gone all glamorous on me. Do you know that?'

The anger inside her was about to burst. She had held on to it tightly for the past hours, all through the droning church service, the walk down the aisle behind the coffin to the waiting cars outside, seeing nobody – except, from the corner of her eye, Bernard Dale sitting alone in the back pew – the ride through the streets out to the cemetery on its windy hill, the standing round the open grave with Wesley's hand on her arm in a public gesture of husbandly concern. How desperately she had wanted to jerk away.

'I'll remind you of where you last saw this costume,' she said, gritting her teeth so hard that her jaw ached. 'The last time I wore it was at another funeral, but the coffin was white and very small that time, Wesley. So very, very small.'

Instantly his anger flared. 'It was my baby too! My little son! Sometimes I think you forget that.'

For a moment she saw her own deep hurt reflected in his eyes, then almost as if she had imagined it his expression changed.

'I'll run you home if you like. Dora and Cousin Ethel are here to help Mother clear up. I've got to get back.'

'Well of course you have,' Amy said, hating herself but saying it just the same. 'She'll be waiting for you, won't she?'

In the end Wesley drove off alone, this time with a wrapped blue vase underneath his arm. Phyllis, according to Dora, had sherry coming out of her ears and would be better going upstairs for a nice lie-down.

'I'll go up with her,' Amy said, leaving Dora and Cousin Ethel to make a start on the clearing up.

Upstairs in the cold bedroom with its dark mahogany furniture and long heavy curtains, Amy persuaded Phyllis to take off her skirt and shoes and lie on her bed beneath the bottle-green taffeta eiderdown. Phyllis looked ill, not at all like herself, with her immaculately set hair mussed up and an untidy wave falling into her eyes.

'It went off very well, didn't it?' She was already half asleep. 'Wesley was so kind to everyone.' She closed her eyes. 'What would I do without him?'

'It was a beautiful funeral.' Amy lingered at the foot of the bed, trying not to look at its twin alongside. 'I thought the vicar spoke very well.'

'Remind me what he said.' Phyllis startled Amy by opening her eyes wide and raising her voice. 'I must ask him if he has a copy – if he has it written down.'

'He talked about Mr Battersby being a man for all seasons.' Amy sat down on the bed.

Phyllis's eyes closed. She felt as if she was falling down and

138

down, through a soft warm cloud. 'Tell me what he meant by that, Amy.'

'It was said over four hundred years ago, Mrs Battersby. About Sir Thomas More . . .' Her mother-in-law was asleep – suddenly and without warning, like a tired child. Amy went on speaking: 'It was so right, so very true. When Mr Battersby laughed he sometimes looked as if he was coming apart at the seams, and yet he could be . . . was so sad. He had a gift of matching the mood of the person he was talking to, of understanding right away what a person was trying to say. He was a very special man, Mrs Battersby.'

'She's gone off,' Dora said, coming up behind Amy. 'I've just settled Cousin Ethel in the guest room for a nice-lie down. She's a pleasant little body, isn't she?'

'She's had a hard life.'

'Who hasn't?' said Dora, following Amy down the stairs.

They worked together, like a team. Amy emptied ashtrays, carried plates through into the kitchen and started on the mammoth washing up. Dora ran the sweeper over the carpets, chunnering to herself all the time about the difference between the dilapidated Ewbank and the shining Hoover at the Marsdens' house. She was tired out as usual, hungry too.

'I know old Ma Battersby's upstairs on her bed in a drunken stupor,' she told Amy, 'but does she care that not a bite has passed my lips all day?'

'I don't suppose she realized.'

'Then she should have flamin' realized!' Dora's feet in the too tight court shoes, worn specially for the funeral, were giving her gyp. Her empty stomach had gone past the rumbling stage and was a yawning, aching void. Amy, she could see, was feeling just as bad, but struggling gamely on. As was her wont. Dora liked the sound of that so said it again – as was her wont.

There she was, her friend Amy, like the good little girl she had been born to be, wiping the sticky marks off the sideboard with a damp cloth, face flushed, the toffee-coloured hair falling round her face, the smart black hat discarded, the Tangee lipstick chewed

139

away. There she was, being sweet and kind, playing the part of a dutiful daughter-in-law, when all the time they treated her as less than the dust beneath their feet. Dora had seen the wonderful Wesley talking to her in the kitchen, and she had also seen him in the little den by the front door, at his father's roll-top desk, ferreting through a pile of papers. Up to no good, she would stake her life on it.

It was almost seven o'clock before they got away, what with Amy insisting they must make sure that Mrs Battersby was up and about and fully *compos mentis* before they left, and Dora spending a long time wrapping things up in greaseproof paper and transferring them to her zipped-up holdall.

'There's still enough left over to see her and her cousin right through next week,' she told Amy, covering plates and putting them on the marble slab in the walk-in pantry off the kitchen. 'If she had a fridge like at the Marsdens' she could have kept this lot fresh till Whitsuntide. Did I tell you about his fridge?'

'American. Bigger than the *Titanic*. Sets jellies before you can blink, with a compartment that makes ice cubes for the cocktail hour at six o'clock. Fancy his wife leaving all that behind.'

'And for such as Wesley, too.'

She looked quickly at Amy, but no offence seemed to have been taken. The telephone rang and was immediately answered from upstairs. Within minutes Mrs Battersby was back downstairs, hair neatly brushed into place and, apart from a cold pinched look to her nose, apparently in full control of herself again.

Amy had always found conversations with her mother-in-law almost impossible. Phyllis said things with such an air of finality that if she'd added 'Class dismiss!' at the end of her sentences, Amy wouldn't have been surprised.

'Thank you, Amy,' she said, patting her hair. 'No doubt we'll be in touch. You've been a great help. And Dora, I'll see you tomorrow afternoon.'

'God willing,' Dora said piously, edging out of the door with the holdall full to bulging. 'Mean old cow,' she said as soon as they were through the gate. 'Not a penny extra for all that work. That one wouldn't give you the time of day if she thought it would cost her anything.'

'A veritable feast,' Bernard said, coming into the house just as they sat down. He put a big brown envelope on the sideboard and turned to go. 'I've put a few pamphlets together, with details of secretarial courses and night classes. It might be worth your while looking through them, Amy.'

'Please sit down.' Amy nodded at the plates of mushroom vol-au-vents, the neat rolls of boiled ham, the fairy cakes in their fluted cases, the almond slices and the iced fancies. 'These are just one or two bits left over from this afternoon.' She blushed a bright scarlet. 'It seemed a shame to let them go to waste, but we made sure there was plenty for Mrs Battersby. We wouldn't want you to think . . .'

'Have a vollyvarnt, Mr Dale.' Dora passed over a plate.

Bernard hesitated. The poached egg on toast eaten well over an hour ago had been a culinary disaster, with the egg set rock hard and the toast as black and brittle as charcoal.

All at once he seemed to make up his mind. 'I've a bottle of something that would go down well with this,' he said, going out and leaving the front door wide open.

'What's all this then?' Charlie Marsden wanted to know, coming in without knocking. 'Can anybody play? Your front door's open. Did you know?'

Amy looked with something akin to dismay at his mobile rubbery face and mirthful eyes.

'Pull up a chair, Charlie,' Dora said. 'It's a free-for-all.'

Charlie had explained to Lottie exactly why he felt he had to go and see Amy Battersby. It was because he couldn't bear the thought of her going home from her father-in-law's funeral to sit alone and brood in that empty house.

'Alone because her husband has run away to a better life with Mother.'

'Well, I don't know about a *better* life, chuck. Certainly to a different one. Don't you ever feel you'd like to see your mother? Say just for a couple of hours? I could run you over in the van. It could be arranged, chuck.'

'I'm not bothered.' Lottie wished her father would make up his mind and go. There were one or two phone calls she wanted to make, and the hairs on her legs needed shaving again so she'd have to borrow his razor. With summer coming, she'd die of shame if anyone saw her looking like a gorilla.

'All right, then. I'll be off . . .' Charlie hesitated, sighed deeply. His stomach was playing him up again so he made himself a glass of hot water and sipped it slowly before putting on his little Tyrolean-like hat and departing, looking upset.

He would be glad when little Dora Ellis came to work at the house. It wasn't natural for a girl of fifteen to spend so much time on her own. Though Lottie could never have been described as 'natural', could she? Not in a month of Sundays. Why didn't she behave like other girls her age and go giggling in groups down to the library every evening? Why wasn't she a Girl Guide or a Sunday school teacher?

He climbed into his van and drove off, filled with pity for himself and his lot in life. He wouldn't put it past Clara walking back one day with her case, just like she'd been on her holidays. It wouldn't be the first time. But he wouldn't have her back, not this time. He couldn't face those last few years with her again. Putting him down in company, flirting with his pals, sticking her chest out at them. Laughing in his face when he accused her of showing him up and spending his hard-earned money like water, as if it grew on trees.

As different from Amy Battersby as chalk from cheese.

He clutched the driving wheel, taking a corner as if he was racing in the British Grand Prix.

Lottie telephoned her friend. 'Could I speak to Olive, please? This is Lottie Marsden. I've left my geography textbook at school and I need to know one or two things.'

Olive's mother reached out a hand behind her and closed the

142

door leading to the hall. She would never have believed herself capable of reading her daughter's diary, but she had. For her sins she had.

Lottie Marsden figured on almost every page. It seemed as if Olive had taken it upon herself to keep a detailed log-book of the Marsden girl's unsavoury doings. A lot of it seemed to be in some kind of simple code, but it hadn't taken much imagination to decipher the unwholesome gist of it. Which was that Lottie Marsden's parents weren't worthy of the name, that they were either drunk or having sexual relations with other people, at times both at once. That Lottie herself was on occasions beaten senseless, and that the only light in her life was her close liaison with a boy called Jimmy who only needed to whistle outside the house late at night for Lottie to rush outside and hurl herself into his waiting arms.

If Olive's mother hadn't had both feet firmly on the ground and known Charlie Marsden for the amiable chap he was, she would have telephoned the RSPCC. As it was, she merely told Lottie that Olive couldn't come to the phone as she was too busy doing her homework, and that she would prefer it if Lottie didn't telephone quite so much.

'Is Lottie Marsden good at English? At writing stories?' she asked her daughter later that night.

'She always comes top,' Olive said. 'She's going to write books one day.'

'That comes as no surprise at all,' her mother said, rolling up her knitting and putting it away.

'Can you come round?' Lottie asked the boy with the husky voice, seeing him in her mind's eye, clutching the telephone close to his ear and blushing bright red.

'Okay.'

'Right now?'

'Okay.'

'He'll be back soon, so we haven't got long.'

'Okay.'

143

Jimmy Dibden had a long way to bend to put on his bicycle clips. So tall he walked with an apologetic stoop, he cycled the short distance to the Marsden house, one hand lightly holding a handlebar, the other one in his pocket.

Lottie let him in at once, led him through into the sitting room, where they fell onto the chintz-covered settee and glued their lips together, only surfacing for long enough for Jimmy to remove his glasses before they set to again.

Wesley drove his father's car with one hand on Clara's silken knee. Now that the funeral was over she felt she deserved a bit of an outing after spending so long on her own, wandering round the shops in the afternoons or going to the pictures. She accepted that she couldn't have foreseen Wesley's father's death, but even so nothing was turning out as she had expected it to. It wasn't that the excitement was wearing off, it was that the excitement seemed to have been lacking in the first place. She glanced sideways at the devastatingly handsome profile of the man beside her.

This was the same Wesley who had set her on fire with his smouldering glances, whose touch had filled her with longing so that their snatched moments together were a mixture of heaven and hell. He had promised her everything, told her they would be out of that poky little flat in a matter of weeks, brought her flowers, scent, told her over and over that she was the most beautiful woman in the world, kissed her all over, even first thing in the morning, then gone downstairs to sell cigars and tobacco flake to men on their way to work.

It wasn't that she hadn't been perfectly honest with him. She had warned him she couldn't cook, wasn't domesticated, would never have made a nurse, but he still expected a meal to be ready at the end of the day, even though she'd told and told him that the gas cooker should have been an exhibit in a museum years ago.

Amy, she supposed, would have a hotpot in the oven, with a rice pudding slowly simmering on the bottom shelf when he got home from work. Amy had massaged his head when he had a headache because he had told her so, and she had darned his socks instead of throwing them away when they got holes in them. Amy had been a paragon of all the flamin' virtues, by the sound of her.

'Did she do this? And this?' she had asked, kissing the corners of his mouth, teasing, caressing, guiding his hand to the buttons of her blouse, to the fastenings of her suspenders, the button at the side of her crêpe-de-Chine French knickers.

He had lost weight, he told her, with so much lovemaking; he was spent, a man almost destroyed by the strength of his passion. She was in his mind all day long, he couldn't get enough of her.

'If you take me home I can pick up a few more clothes,' she said, as they drove past the Hoghton Arms. 'I can see how Lottie is and have a word with Charlie about one or two things.'

'Whilst you're doing that, I'll call in and pick up my flannels and a couple of cravats. I think it's better if I don't go up to Mother's house. Poor dear, she looked worn out when I left this afternoon. I'll ring her when we get back.'

Clara said nothing. Today wasn't the day to have even the mildest kind of confrontation about Wesley's mother, but this poor dear this and poor dear that would have to stop. It sickened her. Just because a woman gave birth to a child it didn't give her the right to own that child body and soul for the rest of its life. Some women – well, most women, she supposed – had children as a kind of insurance against their old age. But not her, not Clara, thank God. The last time Charlie had taken her on holiday to Scarborough there'd been a middle-aged couple in the hotel with two of their grandchildren. Two snotty-nosed whining little brats, for ever wanting to go to the lavatory or demanding an ice-cream cornet or sweets, and she'd thought how awful to have got your own offspring grown up then start all that again with another flamin' generation. Thank God she and Lottie had nothing in common – the umbilical cord had been well and truly severed there. And thank God that after the horrendous experience of Lottie's birth, the doctor had told her they'd done something clever, like tying up tubes, so that she'd never have to suffer that hell again.

When they turned into the well-known avenue, there was a bike propped up against the privet hedge. Clara noticed it as Wesley was

145

driving away, but when she went into the house Lottie was alone. The sofa cushions were any old how, with one down on the floor.

'Mother!' Lottie looked angry, shocked, embarrassed, all at the same time. 'I didn't know you were coming tonight.'

'Apparently not.' Clara rushed to the front door, opening it just in time to see the tail light of a bike disappearing down the long avenue. 'You've had a boy in,' she said. 'As I came in the front he went out of the back!' She sniffed. 'I can smell something funny.' She snatched at Lottie's hand and looked at her fingers. 'You've not been smoking, have you?'

How lovely she was. Lottie had never quite been able to come to terms with her mother's looks. Her eyes were the colour of bluebells, squashed wet bluebells, and her skin had a soft down on it, like a peach, so faint as to be almost invisible. You could look at her and never want to look away.

'You'll get yourself into trouble if you mess about with boys,' Clara was saying now. Her beautiful eyes narrowed. 'You haven't, have you?'

'Haven't what?'

'Been messing about.' All at once Clara lost patience. 'I suppose you'll be telling me next that there wasn't a boy in this room. With you. On that sofa.' She stared at Lottie's mouth. 'Kissing you.'

Lottie's heart was beginning to steady now. She gave a trill of a laugh. 'What boy?' She opened her hands in a dramatic gesture. 'What boy?' she said again.

Clara's blue eyes raised themselves ceilingwards, then she turned to go upstairs. 'Where's your father? Out with the lads?'

'Gone to see Mrs Battersby.' Lottie really enjoyed the way her mother's head whipped round. 'He goes to see her a lot. Now that she's on her own. They're never out of each other's pockets.'

In her bedroom Clara sat down on the peach and white quilted bedspread and drank in – took in to herself – the softness of everything, the paleness, the dreamy peachy colour of the curtains, the thick carpet, the soft wash on the walls. There was a thin film of dust on her dressing table, but she supposed Mrs Tunstall didn't bother to come in here every day.

Lottie had followed her up and was drooping in the doorway, not standing, hunching her shoulders as if weighed down by a heavy yoke.

'I've never done anything dirty,' she said. 'You have to believe that.'

But Clara's mind was on other things. 'It looks to me as if Mrs Tunstall is skimping her work. The stair carpet needs a good brushing and this room hasn't been bottomed in weeks.'

'Mrs Tunstall's left. We're getting a Mrs Ellis any day now. She lives next door to Mrs Battersby, where Father's gone tonight. I expect he heard about her that way.'

'Mrs Ellis?' Clara felt the name should ring a bell. 'What's she like?'

Lottie considered. 'Petite,' she said at last, pursing up her mouth. 'Makes you laugh. Years and years younger than Mrs Tunstall. More glamorous. Wears floaty clothes. No husband. No children. Nicely spoken.'

'So why isn't she working on the perfume counter at Afflick and Brown's in Manchester? A gem like that wouldn't lower herself to housekeep for you and your father.'

'She has a sad past.'

'Who hasn't?' said Clara, getting up from the bed and pulling open a drawer. 'I've remembered the Mrs Ellis you're talking about. She came to the Dramatics once looking like she'd been sleeping rough on a bench in the park for three weeks.' She turned round dangling a cone-shaped bra from her fingers. 'I'd forgotten you could tell lies to music, but I'm not going to ask you why because I gave up trying to fathom you, madam, a long time ago.'

Lottie said: 'Your hair needs bleaching. It's all black at the roots.'

'Thank you very much.' Clara turned back to the drawer in exasperation.

Yet something in Lottie's closed and obstinate face, her telling eyes, filled her with pity. It wasn't Lottie's fault that whatever relationship they might have had was doomed from the start. Clara could never tell her the truth – the truth could easily destroy a girl of Lottie's temperament. Clara didn't need a psychiatrist to tell her that.

'How about going down and making me a cup of tea?' she asked, seeing in her mind's eye the dark young man she had met at a dance all those years ago, when she and Charlie had quarrelled and he had left her to find her way home alone. Dear God, if only she had not been alone!'

Even now when she allowed herself to think about it she felt the same sinking of the spirit, the same disbelief that she could have let a total stranger have his way with her round a corner, leaning against a wall. It was so awful, so stupid, so degrading, her heart still curled in shame when she thought about it. She walked towards the door, cringing visibly at the memory. It hadn't been rape, not quite. Her struggling had been token, that was all. He had tried to give her money when she cried after it was over, but she had run the rest of the way home, never wanting to think, to dream of him again, only to forget, to blot out his memory for ever.

Downstairs Lottie was taking two cups and two saucers from the cupboard, setting them on the table, opening the door of the fridge to take out a bottle of milk. Making a nonsense of the forgetting, forcing Clara to remember the black-haired young man whose name she had not known. Forcing her to realize what in all these years she had tried to ignore – that Charlie was not, could not possibly be Lottie's father. Merely to look at Lottie was to see the stranger again.

'Are you still doing without sugar for the sake of your figure?'

Lottie held the spoon poised over the basin, then dropped it with a clatter on to the table, bewildered, hurt and uncomprehending at the expression of sheer dislike on her mother's face. As though the very sight of her daughter had suddenly turned her stomach, as though just looking at her had made her ill.

'I'm going out for a minute,' Lottie said, going into the long back garden in the dark, leaning up against the empty greenhouse with her face lifted to the sky, her mouth open and her eyes closed. As if she was sunbathing, trying to get a bit of a tan.

Wesley heard the laughter the minute he opened the front door.

They were there round the table, the four of them, with a

148

champagne bottle in the centre. Dora from next door, brushing crumbs from her flat chest, Charlie with his clown's face, Dale the jessie from up the road, and Amy, staring at him mesmerized.

They all went quiet and well they might, sitting there like that having a party, drinking champagne out of cups, enjoying themselves, eating what looked like . . . All at once he found his voice.

'That's funeral food!' he accused. 'My father's funeral food. I recognize the vol-au-vents. Oh, my God! Have you no feelings?'

Amy was on her feet, holding out her hands to him. 'It's not like that, Wesley! It's not a bit what it looks like . . .'

'We buried him today, and here you are – the four of you! God, I feel sick.'

'I can explain, old chap.'

That was Dale, the jessie, the conchy, with his la-di-da voice.

'Don't you "old chap" me!' Wesley felt the anger rise in him, the familiar quick flash of temper he had no power to control. Dora realized what he was about to do, but before she could stop him he grabbed a corner of the tablecloth and yanked it towards him, crashing plates, food and the empty champagne bottle to the floor.

'Out!' he shouted. 'The lot of you!' He stood there like the wrath of God, pointing to the door. 'I'm waiting. Get out of my sight, all of you!'

'Best do as he says,' Dora whispered. 'It's for the two of them to sort this lot out.'

One by one they filed down the lobby, shambling shamefaced, so embarrassed they didn't know where to look.

Bernard turned at the door. Came back. 'If you touch her,' he said quietly, 'I'll swing for you. Gladly.'

Wesley moved quickly, but not quickly enough for Bernard Dale. Before he could strike, his clenched fist was held in a grip of steel.

'I'm warning you, Battersby. Do you hear?'

Wesley's eyes bulged as he tried to break free, but it was hopeless. His struggles merely strengthened the other man's hold on him.

'It was no pre-planned party. Get that quite straight. Amy wished no disrespect to your father, and neither do we. Right?'

The way he dropped Wesley's arm betrayed his contempt.

'That was telling him.' Once out of the house Charlie quickly regained his composure.

'Better than George Raft any old day.' Dora opened her front door and invited them in. 'I'll make a cup of tea. We can hear through the wall if he starts anything.'

'He won't.' Bernard made his excuses and walked away, raising an invisible hat in a polite gesture. Remembering his manners even at a time like this, Dora thought.

Charlie followed her down the hall. 'He's a bit of a funny fella, isn't he? Not from these parts, is he?'

'London.'

'That accounts for him talking like a foreigner, then.' Charlie flexed his muscles. 'I wouldn't like to come up against him in an alleyway on a dark night.'

'Speak for yourself,' Dora said cheekily, putting a cob of coal on the fire and poking the ashes till they glowed a fiery red. She straightened up, putting a finger to her lips. 'Did you hear that? Sounds like the wonderful Wesley is on his way already.'

The humiliation was more than Wesley could take. To be made to look such a fool, such a weakling, in front of people. Charlie Marsden would have a field day reporting it all to the lads at the pub. And look at Amy, calmly picking up some of the mess on the floor, no apology, nothing. Not even some kind of explanation.

'Well, Wesley?' She had met his gaze unflinchingly. 'I appreciate that what you saw when you came in must have given you a bad impression.' She held up a hand. 'No, wait. Hear me out, please. I went along with what your mother wanted today. I played the part of a loving wife and dutiful daughter-in-law, because that was the way she wanted it. But it was just a play, wasn't it? Like the plays you act in, with you the hero, being charming to everyone, even to me because you were in public, because you had an audience.' She shook her head slowly from side to side. 'I did it for love of your father, for love of your mother, if she was interested.'

'But not for love of me?'

He was getting that little-boy-lost look about him and she couldn't bear it.

'Wesley! Oh, you're not really listening, are you?' She lifted her chin. 'You have no right to walk into my house without even knocking, and no right at all to behave as you did.'

Wesley took a step towards her, but she didn't flinch. The white-hot anger had gone from his expression. He was actually smiling, a tight, cold little smile.

'Whose house did you say this is, Amy? Did I hear you say *your* house?'

The crash of the front door slamming made Dora next door straighten up from tending the fire.

9

'I think I'll knock on Dale's door on my way home,' Charlie told
Dora. 'I'd like to shake him by the hand for the way he stuck up for
Amy. I'd have laughed my socks off if I hadn't known it was deadly
serious.'

Dora was still feeling a bit shaky, a lot put out. The scene with
Wesley had left her with a nasty feeling in the pit of her stomach.
For a moment she had glimpsed that other Wesley, the one she had
always known existed, so well hidden beneath the charm and the
dazzling good looks. He'd been livid and, to be honest, she could
understand his feelings. It must have looked bad, them sitting
round the table stuffing themselves with funeral food, even if she
had only brought it home to save it from going off. So in a way it was
all her fault.

'I'd leave Mr Dale well alone if I were you,' she said. 'He's not a
violent man by nature, but he could make mincemeat out of Wesley
Battersby with one arm tied behind his back. He stepped out of line
tonight and he'll need to be alone for a while to sort himself out. He
has to make reasons in his head for everything he does.'

'You seem to know him very well.'

'I used to work for him.'

'So when you work for me you'll have me all fathomed.'

'I've got you fathomed already.'

Charlie laughed. 'I still think I'll give him a knock.'

'No!' Dora stood her ground. 'You'll have to take it from me that
he won't want company tonight. He's private. He lets other folks be
themselves, and expects the same consideration from them.' She
showed him to the door and nodded at the van drawn up at the kerb.
'Go home. Please. I know what's best. Honest.' She gave him a wry
smile. 'I'll be able to start work at your house quite soon, if that's

okay with you. Mrs Battersby will be glad to see the back of me when she hears about tonight.'

'That's if Wesley tells her.'

Dora sniffed. 'He'll tell her all right. He's good at running to his mother with his troubles. He's been doing it for years.'

Charlie glanced at his van, then back to the little woman standing up to him with such determination. They were soon to be employer and housekeeper, but anyone passing would never guess it. They'd think they were on far more familiar terms. He accepted it was his own fault entirely. He should never have asked Dora to call him Charlie. Look how she called the London chap Mr Dale. Authority – that was what he was lacking. He was too matey, too all-pals-together. Too ready for a laugh. Good old Charlie. Undignified –definitely undignified.

He didn't drive off for a full five minutes. Just sat there drumming his stubby fingers on the steering wheel, the black mood on him again. He would never have been a boss-man if his father hadn't died and left the business to him and his brother. Without that inheritance he would still be a jobbing plumber, lugging his tools round the streets, wearing overalls, getting stuck in, doing all the mucky jobs himself instead of allocating them to his workmen. He chewed on nothing for a while.

And yet . . . and yet . . . only the other week it had got back to him that one of his men had said Charlie Marsden was the best gaffer in town. Fair-minded, he'd said, always ready to listen. Worthy of respect, because they all knew they wouldn't be asked to do any job the gaffer wasn't ready and willing to do himself if needs be.

Charlie raised his head, pushed the pea-sized hat to the back and nodded so hard it slipped forward again. Did it matter what Dora Ellis called him? There was respect there in spite of all her cheeky ways. Dora would know not to overstep the mark, and Lottie liked her too – which meant a lot.

He started the engine, let in the clutch, moved slowly forward. Amy Battersby liked him too, he could tell. Now there was a woman and a half for you. He glanced sideways at her house and saw the living room light shining through the ruby-red glass panels in the vestibule door.

Dora hadn't gone straight in there as he had thought she would. It seemed they were all pussy footing carefully round a delicate situation. Not Charlie's style at all. For two pins he'd ignore Dora and go and shake old Bernard by the hand to congratulate him on sticking up for Amy so magnificently. But that wouldn't be dignified, would it? From now on Charlie Marsden was going to be a changed man.

The van rattled round the corner. In this fresh mood of optimism he could see himself being Mayor one of these fine days. Wearing the chain of office and sitting in the Mayor's Parlour. Telling them all down at the Town Hall what to do and how to do it.

Bernard heard the van, held his breath in case it stopped, then breathed again. For a moment he had thought it was going to be Charlie come to talk over what had happened, to tread roughshod over what was better left to lie untouched.

He stared down at a photograph in his hand, ran a finger round the sweet face of the lovely young woman smiling into the camera. He felt the tightening of his heart, the quickening of its beat, asked himself why he had felt the need to take the photograph from its hiding place in his desk to look at it after all this time.

With his gift for self-analysis he knew that the moment he had gripped Battersby's arm the years had rolled back, and he was facing the man who he still believed had been responsible for his wife's death all those years ago.

He got up, went to the desk, took out a yellowed piece of newsprint and smoothed it out. Usually, to read small print, he wore his glasses, but not this time. He could have repeated it word for word without even glancing at it.

TRAGIC ACCIDENT AT BATTERSEA FLAT

On Thursday evening at half-past seven, Anna Dale (29), wife of Bernard Dale, a local government clerk, fell to her death down a flight of stone stairs. She suffered a head injury from which she never regained consciousness. A man who witnessed the fall was taken in for questioning but released later. There are no suspicious circumstances.

154

Bernard had trained his mind over the years not to think on things destructive. A spiritual man rather than a religious one, he had accepted his wife's death while never really coming to terms with it. But he had discovered that in spite of his resolution it only needed one small thing, the way a woman turned her head, the apprehension in her eyes, the vulnerability of a woman when life kicked her in the teeth . . . He put the photograph and the cutting back into the document drawer of his desk, grabbed his coat and hat from the pegs at the foot of the stairs and went out, crashing the door behind him.

For almost an hour he walked hard and fast, climbing the steep streets, away from the centre of the town, till he could look down on twinkling lights, the pencil shape of mill chimneys pointing to the sky, while behind him stretched over thirty miles of fields and woods to the sea. He stood, hands deep in the pockets of his raincoat, aware of the darkness, the unheard pulsating life of the town, his own heartbeats. Above him the sky was alive with stars, but he did not look up. He knew that he was going to have to relive it all once more in his mind, hoping that one day it would make some kind of sense. Turning, he retraced his steps, walking slowly now, head bent, shoulders hunched, lost in memory.

He married his Anna in 1925, a marriage long delayed because as the only child of ailing parents it was taken for granted she would stay at home and look after them. When Anna's father died, the wedding took place and they moved in with her mother, not the best of arrangements, they both agreed, but Bernard liked his mother-in-law, admired her independence and the way she fought to the last ditch not to move in with them to the new flat he found in Battersea, finally accepting with great reluctance that she was far too frail to manage on her own.

Without needing to close his eyes Bernard could 'see' the flat with its front door built in to make it look like a house – very important, according to Anna. The flat was filled with new and wonderful amenities, such as a white-tiled bathroom and toilet, a separate balcony, a separate space for clothes drying, and out in the small back garden a coalshed with an attached lean-to for Bernard to keep his bicycle and the lawnmower they would buy one day. There was a wide cream fireplace with a raised tile hearth, walls distempered to a pale peppermint green with a picture rail to break the monotony of completely bare walls. The outside was pebble-dashed with a slate roof, and the elderly couple living downstairs were so quiet Anna felt obligated now and again to knock on their door, just to check that they hadn't quietly died without telling anybody.

He had walked the whole length of a long road without noticing, registering nothing but remembering that Thursday evening of twelve years ago as if it was yesterday.

He was relaxing after work, sitting in his chair with a book open on his knee, watching Anna opposite to him, busy with her sewing, hemming something or other with quick busy fingers, looking up now and again to smile at him. Her mother had gone to bed straight after tea, reeking of wintergreen, clutching a stone hot-water bottle to her chest, suffering from a summer cold which she swore was ten times more upsetting than the winter variety, always destined to settle on the chest unless ruthlessly dealt with from the first sneeze.

Why hadn't he been the one to jump up and go out to the corner shop when he found he had run out of cigarettes? Why had he let Anna go? Why, in God's name, why? She had said she needed a bobbin of white cotton and would get that at the same time; she had said it was such a lovely evening she wouldn't bother with a coat, and she had said she would be back in a few minutes.

The recollection of those few minutes sent him reeling into a dusty privet hedge, off balance, consumed by the hurt that he sometimes felt would never go away.

There had been noise, a neighbour came in, said something. Bernard ran to the top of the stairs and saw Anna lying at the bottom with an arm across her face, the position she often slept in. The man bending over her looked up, his handsome face shocked into an ugly mask of horror.

Anna was dead. Bernard knew that the minute he touched her. Guessed that her neck was broken. His reaction had been swift,

156

immediate, taking the man so much by surprise that he made no attempt to defend himself.

'I didn't touch her,' he found the breath to say. 'I spoke to her, that was all, and she tripped. I swear to God I didn't touch her.'

Bernard had lifted the man off his feet by the lapels of his jacket, jerked him up, held him dangling, shaking him in the way a terrier shakes a rat.

'You knew she was afraid of you,' he hissed through clenched teeth. 'You knew she couldn't stand you touching her – you knew!'

Nothing was ever proven, and even Bernard himself didn't believe that the man who had convinced himself he was God's gift to women had done any more than tease Anna, maybe stretch out a playful hand. So that she had jerked away, missed her footing, stepped off into space, into a void of nothing, with a concrete floor to break her fall.

Bernard blinked the tears from his eyes, straightened up and walked on, calmer now he had forced himself to live it through. It was a long time ago and a hurt so deep cannot be sustained for ever, but back there in Amy's house he had looked into her husband's face and seen again the face he had tried to forget, the handsome weak face of a man who sees himself as irresistible, who cannot bear to think he could ever be rebuffed.

Bernard had come to the end of the long road. Round the corner, laid out beneath the night sky, was the town with its ribbons of light, the blackness behind that was moorland and hills, little running streams, stone cottages and drystone walls. A countryside he loved, a place that had brought him to a kind of peace.

Wesley and Clara were silent on the way home. He was still smarting from the shame, the humiliation of being bested by a man he considered to be beneath his contempt. Dale had seemed quite at home sitting round the table with Charlie Marsden and the sharp-tongued Dora, all laughing their heads off and tucking in at food bought specially to see his father off in style. Amy had disappointed him – appalled him would be a better word.

157

'How was Amy?' Clara seemed put out too. 'I believe Charlie was with her, or was that another of Lottie's flights of fancy?'

'He was there all right.' Wesley pressed his foot down hard on the accelerator. 'Amy was having a party, a champagne party. The last person she expected to see was me.'

'Amy? A party? With champagne?' Clara laughed out loud. 'Good for her! I've thought before that let off the leash your wife could be a bit of a lass.'

'Let off the leash?' Wesley turned a corner practically on two wheels. 'What do you mean by that?'

'Well, you kept her down, didn't you? Most people guessed that. Just because you did the right thing and married her when you got her pregnant in her gymslip, you saw to it that she was subservient to you, out of what you felt should be gratitude. I bet she cleaned your shoes.'

'Only because she wanted to!' Wesley overtook a red Ribble bus with no more than an inch to spare.

Clara closed her eyes and decided that if she was to arrive back at the flat in one piece it might be advisable to change the subject.

'Lottie had a boy in with her, but he skedaddled the minute he heard my key in the door. She denied it of course, but it appears she was telling the truth for once when she said that Charlie was at Amy's house.'

'*My* house.' Wesley jerked at the steering wheel, causing Clara to clutch at the door handle for support. 'My house, given to me by my father on my wedding day.'

'To you, or to both of you?'

'To *me*! To *me*!'

It was no good asking him to slow down, not in the mood he was in. Clara tried again: 'Lottie told me that your next-door neighbour, Dora Ellis, is going to work for Charlie as his housekeeper. Do you reckon there could be any truth in that?'

'No.' Wesley was sure about that one. 'Dora Ellis works for my mother, has done for years.' He gave a hard laugh. 'But she won't be working for her much longer when I call in on Mother in the morning and tell her what I found. Mother will be shot of her so quick Dora won't know what's hit her.'

Clara shut up. Something had rattled Wesley badly, something much more than finding Amy having a bit of fun with friends. Maybe it wasn't in the best of taste on the evening of his father's funeral, but life was for the living, to be enjoyed, not endured. She felt no personal sense of loss at old Mr Battersby's death, never having met him, but he was an old man, into his seventies, and he and Wesley hadn't exactly been buddies.

She couldn't remember her own father, but she had gone to her mother's funeral in a red hat, and why not? Why pretend feelings that weren't there in the first place just to put on a show? When she died she wanted a jazz band at her funeral, no mention of God, no hymns, and anyone who cared to come wearing bright colours. She didn't want to live too long, growing old and decrepit, losing her hearing, her sight and, God forbid, her teeth.

Wesley slammed on his brakes to avoid running into the back of a taxi, almost catapulting Clara through the windscreen.

That night his lovemaking was filled with a frantic urgency, an aggression that Clara found exciting, awakening a response that surprised even herself.

'You'll have to go and see Amy more often,' she told him, when it was over and they lay exhausted in each other's arms. 'If this is what seeing her does for you.'

But he was asleep, seemingly from one breath to the next.

Amy's mother called round early the next morning on her way to the Co-op. 'You look shocking,' she said, 'but I thought you looked very nice at the funeral yesterday. You suited that hat. I've not seen it before.'

'It was nice of you to go to the church, Mam, especially as Mrs Battersby hadn't thought to ask you back to the house.'

'She thought all right, thought I wasn't good enough for her la-di-da relations. What does she think I'd do? Talk about passing wind, or spit in the fire? I can be as refined as she thinks she is when I want to be.'

Gladys's nostrils twitched with suspicion. Something was up with Amy, something on top of all her other worries. She had that shut-in look about her, that air of obstinacy, of keeping things to herself. Gladys wished her husband was alive. He could have wheedled out of Amy what was wrong with her.

Standing there in her daughter's living room, with her basket over her arm and her shopping coat and hat on, she had a clear recollection of her husband's Jesus sort of face, his large kind eyes and his skin that looked tanned even when he hadn't been on his holidays. She wondered if Amy missed him as much as she did? Wished she could find the words to ask her.

'You want to get some Acdo on that mark on the carpet,' she said instead, looking down. 'Did you drop your tea on it last night? I would have thought there'd be plenty to eat at the funeral.'

'Do you remember what was said about this house when Wesley and me got married?' Amy didn't even bother to look at the mark. 'Can you remember *exactly*?'

'Mr Battersby bought it outright for you.'

'For Wesley?'

Gladys cottoned on quickly that something was very much up.

'For both of you. For you to live in to give you a good start. So you didn't have to move in with me.'

Amy was flabbergasted. 'Would you have had us living with you?'

'Well, *she* wouldn't. That was made clear from the beginning. She wouldn't have had her house messed up with a baby's things. Not Lady Muck.'

'But there was no baby, was there?'

'Wasn't meant to be,' said Gladys stoutly. 'The Lord works in mysterious ways.'

Amy sat down suddenly. 'He could have been coming up to twenty now.'

Gladys wasn't standing for this sort of talk. 'Yes, he would. And he'd be just the right age for the next war. Though if there is one we'll all be dead anyway. They haven't opened that gas-mask factory not all that far from here – though it's meant to be 'ush-'ush – for nothing.'

'Mam?'

'Yes?'

160

'There's nobody can cheer me up like you.'

'It's my disposition.' Gladys almost literally warmed herself at Amy's smile. 'How about me fetching you a small tin of Heinz soup? Cream of tomato would be nice. It's reduced to fourpence this week. If you do a couple of slices of toast to it you won't come to any harm.'

She walked down the hill to the Co-op with her mind in a turmoil. What Amy had said about the house wasn't just idle chatter. Amy was nearly out of her mind with anxiety, and what about that big stain on the carpet? It wasn't like her to go throwing her food around. Look at what a neat and tidy baby she'd been. Screamed the house down if she got as much as a spot of food on her towelling bibs, and if you dropped her dummy on the floor she wouldn't have it back till it had been well rinsed under the tap.

It was all to do with Mr Battersby dying. Gladys waited for a coal cart to pass before she crossed the road. While he was alive Amy was safe in that house. But with him dead and gone? Everything was going wrong since Wesley went away.

The shop door pinged as she opened it. Everything looked nice and normal, with the manager patting half a pound of best margarine into a decent shape, and Mrs Beal from Ribble Street sitting on the stool at the counter watching her weekly order being made up.

'Good morning, Mrs Renshawe.'

Gladys nodded. 'How's your husband, Mrs Beal?'

'Fair to middlin', I'm glad to say.'

The manager took out his long black book of divi stamps with its flimsy pages and slipping carbons, pencil poised.

'I'll not be a minute, Mrs Renshawe. Your Amy all right?'

'Champion. I've just left her.' Gladys nodded. 'Aye. She's champion.'

Was Mrs Beal looking at her funny? Was it getting about that Wesley had done a bunk? Could it be on the cards that he would turf Amy out of that house and move in with his fancy piece? Gladys went stone cold. She could just imagine what would be said, especially after she'd been so openly proud of Amy marrying into money, almost into the gentry.

'I'll have two ounces of tea and three rashers of bacon,' she said, when the door had pinged behind Mrs Beal. She hardly knew what she was saying or doing. If what she was afraid of came to pass, it would be worse than dreadful. The gossips would have a field day. What had been said about the pinched-faced Prince of Wales and that American woman, Mrs Simpson, would have been no more than tittle-tattle compared. Amy's name would be mud, or worse, folks would pity her. For no reason at all a line of a song shouted in the streets by children at the time of the Abdication popped into her mind:

> Hark the herald angels sing,
> Mrs Simpson stole our King.

Coming out of the Co-op, Gladys saw two women she knew talking together on the corner. It seemed to her they darted funny glances at her as she passed.

'I don't know how you have the nerve to come here today, Dora.'

Phyllis Battersby had been at the bottle. You didn't need to be Sherlock Holmes to know that. She was wearing a dusty pink dress with a cardigan buttoned wrongly so that there was a left-over piece dangling down. She looked sticky and sherry-sodden, and Dora knew that the wonderful Wesley had already been and done his worst. Ethel, it seemed, had gone into town to do some shopping.

Dora knew there was no point in explaining that she had taken the food because she couldn't bear to see it go to waste. No point in explaining that Amy hadn't expected either Charlie Marsden or Mr Dale to drop in. Useless to point out that laughter on the day of a funeral was a natural relief from the awfulness of it all. Wesley would have put the worst interpretation on it, for reasons of his own.

'I'm starting that other job on Monday, Mrs Battersby,' Dora said quickly, getting it in before Phyllis had the chance to give her

162

the sack. 'You won't have any trouble finding someone else, I know at least three women who would jump at the chance.'

Phyllis merely shrugged her shoulders before reaching down to the side of her chair and coming up with a three-quarter full glass of sherry.

She had put it there not knowing who was at the door, Dora realized. She was a grief-stricken widow, with a cousin from St Helens staying with her – but for how long? She needed help, friendship, company, an outstretched hand. Dora half stretched her own out, then drew it back. She sat down suddenly without having been given permission to do so.

It was no good. Dora had known and accepted a long time ago that she would never get to heaven when she died. She'd done some awful things in her time, but this was surely one of the lowest and meanest. Old Ma Battersby might have treated her less than the dust, paid her peanuts, worked her till she was fit to drop, but this wasn't the time to desert her. Charlie Marsden would understand, Dora knew that instinctively. He'd be disappointed, but he'd understand.

'I've been thinking about what I just said, Mrs Battersby.' Dora's small face shone with pious zeal as she made her supreme sacrifice. 'And I've changed me mind. I'll stop on here. In fact, I'll go through in the kitchen right this minute and make you a cup of tea. You look done in.'

'No thank you, Dora!'

In an instant the old Phyllis was there. 'I was going to tell you not to come any more if you had given me the chance to speak.' Phyllis's thin mouth with the lipstick blurred round the edges set hard. 'I will be leaving this house as soon as possible.' She waved a hand round the vast expanse of carpet. 'My son is arranging for me to move into something smaller. Eventually. When Ethel's gone back. He has everything in hand. He's got a good business head on his shoulders. Not that his father would ever admit that.' Her eyes were suddenly bleak with despair. 'They never got on, you know, Dora. My husband never let my son in on any of his business transactions.'

She had great difficulty forming her mouth round the last word, and Dora knew then that old Ma Battersby had had more than a skinful, because never in a million years would she have dropped her guard like this.

'Was it my fault, Dora?' Great glycerine tears welled in her eyes. 'Was it true that I thought more of my son than of my husband?' Her voice rose to a wail. 'I'll tell you something I've never told anyone before – if someone had given me a gun and ordered me to shoot the one or the other, I'd have shot my husband without pausing to think.' She drained her glass and looked at it in bewilderment. 'I feel guilty, Dora. So very, very guilty.'

'I put *my* husband away,' Dora said, 'an' I'll never stop feeling guilty till the day I die.' At a sign from Phyllis she went to the sideboard for the sherry decanter. 'How do I know my Greg wasn't forever calling out for me during the night?' She refilled the wine glass that Mrs Battersby now used for sherry. 'How do I know whether they ignored him night after night, when he lay there not able to go to sleep? I used to get up and sit on his bed, Mrs Battersby, and let him talk to me about the war. Yes, thank you Mrs Battersby, I will have a drop. Yes, I know where the sherry glasses are. Thank you.'

Holding a glass roughly half the size of her employer's, Dora sat down again to keep Phyllis company. Poor old sausage.

'Greg never got to be more than a lance corporal,' she confided. 'He would have ended up a sergeant, I know, if he hadn't got wounded early on. He was in hospital on and off for nearly two years.'

'Wesley still has a piece of shrapnel in his thumb,' Phyllis said. 'He can move it round and round with his finger.'

'It was the second battle of Ypres where Greg was wounded. He said the firing was like all hell let loose. Bloody Germans.'

'Down with the Kaiser,' Phyllis agreed, sipping her drink in a very refined way.

Dora did the same. 'It rained for twelve days out in Belgium and that was June. They never got dry in all that time, then in early July they were in the thick of it. High explosives, shrapnel and gas-shells. Greg said the gas smelled like coconut oil. He said they were wading up to their knees in mud, and that when their water supply came on the cart it was purple. But when the tea was made it was green.'

'I don't suppose you've ever tasted Earl Grey, have you, Dora?' Phyllis said, attempting a hostess smile. 'It's not usually given to domestics but I think we'll have a cup. Sherry gives me a dry tongue.'

'And a shredded liver,' Dora said, going into the kitchen to make a pot of the tea she had tasted once on the quiet and decided that if someone gave her a cup of hot water with Ashes of Roses scent sprinkled in it she'd have a job to tell the difference.

'I said I would give backword to Charlie Marsden and stop on with her,' Dora told Amy. 'But though I felt heart-sorry for her, she's never going to change. She told me that Wesley is looking around for something smaller for her, more manageable, and that for the time being Ethel will do the housework, so she doesn't really need *me* any more.'

'You mean Wesley's looking around for a smaller house? Like this one?'

Dora shook her head. 'Well, yes, I suppose. More like this one, but in a better district, I suppose.'

'This isn't exactly a slum.'

'I should think not, but can you see old Ma Battersby living here? Next door to me, and across the street from Mrs Rakestraw? No garden, and a lavatory down the backyard. That would be a bit of a come-down, wouldn't it?'

'He's going to try to get me out,' Amy said. 'I'm convinced of it.'

'But it's *your* house!' Dora was outraged. 'Mr Battersby gave it to you on your wedding day.'

'To both of us? Or to Wesley? I've never seen the deeds, Dora.'

'Oh, my sainted aunt!' Dora sat down with a thump on the piano stool. 'That's what he's looking for in his father's desk. He'd been at it again this morning. Hadn't even bothered to roll the top back again. Papers everywhere. He wouldn't tell you to get out. Surely?'

They stared at each other for a long time without speaking.

And knew he would.

Twice during that long, endless night Amy had read the pamphlets Bernard had left on the sideboard.

She leaned against the draining board in the kitchen, drinking tea and worrying herself to death. If Wesley was to repossess the house, or whatever they chose to call it, there would be no point in her training for anything. She would have to find money now, this minute, and fast.

Anyway, the pamphlets were about secretarial courses not due to start until September, though Bernard had kindly included a leaflet advertising private typing lessons, at half a crown a lesson, which she could start straight away. Half a crown a lesson. Dirt cheap at the price.

Amy looked up at the ceiling and sighed. Soon every last penny of her nest egg would be gone. Soon there would be nothing worth while and portable left to sell to the little man with the second-hand stall on the market. The gilt carriage clock and the pair of matching vases had fetched a reasonable price. The stallholder had whipped the vases out of sight before counting three grubby pound notes into her hand. Amy, who had never liked them, thought there was no accounting for taste, and put the money away in her purse.

She opened the back door to take in a sniff of the damp night air. Her father had died owing no man a penny, and her mother had a set of little boxes in a kitchen drawer marked gas, rent, doctor's man, clothing club, Christmas club and, optimistically, holidays, though that one was always empty when the July Wakes week came round.

'Neither a borrower nor a lender be,' Amy could remember her father saying, and once, when a mistake had been made down at the Town Hall and the gas bill came in grossly overcharged, Gladys had come round with tears streaming down her cheeks, sure she was headed for a debtor's prison with all the neighbours reading about her in the newspaper.

Amy put the leaflets on further education away at the back of a drawer in the sideboard. As she trailed upstairs she whispered a sad farewell to her fantasy of herself as a secretary with a clean white collar tacked to the neck of her navy-blue dress, and her hair screwed up into a little bun on top of her head. In films Joan Crawford never seemed to have the slightest difficulty in finding herself a job in an office. She would pause outside the door just long enough to pin a white gardenia on the lapel of her dark suit, put on the white gloves kept in her handbag, check that her stocking seams were straight, lick a finger and smooth her eyebrows in the right shape, dip a scoop-shaped hat over one eye, square her already squared shoulders and march in, coming out half an hour later with the job hers and the boss already crazy about her.

Amy walked over to the window and drew back the curtains. It was raining hard, pouring in a torrent from a gap in the guttering, dropping like a frenzied waterfall to splash noisily and rhythmically in a pulsating beat. She got back into bed, turned her pillow over and pulled the heavy blankets over her head. But they failed to muffle the sound of the rain.

'You fool, fool, fool,' it was saying. 'How could you be such a fool as to think the vases and the clock were yours to sell? How could you be such a fool as to think you could go on living in this house? Did you really believe it had ever been yours? You fool, fool, fool . . .'

By nine o'clock the next morning the rain had gone and she was in the queue at the Labour Exchange, willing to go down on her knees for the chance to scrub the Town Hall steps at five o'clock every morning if needs be.

Wesley drove into town not long after that. He was finding it easier and easier to leave the Preston shop now that Clara had stopped grumbling so much at having to take a turn behind the counter. That she wouldn't have felt the same about a shop patronized mainly by women never occurred to him. It was men buying the cigarettes, cigars and tins of tobacco, and the majority could always spare a few minutes to exchange banter with the tall blonde who had more than a passing resemblance to Jean Harlow. When she climbed the flimsy ladder to reach a box of cigars from the top shelf their eyes stood out like chapel hat-pegs as her tight skirts rode up to show her stocking tops.

The commercial travellers were equally taken with her, though young Arnold Porrit considered the whole performance to be pathetic. This one wasn't a patch on the real Mrs Battersby. This one looked like death warmed up when she didn't have all that stuff on her face. It must be awful kissing her through all that purple lipstick, like sucking damson jam off a spoon.

Wesley found the outer door of the office in Richmond Terrace on the latch. Taking off his hat he stood there for a moment in the narrow hall, staring up, far up through the well of the house, which not all that long ago had been a gentleman's residence with gas lamps flickering on the walls, and thick carpets instead of well-trodden linoleum the colour of beef tea.

The banister rail was smooth to his touch. The door to the solicitor's office was open a fraction, so he went in.

No, the girl with water-waved ginger hair told him, Mr Thomson wasn't in but if he cared to sit down he wouldn't have long to wait. Mr Thomson never came into the office before ten o'clock these days.

Wesley thanked her and sat down, holding his hat on his knees. Why didn't the old codger retire, he wondered. With all the unemployment in the town what had possessed him to pick this girl with the biggest freckles he'd ever seen all over her pasty face, and close-set fishy eyes. She wasn't much cop as a typist either, picking at the keys and darting little glances at him when she thought he wasn't looking.

The minutes ticked by – five, ten, fifteen. Wesley sat without moving as the girl, a bundle of quivering nerves by now, rubbed so hard at a typing error she made a hole in the paper and had to start again.

The last time she had seen Wesley Battersby he had been playing the lead in the Operatics, striding about the stage waving a sword and singing of his love, his everlasting love which knew no bounds. He was the best-looking man she had ever seen in her life, with his jet-black wavy hair and his slumbering, come-to-bed eyes. Her skin

168

suddenly crept with devastating embarrassment as he smiled straight at her.

'Would it upset you if I smoked, Miss . . . ?'

'Fish,' she said, going blood red. 'Miss Fish. No, it won't upset me at all if you smoke.' She pushed an ashtray towards him. 'Thank you very much,' she finished, totally overcome.

'What a lovely day,' Wesley said, thoroughly enjoying the effect he knew he was having on her. 'I hope they have a day like this for the Coronation on the twelfth.'

Miss Fish was racking her brains for something meaningful to say about the new King and Queen, but it was no good. She could only stare with her thin mouth agape, groping around in her mind for the words that refused to come. If they'd been in a film, which they weren't, he would have sung at her and she would have jumped on the desk, lifted her skirts and done a tap dance, before he lowered her slowly down into his arms, gazed into her face and kissed her.

'I hope they have a lovely day, too,' she said dreamily at last, as Wesley, hearing old Thomson's heavy tread on the stair, stood up in relief.

Ten minutes later Miss Fish couldn't believe her eyes when Wesley came out of Mr Thomson's inner sanctum, bashing his way past her desk, camelhair coat flying, a look on his handsome face like the wrath of God, sparing her neither a glance nor a civil good-day.

Polite as ever, Mr Thomson hovered behind him, hands clasped together in his customary pose, gold-rimmed spectacles and watch chain gleaming in a sudden shaft of sunlight filtering in from the high windows.

'A beautiful day, Miss Fish,' he said, beaming at her with satisfaction. Obviously chuffed to little mint balls about something or other.

'Let's hope it keeps up for the Coronation,' she said, beaming back.

'Indeed. Indeed,' said Mr Thomson, going back into his room and closing the door with an unmistakably triumphant click.

10

'God, I need a drink!' Wesley flung himself at the sideboard and poured himself a large whisky. 'Where's Amy?' he shouted, just as if his mother would know. 'I've been at the house and she's not in.' He gulped the whisky down. 'I'm going back there now. She'd better be in this time.'

'Will you be staying for a spot of lunch, dear? Ethel will be back from town in time to make it. She won't let me lift a finger.'

Phyllis was talking to him in a prissy voice with her mouth wobbling itself round the words. She lifted her head and narrowed her eyes to get him into better focus. He looked as if he'd run all the way from Preston, but how could that be when she could see the car on the drive outside?

'You look very hot, dear,' she said, standing up then sitting down immediately as the carpet came up to smack her in the face. 'Feverish,' she added. 'I hope you're not going to be ill.'

At the very thought of him becoming ill she covered her eyes with a hand, only to take it swiftly away at the sound of Wesley's loud voice.

'Did you know that Dad went down to see Harold Thomson not long before he went into hospital?'

Phyllis shook her head violently from side to side. Which was a mistake.

'You mean he didn't tell you?'

'Tell me what, dear?'

Wesley stared at her balefully. 'Well of course he didn't tell you! I don't suppose he discussed an unimportant thing like that with you, did he? He could have signed everything away without telling *you*.' He put his drink down and stood up. 'Think yourself lucky, Mother dear, that he didn't.' Wesley was looking as bad as she felt. Red and sweating, his eyes dark as pits, he began to pace about, beating a fist into the palm of a hand. 'How often did he go down to see Amy? Once a week? Twice?'

'I don't know . . .' Phyllis was going to cry if she wasn't careful. It wasn't nice Wesley speaking to her like this. As though she had done something wrong. He had stopped by her chair and was standing over her, looking as if he hated her. Phyllis cringed away from the sight of him, even as her mind told her how silly she was to be afraid of Wesley, her boy, her lovely, loving boy.

His voice was rough with rage. 'Harold Thomson told me this morning that Dad had been to see him not long before he went into hospital. I'm asking you again – did you know that?'

Phyllis tried in vain to remember, but before she needed to admit that she knew nothing at all about it, Wesley exploded into a torrent of words, stabbing the air with a finger, rolling his eyes, a tic jerking away in his left cheek.

'He went to see his friend Thomson and signed my house over to Amy! Do you realize what I'm saying, Mother? I'm talking about the house he gave *me* as a wedding present. To give us a good start, he said. *My* father, *my* house! Did you ever think differently from that?'

'Your house, dear?' Phyllis's fuddled brain was struggling to understand, to make some sense of what he was saying, when all she wanted was to lie down and go to sleep, preferably right there and then.

'Of course I mean *my* house!' Much to her relief he backed away slightly. 'I had plans for that house, and they had nothing to do with Amy. She's forfeited any right to any part of that house.' He walked to the door and turned. 'You've no need to worry, Mother dear. *This* house is safe, plus your annuity, plus the profits from the shop in town and the Darwen one.' He wrenched the door open, almost severing it from its hinges. 'Oh, he hasn't left me out, not quite. From the generosity of his heart he's left me the Preston shop. Oh, yes, the bloody Preston shop, which is – as he well knew – running at a loss at the moment!' He paused for breath. 'So never, ever again try to tell me that my father loved me. He didn't even *like* me. He's proved that, right enough!'

171

'Stay for a spot of lunch, dear. Ethel will be so sorry to have missed you.'

Phyllis stretched out a hand, then watched it drop back into her lap. She was so tired she could hardly summon the strength to blink, let alone think. Ethel would never forgive her for having a little drink or two. Or was it three? She honestly couldn't remember.

Wesley had been in a real paddy. Something to do with a house and his father. She mopped her face with the lace-edged handkerchief she always kept tucked up her sleeve. The naughty boy had been almost beside himself with temper. Her mouth tightened into a bleak smile. Once, when Wesley was a little boy he had jumped on his teddy bear in his spiked football boots till it burst, scattering the flock stuffing all across the kitchen floor. What a tiresome little boy he had been at times.

Before Wesley had driven his father's car to the end of the road she was asleep, head lolling, mouth open, in the stuffy room with the fire blazing away up the chimney, even though the May morning sunshine slanted through the tall window.

Bernard just happened to be looking down through his office window when he saw Amy going into the library across the street. She was wearing the black suit she had worn at the Battersby funeral, but with a dusty-pink beret-style hat. Even her back looked dejected.

It was eleven o'clock in the morning. That afternoon Bernard had two meetings, one with the Town Clerk in his Town Hall round the corner, and the other with a distraught father of a brilliantly clever boy, who feared he was going to be forced to take his son away from school to earn a pittance that could make all the difference between the family living and merely existing. Both meetings were important in their own way – equally so, in Bernard's mind, but his notes were halfway dictated and if he didn't hurry he might miss Amy. After last night he needed to be reassured that she was all right.

There was a strange urgency about him, an almost feverish desperation in the way he left his room, ran down the stairs and across the street. He had acted without conscious volition and when he found her in the reading room he stopped in the doorway, fully aware that every head was turned in his direction.

'Amy!' He went straight to her, remembering to keep his voice to a whisper. 'Come outside. I have to talk to you.'

All the heads in trilbies or flat caps turned away, back to their newspapers. The room was too cold, in spite of the sunshine outside, their general apathy too well established for the majority of the men even to begin to wonder what was going on. The Silence is Requested notice on the wall was quite unnecessary. Only an elderly man in a bowler hat and a black coat with a velvet collar paused before going back to thumbing through a small notebook on the sloping table in front of him. Something about the way the man had taken the young woman by the arm and led her out, something in the way he had looked at her, had reminded him with an unexpected jolt of himself as a youngish man in love with a girl like that with butter-brown hair. So terribly, so much in love. Sighing, the old man bowed his head over his writings and in a spidery hand began a new line.

'Amy . . .' Bernard walked her round the corner into the shadow of the library with its church-like windows. 'How are you? You look tired. Where have you been?' He let go her arm. 'I went for a long walk last night and I nearly knocked at your door on my way back, but it was too late.' He lifted a hand to his hair. 'I should have knocked. I know now. Yes, I should have knocked.'

The wind ruffled his brown hair. Amy knew it irritated his sense of tidiness. He was strangely impatient, not with her but with the whole notion that he could be behaving in this way, marching her out of the library, dragging her out, he supposed, if one was a stickler for the truth.

'I'm all right,' she reassured him. 'If I look a bit fed up it's because I am. I stood in a queue at the Labour Exchange for two hours only to be told I was too old, too lacking in qualifications – the wrong shape, I suppose.' She smiled. 'Married women of my age don't look for jobs, they let their husbands keep them. Married women only go out to work to provide for their children and only then if their husband

173

is out of work or ill or dead.' She shrugged her shoulders. 'I don't fit into any of those categories, and I won't apply for charity, so there we are. It's a case of where do I go from here?'

He thought he saw the sparkle of tears in her eyes and was immediately cast down. Did all this mean that Battersby wasn't providing for her? Sustaining her? Supporting her? The chivalrous side of him made him see red. He had thought Dora was joking when she hinted that if Amy didn't find a job soon she would starve. Starve? Oh, my God! A thing like that couldn't quietly happen in this day and age. Could it?

'I must go,' he said quickly, as abruptly as if she had been trying to detain him. 'But I'll . . . will you come to my house for tea on Sunday? We can go through those pamphlets together.' He walked backwards, away from her, still smoothing his hair. 'You will come, won't you?'

'Yes,' Amy said. 'I'll come.'

She made her way back into the library, seeing, out of the corner of her eye, Wesley's father's friend, the solicitor Mr Thomson, coming out of the front door of his office right across the street. She had only met him once or twice at The Cedars and was surprised that he even recognized her. Yet there he was, waving his newspaper at her, beaming all over his whiskery face, before striding off in the direction of the tram stop.

Everyone was behaving in a peculiar way. Perhaps it was the unexpected warmth of the sun addling their brains.

Inside the reading room it was as though no one had moved. The men in their outdoor clothes still read their newspapers, turning the pages slowly, as if living on the dole had defeated them, drained all hope from their souls. It might be spring outside, but not a single ray of sunshine touched this cold grey room.

Amy shuddered, turned on her heel and walked out again into the street, unaware that an elderly man with a velvet collar on his threadbare overcoat watched her go with the suspicion of tears in his eyes.

Dora was standing on her doorstep when Amy went past. She had never been a stander on doorsteps like some women along the street, arms folded over flowered pinnies, calling out to a neighbour cleaning her windows or mopping her front flagstones. But she wanted to know how Amy had got on.

'I can see you've not been offered a managerial job,' she said, 'but I've had an idea. If you'd like to come in for a minute I'll tell you.' After she'd handed Amy a steaming cup of tea, she went on: 'Mrs Green and her daughter. The married daughter. They're both looking for help. Mrs Green knows you from your last job. All right,' she said, before Amy had had a chance to speak, 'I know it's beneath your dignity to go out cleaning, but it would put you on till you've qualified as something more in keeping.'

'In keeping with what, for heaven's sake?' Amy thought how well Dora was looking since she'd stopped running, stopped hurling herself from one job to the next. She wouldn't swear to it, but she was almost sure that Dora had been putting powder on her nose.

'They want cast-iron references.' Dora ignored Amy's last remark. 'Preferably signed by God. There's enough good stuff in those two houses to set up a shop. Even the chamber pots are bone china, and there's a lace doily with a Busy Lizzie plant on it on top of the lavatory cistern. It's a low-flush suite, of course. Talk posh,' she advised, as Amy rushed away to the phone box at the end of the street. 'Tell her you're well connected.'

'If I tell her I'm acquainted with you she'll know that,' Amy said over a disappearing shoulder.

Less than a quarter of an hour later she just had to call and tell Dora the news that both jobs were hers, which delayed her for another half hour. So that when she walked into her own house it was almost two o'clock and Wesley's patience was at snapping point.

He rose from the chair that had once been his and went straight into battle.

Shock at seeing him left Amy speechless. She stood there by the door, smart as paint in the little black costume and the dusty-pink velvet beret, the colour coming and going in her cheeks.

'I have been to see my solicitor this morning.' Wesley fired each word, each syllable at her, snapping them off at the ends. As if he were auditioning for a part in a Shakespearian play, Amy thought, too flushed with her recent success at finding a job to recognize the venom in his words.

'Mr Thomson?' she asked. 'He waved to me this morning. I saw him coming out of his office.'

Wesley ignored her. 'Shall I tell you what he said to me? In his exact words?'

Still mystified, Amy nodded.

Wesley took up a legal stance. 'The *exact* words, Amy?'

Again she nodded. 'If that's what you want, Wesley.'

'Right! He told me that I must appreciate that probate of my father's last Will and Testament has yet to be granted, but as a family friend he saw no reason why he could not inform me that this house, my house, Amy, has been bequeathed to *you*! Plus a certain amount of the ready.' He flared his nostrils. 'Now try and tell me you knew nothing about it. Try and tell me that your friendship with my father blossomed at just the right time because you were genuinely fond of him. Go on! Say something, even if it's only to tell barefaced lies.'

Amy felt the blood drain from her face and her legs turn to water. She was going to faint – she was going to keel over right there and then, so she must take deep, deep breaths, look straight ahead, not up nor down, and convince Wesley in no uncertain terms that this was as much of a shock to her as to him.

'No wonder I couldn't find the deeds,' he was saying. 'The old man must have taken them down to Thomson not long before he died.' He took a step forward, then shook his head sadly as Amy instinctively backed away. 'I'm not going to touch you, Amy. The way I feel goes far beyond anger.' He sat down at the table and buried his face in his hands. 'My father came to see you on the day he went into hospital, didn't he? Was that the time you wheedled the promise out of him? When he was ill, in pain, and hardly knew what he was doing? My God, Amy, I don't know you these days. I'm discovering that I never really knew you.'

Amy stared at him in horror. There were tears in his eyes,

176

genuine tears this time. His face was crumpled with hurt, and his beautiful voice broke on a sob. She felt a sense of disgust, knowing that he was now going to play the scene differently – quite, quite differently. She held her breath.

'Do you remember the day we got married? That cold grey day, with me in khaki, knowing that within a week I would be back at the front. Lying in a filthy waterlogged shell hole, knowing every minute could be my last.'

Amy widened her eyes. Wesley had never been at the front, never got further than Boulogne, Charlie had told her that. Wesley had been a clerk in an army office working long hours as a pen-pusher, eating and sleeping at his makeshift desk, his fingers so cold, so swollen with chilblains that for years you could still see the scars on them. There had been no need to lie. Wesley had had an uncomfortable if not a dramatic war.

'I remember our wedding day very well,' Amy said, relaxed enough now to pull out a stand-chair and sit down opposite to him. 'Go on, Wesley, have your say, then hear mine.'

'We had nothing,' he reminded her, spreading his hands. 'When my father told me that this house was his gift, I was so overcome, so overwhelmed . . . you just don't know.'

'He gave it to us,' Amy whispered. 'To *us*, not just to you.'

'It was the first time my father had given me anything.' Wesley twisted his hands together as if lathering them with soap. 'Nothing I ever did pleased him. You didn't know I'd run away from home four times as a child, did you?' Wesley's voice throbbed with sincerity. 'He wanted to set me in his mould, do the things he wanted me to do. Go to university, get a degree, join the tennis club, get a bloody medal and a commission in the war, be a businessman, think of nothing but increasing profits, get on in the world. Your father loved you, Amy, he was proud of you, whereas mine . . .' He turned his head to stare into the empty grate. 'My father was ashamed of me.'

'What has all this got to do with the house, Wesley?' Amy watched the performance with a totally blank expression. At one time, not all that long ago, the sight of his handsome suffering face, the sound of heartbreak in his voice, would have moved her so much she would have had to stretch out a hand to him, tell him she understood, promise to stand with him against the world. 'What do you want me to say? That I don't want it?' she asked. 'That I realize your father did this while he was ill? Not in his right mind? That I renounce it in your favour?'

This was so exactly what Wesley *did* want that he wasn't quick enough to hide his expression. 'I knew you'd see it like that. I told Harold Thomson you wouldn't accept when you realized the unfairness of it.'

'What did Mr Thomson say?'

Wesley would never tell anyone what his father's old friend had said.

Harold Thomson hadn't minced his words. The memory of Edgar Battersby sitting crumpled with pain not all that long ago in the very same room was too recent; it still filled him with sadness. Edgar's pride had stopped him for enlarging on his reasons for wanting the name on the deeds changed, but his old friend knew all right. The tall young man with his film-star looks had brought his father nothing but trouble. Twice at least Edgar's money had bailed him out from some tricky situation. Wesley sailed just this side of the wind, always had, even as a young lad. Always been a wrong 'un, and always would be. So there was no way, he told Wesley, no way at all that anything could be changed or altered in the slightest as far as the deeds were concerned.

'He was astonished, to say the least,' Wesley lied. 'He's known me since I went to kindergarten with his son. I expect he tried to reason with my father, but you know how stubborn the old man could be.'

Amy had a clear picture in her mind of a beaming Mr Thomson waving his newspaper at her from across the street. She hesitated, biting her lip as Wesley got up and went over to the window to stare out at the sloping backyard with its meat safe on the wall, flanked by the zinc hip-bath which had been there before the bathroom was put in.

'Come here, love . . . Please . . .' Wesley whispered.

She was acutely aware of the utter dejection of him, the droop of

178

his shoulders, the way his thick black hair grew to an endearing point in the nape of his neck. It was a sight as familiar to her as the palm of her own hand, a sight that had always moved her, made her ache with love for him, especially the times when he had sat at the piano and played for her.

Slowly she pushed her chair back and went over to stand behind him. She had thought she hated him, but she didn't. You couldn't live with a man for over twenty years, lie in bed next to him, hold him close, respond to his lovemaking and feel nothing.

'Yes?'

'I'm sorry, love. I've done a lot of thinking lately. I've taken a good hard look at myself and I don't like what I've seen.' He put up a hand. 'No, don't argue. There was an awful lot wrong with our marriage, but not in the way we cared for each other. I'm still very, very fond of you.' He lifted his head. 'I can tell you now that every time in the past when I thought of a good reason to leave you, you did or said something that made me want to stay.'

Before Amy could even think of moving, he turned to face her, pulled her roughly into his arms and kissed her, opening his mouth over hers, tearing at the buttons on her jacket, cupping her breasts with his hand, squeezing, kneading.

All the blazing anger so carefully subdued up to now was in his kiss; there was nothing of tenderness in it, nothing to attune with the words he'd just spoken. Amy pushed at his chest, jerked herself away from him with such force that he had to feel behind him for the arm of the settee to regain his balance. She wiped her mouth with the back of her hand before pulling at her blouse to straighten it.

'I'm saying nothing this time to make you want to stay,' she said in a clear firm voice. 'You're right. There was an awful lot wrong with our marriage, but God help me for not realizing till the moment you walked away through that door.' She stepped aside. 'You must go now, Wesley, this isn't the time to talk about the house. I need to believe it first, ponder it.' There were sudden tears in her eyes. 'If it's true, can't you see that it's the most marvellous thing that's ever happened to me? It's security handed to me on a plate, Wesley. I wish I could say it more poetically than that, but it's what I mean. It's the security your father knew I'd never had with you.'

'Are you telling me you don't love me any more?' His face was the face of a whipped child. The sight of her wiping his kiss from her mouth had filled him first with shock, then with disbelief. His mind was whirling round like a moth caught in the bowl of a light fitting. He knew Amy through and through, and losing his temper now could destroy everything. Let her go ahead and ponder on the house, see it as hers for a while, enjoy the feeling of possession, before coming down to earth and accepting the unfairness of it.

Wesley swallowed hard. God damn it, this was *his* house, given to him by his father, and Amy would, in her own time, see that. She hadn't said she no longer loved him. It had been a mistake to kiss her like that, but God help him, he was only human. Yes, this was the way to do it, to go away and leave her to wrestle with her principles. Amy had always set great store on principles, felt strongly about injustices. She would come to accept how wrongly his father had treated him.

But on the way out he had to pass the piano. His piano with its smooth ivory keys, its mellow tone, given to him on his tenth birthday by a doting godmother.

'The house as it stands, the house and its contents,' Harold Thomson had said, stabbing with his finger on the pink blotter on his desk. 'Your father made that very clear.'

Wesley touched the smooth mahogany of the closed lid, trailed a finger along it, then as the tight control slipped away from him lifted the lid and crashed it down, remembering she had destroyed his music. Closing his eyes he saw rage, red as molten lava behind his eyelids. God Almighty, if nothing else was to be his, this was. He had missed it, yearned for it in that awful dreary flat over the shop, would have had it brought there if there had been room.

Flinging himself down on the stool he opened the lid again and began to play, jamming the loud pedal down hard, almost to the floorboards. There was no tune, no attempt at one, just a crashing of unmelodious chords, a thumping of the keys that brought Amy's hands up to her ears in an attempt to blot out the terrible sound.

Wesley was possessed. His hair flopped over his forehead, his eyes narrowed with an anger that consumed him. He had been thwarted, slighted, rejected, and he couldn't bear it. He trailed the keyboard from one end to the other – and saw again the shocking sight of Amy wiping his kiss away.

Next door, through walls hardly more than plywood thick, Dora heard the din in disbelief. Amy couldn't play the piano, not even a simple tune with one finger. Once or twice, to Dora's knowledge, she had tried until Wesley had laughed her out of it. So what was going on? Dora put down her sewing and sat stone still, listening, trying to make sense. She stood up. That piano was being played by a madman, venting his fury on the keyboard, and if it didn't stop soon anyone forced to listen would go mad too.

Wesley! The wonderful Wesley . . . Within two seconds Dora was down the lobby, out of the house, on her way next door. To be pushed roughly aside by Wesley as he left, muttering to himself, striding off to his car parked just round the corner.

'I've been left the house,' Amy said straight out. 'Wesley just found out today and he doesn't like it.'

The statement was so calm, so Amy-like in the face of what had just happened that Dora burst out laughing.

'I didn't like that tune he was playing,' she said deadpan.

'It wasn't exactly "In a Monastery Garden", Dora.'

'Perhaps that was just the verse, Amy. Perhaps the chorus would have had more tune to it.'

They stared at each other, quiet and unmoving for a full minute, Dora's eyes wary, Amy's brimming with the unexpected joy bubbling up from somewhere inside her.

'This house is to be mine!' she said again. 'Mine, Dora, mine!' Suddenly she flung both arms wide. 'I own a house, every stick and stone. I thought nothing good was ever going to happen to me again, but it has! Whether it's fair or not, I'm taking it. I'll work to keep it going, Dora, no matter what I do. Then at night I'll close the front door and come inside, and no one can ever take it away from me.'

181

'Mr Battersby willed it to you? Legal and signed on the dotted line?'

'Yes, Dora, yes!'

They had been friends for years, yet they had never held hands, never embraced; but when Dora held out her arms Amy went into them and they rocked backwards and forwards together, over-whelmed by their mutual delight.

11

Amy wasn't going to tell a soul, not until everything was out in the open and cleared, but how could she keep quiet when her mother looked so worried?

'You're going thin,' Gladys accused. 'You're going to skin and bone. I can see your ribs sticking out through that jumper and your skirt's dropping off you. If you fell down a grate you wouldn't even bark your shins.'

She was so worried, so struggling not to show it that Amy told her about the house and the money to cheer her up.

'Mr Battersby has left this house to me in his Will, Mam.'

Instantly Gladys was all outraged suspicion. 'Who told you a thing like that?'

'Wesley.'

'Who told *him*?'

'The solicitor.'

'What solicitor?'

'Mr Thomson.'

'With a brother who used to be the Mayor?'

'Mam!' Amy couldn't wipe the smile off her face. 'It's true! Did you ever dream Mr Battersby would do a thing like this? For me?'

'What does Wesley have to say about it?'

'He doesn't like it. He's livid.' Amy's smile wavered. 'Mam, how can I be so glad about something that's happened only because a dear old man died?'

'What does his mother have to say about it?'

'I don't know, Mam. I don't care! Just at this moment all I can think is that I own my own house.'

'What about the rates?' Gladys was so affronted she couldn't contain herself. 'And the upkeep? Houses eat money.'

'I can work, Mam! There won't be the rent to pay, and there's a bit of money to come as well when things are sorted out. Mam, I own a house! I can do what I like with it. I can take a lodger if I want. I can paint the front door purple, I can sell it if I want to.'

'How much for?' Gladys was totally out of her depth. 'There's got to be a catch in it somewhere.' She had gone quite pale.

Amy felt her new-found exhilaration begin to slip away. Her mother was right. There had to be a catch in it somewhere. Houses weren't handed over like a tram ticket. Wesley had implied that she had wheedled it out of his father when he was too ill to know what he was doing. Maybe he would be able to claim it back?

She looked at her mother, cowed down, unable to believe that sometimes round the corner there could be a stroke of good fortune waiting to happen. Poor Mam had never hoped for the best, always been sure that even when the sun shone there was always the chance that it would rain the next day. Poor Mam had never believed in a silver lining.

Amy remembered as a little girl walking with her mam and dad along a winding country lane, with great feathery masses of bread and cheese growing in the hedgerows. It had rained and they had sheltered beneath the sloping roof of a barn, coming out into a magic world where raindrops had set the greenery to sparkle like diamonds, and where away in the distance a rainbow wavered into beauty, a shimmering arc spanning the grey sky. Amy's father had pointed it out to her and they had stood entranced, but Mam hadn't seen it, couldn't see it at all.

'There!' the small Amy had shouted, wanting her mother to see it, trying to make her see it. All in vain.

'We'll miss the bus if we don't look sharp,' Mam had said, trudging along with her head down, watching carefully where she put her feet because this was the countryside where you never knew what you'd step in next.

Charlie couldn't take his eyes off Amy when he called that afternoon. He left his hat on as he was only going to stop for a minute and his face, beneath the smallish brim, was illuminated with a shiny glow of admiration for this bonny woman who was coping so well on her own, with never a grumble.

She was wearing a green-flowered print dress with a sweetheart neckline, set off with a floppy white organdie bow. Charlie couldn't have described it in such terms; all he knew was that the pale green suited her down to the ground, showed off the burnished sheen of her hair, brought out gold flecks in her eyes.

'I'm very fond of you, Amy,' he said all at once. 'More than fond, as a matter of fact.' He began to walk backwards and forwards, the hat still on his head. 'You give me ideas every time I look at you.'

'What sort of ideas?' Amy was foolish enough to ask.

Charlie stopped his perambulating and took the hat off. 'I'm a very passionate man, Amy, and I've been celibate for far too long. Clara isn't going to come back this time, not that I'd have her if she did, and Wesley's not exactly camping on your doorstep, is he?'

Amy looked at him coldly.

'We could be such a comfort to each other.' He drew in his lips as if to stop them trembling. 'We're not children and some day, when the divorces come through, we'll be married. Lottie needs a mother and oh, heaven help me, Amy, but I need you.'

By executing the smartest of sidesteps, Amy managed to avoid the short outstretched arms. Putting the width of the table between them, she spoke to him firmly.

'Charlie. Listen. No, stay where you are and just listen.'

'I can't help it, Amy. I think about you all day long and dream about you all night.'

He seemed to be gathering himself together, and for a wild moment Amy wondered if he was going to leap over the table. He was breathing heavily and his face had gone blood red.

'Stop it, Charlie!' Amy glanced over her shoulder to the foot of the stairs, wondering if she could make a run for it. Was this one of Charlie's jokes? Wesley used to tell her that old Charlie was funnier than any comic on the halls when he got going. Was he going to burst out laughing any moment now, slap his hand against his thigh, chuffed with himself for having had her on so successfully?

185

'Stop behaving like a clown, Charlie,' she said firmly. 'You're not the right shape for a Romeo.'

He blinked as hard as if he'd been sloshed with a bucket of cold water. Too late Amy realized he'd been in deadly earnest.

'Charlie . . .' she said softly, 'I'm fond of you, too. Very fond.' She wondered if she dare go to him and touch his arm, or even kiss him on a red-veined cheek, then swiftly decided better not. 'I admire you very much and if I wanted to have an affair, I can't think of anyone nicer to have one with. But . . .' She stared at him, biting her lips. 'I'm sorry, really sorry.'

He put the hat back on his head, pulling it too low down over his bushy eyebrows. 'Okay, if that's the way it is, I guess we'll forget all about it. Crack on it never happened.'

In his mind he was John Gilbert or Ronald Colman, whispering a brave farewell to the love of his life. But even as he walked out of the house, his step as jaunty as ever, he knew in his heart he was much more of an Oliver Hardy.

'You've been giving me all the wrong signals,' he felt bound to say in his own defence, salvaging his pride. Just a little.

Wesley was worried about what Clara would say when he told her the news about the house, but her attitude almost knocked him for six.

'Oh, let her have it, for goodness' sake. What is it after all but a little terraced house with a lavatory in the backyard? She'll probably sell it and go and live with her mother.' Clara raised plucked eyebrows almost to her hairline. 'What do you reckon it's worth on today's prices? Three hundred? Three hundred and fifty?'

Wesley couldn't believe what he was hearing. 'It's *my* house, for God's sake! It's a little gem, everybody who saw it said so. We had a bathroom put in, a bay window at the front and a tiled fireplace in the living room.'

'I know, I've seen it,' Clara said. 'With a mantelpiece so narrow there's nowhere to stand your glass.'

Was she being serious, or was she taking the mickey? For once he could smell something cooking in the oven out on the wide landing, and looking properly at her for the first time since he'd come storming up the stairs saw that she was wearing a little jewelled slide in her hair and had painted her nails a strong fuchsia shade. She was sitting on the floor by the gas fire. She had taken her shoes off and through her silk stockings he could see that her toenails were painted to match. He felt choked.

Couldn't she understand that he needed some of the money from his house so that he could pay a deposit on one with a garden and an inside toilet? Couldn't she see he was half out of his mind with worry about money and how he was going to keep her in the style to which she had become accustomed? His mouth twisted as he remembered how he had promised her the earth if only she would leave Charlie and move in here with him. He would climb up and get the moon for her, he had said.

'I called in on Mother today,' he said, missing the way Clara's eyes narrowed. 'I told her about Amy getting my house, but I don't think it sank in. All she wanted was for me to stay and have a spot of lunch with her.' He frowned, seeing a picture of his mother's flushed face and watery eyes. 'She didn't look well at all. Puffed in the face – blotchy.'

'She's an old lady, love.'

'Not *that* old. Sixty-eight. She was six years younger than my father.'

'That man who looks like the village squire came in the shop this morning.'

'Which man?'

'The man you said was in his sixties, though God knows he doesn't look it. The one whose wife died last winter. The one with a double-barrelled name.'

'Mr Brown-Davies? What made you think of him?' Wesley put out a hand and touched the silky hair curling that day in tight little sausages round her head. He sighed and closed his eyes.

Clara paused for a moment, then went on: 'He can't get over losing Mrs Brown-Davies. He really bared his soul to me, poor old sausage. He can't cope. Has no idea. He comes in every day for his Balkan Soubranie, just for an excuse to drive into town and have a

187

walk round. He says I make him laugh, make him feel twenty-one again.'

'He's loaded,' Wesley told her. 'His father was in textiles when textiles were a good thing to be in. I can understand him missing his wife, she was a lot younger than him and a right bobby-dazzler. There'd been one before her too. I think the old codger's been quite a ladies' man in his time. I always find myself waiting for him to twirl his moustache!'

'Look who's talking! Talk about the pot calling the kettle black. You'd be forever twirling yours if you had one.'

Wesley liked that. Clara leaned back against his knees, the gas fire spluttered and the meaty smell from the landing was making his mouth water. Clara was right. Let Amy have the house, give in gracefully and that way he'd be free of any further obligation to her. In a few weeks, when his mother was more herself, he would have a long talk with her about her financial position. Once the Will was read and probate granted she would begin to realize she was quite a rich old lady. When she was over the worst of her grieving she would listen to him. He would point out to her that having a son living over a shop wasn't exactly compatible with her idea of gracious living. In a few weeks' time he would bring her over – it was time she met Clara.

He reached into his inside pocket for his cigarette case. Yes, Clara's attitude about the house was exactly the right one. He watched her lay knives and forks out on the card table by the window. What a woman she was! Hard as nails, some would say, but he knew better. Calculating, some would say, but he could contradict that, too. Think what she'd left behind to follow him. Just think about that well-kept, red-brick house with all the mod. cons, and a lot besides. He bet there were more controls in Charlie's kitchen than on the flight deck of an airship. Charlie had always been a gadget man.

Wesley blew a perfect smoke ring up to the rather dirty ceiling, his badly shaken confidence trickling back, his innate belief in himself fully restored. His mother hadn't been herself at all this morning but give her time, give everything time. It was early days.

She would be only too glad to hand over the shops to him, only too glad to have him sort out her papers. In time she would be more than willing to let him explain things to her, advise her on what to hold on to and what to let go. When she was more herself, not in such deep shock.

He put out his cigarette, sat down at the rickety makeshift table and helped himself from the steaming dish brought in by a scowling Clara.

'I hate cooking!' she burst out. 'If you say you don't like it I'll empty the lot on your head.' She watched him carefully.

Was it stew? Hotpot? Were these pieces of gristly meat beef or lamb? Shouldn't the gravy be thick rather than watery? And what was this hard lump? A piece of carrot or something dropped in by mistake? Wesley put a forkful into his mouth, chewed valiantly for a full minute, subdued an almost overwhelming urge to spit it out. He swallowed hard, feeling the food stick halfway down.

'Very nice,' he forced himself to say, smiling at her with watery eyes. 'Really delicious.'

Clara put her knife and fork down with a thump. 'It couldn't taste worse if I'd boiled up the dishcloth.' She narrowed her eyes at him. 'You don't always have to act flarchy, you know.'

'Flarchy?'

'Oh, come on, Wesley. Didn't they teach you a word like that at the Grammar School? It means turning on the charm, saying things you don't mean. Lying, I suppose, with charm. Always with charm.'

'I've never lied to you. You'd have found me out if I had.' Wesley's smile was intact as he stretched out a hand across the table. 'That's just one of the many things I like about you, your direct honesty. It takes my breath away at times, but I wouldn't have you change in any way.'

Clara got up swiftly and began to scrape the plates into the brown dish. 'You lied to me about this flat. You told me we'd be living here for no more than a month at the most. You made me believe that this shop was yours, when all the time you were nothing more than a so-called manager with a staff of one – a half-baked lad with a slate missing.'

189

He couldn't believe what he was hearing. 'If the old man hadn't died . . . there were all kind of negotiations in the pipeline . . .'

'Stop blustering, Wesley! Your dad had your measure, I'm beginning to realize that.' She marched out with the dish, then marched back, pink-cheeked and furious, with the little jewelled slide slipping from her yellow hair. 'He knew what he was doing when he left the house to Amy, and bloody good luck to her, I say. You haven't given her a penny piece since you walked out, have you?'

'Clara! Love . . .' His face was a mask of hurt. 'Why are you being like this? Tell me why?'

'Give Charlie his due,' she said, 'he's never missed a week. His money has come through regular as clockwork. He'd have me back tomorrow, would Charlie.'

'But you wouldn't go? You'd never leave me? You couldn't . . . not after . . .'

There was a trembling in his voice and for the life of her Clara couldn't make out whether it was real or whether he was play-acting again. He certainly looked hurt, deeply wounded – bewildered even. Like a small boy being punished for something he hasn't done. Clara sighed, feeling the anger draining out of her. What right had she to pick faults in him? Chastise him for telling lies? God help them, they were two of a kind if you went down that road.

There was a sweetness about him that caught you unawares at times. He would have eaten the atrocious stew to please her, and he had to be the best-looking man she had ever set eyes on. His voice alone was enough to seduce a Mother Superior, and that was before he even touched you. And to feel the clean springiness of his thick hair, trace the outline of his curvy mouth, experience the strength of his arms, the fierce passion of him when he made love . . . After all, who on this rotten earth was perfect? Certainly not her. Definitely not yours truly.

Slowly she moved towards him and as his arms came round her and just before he kissed her, she saw the fear in his eyes change to relief.

'Clara, oh Clara . . .'

190

His hands were gentle at first, holding her to him so that she felt his hardness, then he was lifting her up into his arms, carrying her through into the room across the landing, still kissing her even as he tore at the buttons on her blouse. She heard herself cry out with impatience, tangled her fingers in his hair, closed her eyes . . . and heard the telephone shrill out, intrusive, shocking, jerking them back to reality.

'Ignore it,' she whispered, winding her arms round him and pulling him close again. 'It'll stop soon. Wesley . . . oh, Wesley . . .'

But it was no good. The ringing went on and on, louder it seemed with every second. When Wesley rolled away from her and went downstairs to answer it she lay there staring up at the ceiling, in the bed surrounded by packing cases, not bothering to cover herself, waiting for him to come back to her.

'Is that you, dear?'

Ethel's voice was uncharacteristically loud so that Wesley had to hold the telephone away from his ear. He had stubbed his toe rushing down the stairs, and the pain was so bad it was making him feel sick.

'Of course it's me. Is something wrong with Mother?' He stood on one leg, hopped slightly round the counter trying to avoid the draught coming at him from beneath the shop door. 'You sound a bit upset, Ethel.' He controlled his temper with difficulty. Getting any sense out of Ethel had always been like getting blood out of a stone.

She was whispering now: 'Your mother says your father is sitting on the top stair. She wants to go up to her bedroom but he won't let her pass. She says she's very cross with him.' The whisper faded almost to nothing. 'I'm ringing from the upstairs extension, dear. She looks very ill, most peculiar, but I don't think she would want the doctor to see her like this.'

'How did *you* manage to get past Father on the stair?' Wesley felt bound to ask.

'Oh, he's not there really, dear,' Ethel explained. 'I wish you'd drive over. You're so good with her.' The faint voice wobbled. 'I'm at my wits' end, dear. I don't know what to do.'

Clara said in a sarcastic way that of course she understood that Wesley must go to his mother's house right away. He had his priorities right, hadn't she always known that?

Wesley dressed angrily, pulling on his jacket, not bothering with a tie, wincing as he forced his bruised foot into his shoe. He saw the hard-set expression on Clara's pretty face and went to sit beside her on the bed.

'Look, love. I don't want to go. The last thing I want to do right this minute is leave you. But she is my mother and I can't not go. For God's sake, Clara, she's hallucinating! She thinks my father's there. She might do something silly.'

'But she won't, will she? Not now she knows Wesley is on his way.' Clara actually gave him a push. 'Oh, go to Mummy. Stay the night with her if you wish.'

Wesley stood up. 'For God's sake! Aren't you listening? She thinks my father's there, sitting on the stairs.'

'Give him my kind regards,' Clara said, swinging her legs over the side of the bed and reaching for her dressing gown.

It was two o'clock the next morning when Wesley arrived back at the flat, exhausted. The sight of his fastidious mother in the state she was in had disgusted him. She looked beaten, she smelled of vomit, and it was obvious she had somehow tricked Ethel and managed to drink the best part of a bottle of sherry.

'It won't happen again,' Ethel had vowed, wearing her Band of Hope expression. 'I've cleared the house of drink.' She winked at Wesley. 'Poured the lot down the sink!'

'Oh, my God,' he said.

'Oh, my God,' Clara said when she woke up the next morning in a much better mood. 'What a waste.'

'Cousin Ethel's so filled with virtue she could make Al Capone himself see the light.'

'So your mother wasn't too bad after all? I bet she forgot all about seeing your dad sitting on the stairs.'

'Oh no.' Wesley grinned. 'When we finally got her to walk upstairs to her bedroom she stepped aside on the third step from the top and bowed politely. "Excuse me," she said.'

'Is that meant to be funny?' Clara wanted to know, back in a black mood again.

Amy called round to see her mother-in-law after her stint at Mrs Green's house. She found Ethel in the kitchen.

'Amy! How nice to see you, dear.' Ethel was busily beating a raw egg into a glass of milk. 'If I have to hold her nose and spoon it down her throat I'll see she drinks it,' she said gaily. 'Both my parents had this every morning of their lives once they'd turned eighty, and as you know they both saw ninety before dying as fit as fiddles.'

To Amy's surprise the little round woman turned to face her, her plump face as red as fire.

'I have to say this, dear.' She twisted the corner of her apron into a rope. 'Your mother-in-law is being very difficult. I've had to be firm with her at times, but I've got the better of her now.' She lowered her voice, obviously overcome with embarrassment. 'For instance, I got it out of her when she was a bit muddled one day that you and Wesley aren't living together. That he's living in sin at Preston. I know it happens,' she went on, 'and never having been married I don't feel qualified to speak about such things. You don't expect to come across it in your own family, but what I want to say to you before Wesley's mother comes downstairs is that I'm on your side, dear. I won't give my reasons, but I am. When I see what goes on in some marriages I'm glad I was never tempted.' Her smile wavered. 'Though I have to say I always thought you and Wesley were such a lovely couple. A perfect foil for each other, somehow.'

She was so kind, so obviously trying to say the right thing that Amy gave her an affectionate hug, just as Phyllis walked in looking much better than Amy had expected her to.

'Be a dear and bring my spectacle case down from the bedroom, please, Ethel. I left it on the table by my bed.'

'No trouble, dear.' Ethel trotted off, eager as ever to be of service, her round face shining with zeal.

'That's for me, I take it?' Phyllis nodded at the egg and milk, opened her handbag, unscrewed the top of a flask and poured a generous slosh of whisky into the custardy mixture, then with obvious satisfaction drained it down.

'I'll soon have her built up,' Ethel said, coming in with the spectacle case. 'I would have done that, dear,' she fussed, as Phyllis rinsed the glass and upended it on the draining board. 'She doesn't need to lift a finger while I'm here,' she told Amy. 'She's down to rock bottom, but I'll soon have her fully restored. You can see my egg and milk mixture doing her good already. Just look at the way it's brought the colour back to her cheeks.'

'What did old Ma Battersby have to say about the house?' Dora had come in and caught Amy listening to a talk on the wireless by an earnest young man called Godfrey Winn. It was all about the rights of the modern woman, and Dora made it clear she had no time for him. 'Switch him off,' she advised Amy. 'He's talking through his hat. Women never had any real rights, and he should know it. He probably only knows rich women, anyway.'

Amy could see that Dora was in a good mood. Lately the tired look had gone from her eyes and she could sit still for five minutes without dropping off to sleep.

'Okay,' she said, reaching for the switch. 'Let's have him off, then I can tell you.' She settled back in her chair. 'The house wasn't mentioned. Cousin Ethel was there for one thing, and for another I'm taking Bernard's advice and playing it all low key till I've had it in writing.'

'You told Bernard?'

Amy blushed. 'He seemed concerned about how I was managing.' She nodded at a shrouded object on the sideboard. 'He brought me an old typewriter to practise on, and a manual. He says typing skills are never wasted.'

'I should think not,' Dora said. 'The first thing Greta Garbo was asked when she arrived in Hollywood was could she type.'

Amy said that for the first time ever she had realized that there was a side to Wesley's mother she hadn't seen before. In fact, for a few moments she had actually felt very fond of her.

'Was that when she told you she wished she'd had Wesley drowned at birth?'

'It was when she got Cousin Ethel out of the way so she could slosh whisky into her egg and milk. She's human, Dora. Plus being quite capable of stopping drinking when she wants to. She's not the type to drink herself to death.'

At that moment, in her state of well-being, Dora couldn't care less if Wesley's mother lay down on the Boulevard in front of Queen Victoria's statue and had to be marched off to the police station, shouting rude words and waving her arms about. Things were definitely looking up for her and Amy, and she wouldn't be surprised to see her friend typing so fast on that machine eventually that the carriage smoked. There wasn't an ounce of envy in her whole body. She had always known that Amy deserved better, and with her own life transformed so completely she could afford to be magnanimous. Besides, any good that came Amy's way was one in the eye for the wonderful Wesley.

She was positively pink with pleasure as she described the washing machine in Charlie's kitchen yet again. She hadn't known about the drying cabinet, or the ironing board you could sit down at, or the fact that the Hoover meant an end to wet tea leaves sprinkled on carpets to stop the dust rising when you swept them.

'It nearly sucked the cat up this morning,' she declared. 'Charlie laughed his socks off when I told him.'

Amy found it difficult to talk naturally about Charlie ever since he had declared his feelings and almost made a dive for her across the width of the table. She also accepted that unthinkingly she had wounded him deeply.

'Charlie reminds me of Greg – of the way Greg used to be before he was wounded,' Dora was saying. 'I don't mean in looks. Charlie is much better looking. Greg was no oil painting, was he?'

Amy was fascinated. 'You think Charlie is handsome?'

'Suave,' Dora said at once. 'With a sort of Bulldog Drummond look to him. He'd be the living spit of Ronald Colman if he had darker hair, a moustache, was quite a bit thinner and spoke in a posher voice.'

Amy hoped her eyebrows were still where they belonged. 'Do you think Wesley is handsome?'

'Not in the same class.'

'As Ronald Colman?'

'As Charlie.'

Dora nodded, smiling at nothing, sure that her ship had come in at last, determined not to let the niggling worry about Charlie's daughter Lottie spoil her new-found happiness. Lottie was seeing a boy, having him in the house when her father was out at the pub in the evenings. Dora had found a pair of bicycle clips underneath the sofa cushions, besides which she knew a lovebite when she saw one.

'What's that mark on your neck?' she'd asked.

Lottie had come back quick as a flash with the story that she'd been using the curling tongs when they'd slipped and burnt her neck. 'But I washed the curls out because my friend prefers me with straight hair, says it becomes me more.'

'Which friend?'

'I forget at the moment. I've got so many.'

'Was it the boy I've seen you talking to on the corner?'

'Oh, that would be Mollie, a girl I know who's had her hair Eton-cropped. Everyone thinks she's a boy.'

Dora had given up.

Amy frowned. 'You look very serious all of a sudden. A goose walking over your grave?'

Dora nodded. 'Wearing bicycle clips,' she said.

After Sunday tea Bernard suggested that they went for a walk and, though they had no intention of going to the cemetery on its windswept hill, that is where they went.

Amy had been greatly touched by the way he had removed the crusts from the egg and cress sandwiches, cutting them into triangles, layering them on to a big flowered plate. Like fish scales, she had thought. His apparent expertise was a revelation to her, and rather tactlessly she told him so.

'Wesley could burn a cup of tea, and my father only used the kitchen as a short cut to the backyard,' she laughed.

He was walking a small distance from her, his hands thrust deep into the pockets of his tweed sports jacket, his head down as if he searched for something he had lost.

'I've had to fend for myself for a long time,' he muttered, kicking at a loose stone. 'After my wife died I cared for her mother, and she was bedridden for the last long endless year of her life. So I had to learn to be domesticated. To cook, in a fashion.' He began to walk more quickly, angry with himself for giving so much away, and for moving so swiftly on to the defensive.

Amy was wearing a pink and white print dress with a white angora cardigan round her shoulders. She walked the steep hill easily without leaning forward, and he thought she looked like a flower. Thinking this he grew even more angry.

'I'm sorry. I didn't know. I had no idea. I didn't mean . . . I knew about your wife, but not about . . . It must have been awful for you.'

'It doesn't matter.' Suddenly he turned his head and smiled at her. 'I know why you've chosen the cemetery for our walk.'

'I didn't choose it consciously.'

'I know that.'

They sat down on a bench lopsided with age, weathered and scarred, flaking rust. Across the wide expanse of graves an elderly couple trod carefully, bending to read the inscriptions on the headstones. The sun was slowly fading away, the air was still and grass-scented all around them. When the couple disappeared over the brow of the hill, Amy moved a small indefinite distance from him, subduing a sudden and overwhelming desire to lean against him, to feel the peace and strength of him.

He was smiling at her, his eyes teasing. 'We've come up here because all the Sunday walkers have gone. There are no nosey parkers to see you walking out with me, a man who is neither your husband nor your sweetheart. You are afraid that people would talk.' He took her hand, leaned towards her and kissed her on her closed mouth. 'So there you are.' He shook his head from side to side. 'I had no intention of doing that.' He had kept hold of her hand

and was jiggling it up and down. 'I never thought I'd feel like this ever again. Down all the years since Anna. Never once.' He held her hand to his cheek for a moment. 'What shall I do with myself, Amy? You remind me so much of her – even your name, the sound is vaguely the same.'

Because she didn't know how to deal with the situation, Amy spoke too loudly and too quickly. She felt she had to stop him from saying more.

'Don't talk like that! You don't even know me all that well.' She was gabbling now, embarrassed to the point of incoherence. 'I was thinking only the other day that every single time we've met I've been in the middle of some crisis, some kind of desperate situation, charged to the hilt with emotion, tears never far away.' She paused. 'You've always been so kind to me, so very, very kind to me. You've pitied me. Yes, you have, you've pitied me.'

She looked away from him, suddenly remembering what Dora had told her about this man – how he'd come into the house, taken her by the hand and led her upstairs, to make love to her in his bed. Because he was sorry for her, too.

'You see me as a poor little woman with a husband who has left her to live with someone else. You're sorry for me.'

'No, Amy. I see a very brave woman who lost two babies at birth, and others too before they'd had time to grow. Isn't that why your footsteps led you to this place? I also see a woman who is so afraid to show her feelings, to be herself, that she thinks people are fooled by her smart talk and her way of turning everything into a laugh. I see a woman so vulnerable that there's an invisible sign on her forehead asking me to kiss her.'

She stood up abruptly. 'Don't say things like that to me!' Her eyes pricked with tears of fury. 'Damn and bloody blast you for saying things like that to me!'

The swearing was so unexpected, so totally uncharacteristic of her that he caught her by the arm and pulled her down to sit beside him again.

'Good,' he said. 'That's more like it.'

198

She gazed at him coldly. 'I feel sick with disgust of you. You think you can kiss any woman who takes your fancy, especially if she's unhappy and in trouble. You think your charms are irresistible.' Her voice rose. 'Charm doesn't fox me, oh dear me, no. I could write a book about charm, a whole shelf-full of books on that subject. I'm not as easily swayed as some women in your shady past might have been.'

'Dora?' He sounded quite detached. 'I thought somehow she would tell you.'

She tried to move away, but his grip on her arm tightened.

'Go on! Just dismiss even that as though it meant nothing.'

Bernard shook his head. 'You're wrong, love. It meant a great deal at the time. To both of us. Dora is a fine and good person.'

'And you weren't ashamed afterwards?' Amy was consumed with such a curiosity that her anger began to evaporate.

'Amy . . . Amy . . .' Gently he shook her. 'If we'd been filled with guilt, ashamed, it *would* have been wrong. Dora would have been as sick with disgust with me as you say you are now.'

Amy remembered the look on Dora's small pinched face as she told what had happened between her and this man. Her whole expression had been smoothed into tenderness, into the quiet joy of remembering.

'I don't understand,' she said slowly. 'God help me, but I think there's a lot I don't understand.'

She could have walked away and left him, knowing that he would have let her go. But she sat on, pulling the soft white woollen cardigan closer round her shoulders, feeling the day closing in around them.

'What will happen now?' she said, as they walked, still with that small distance between them, down the stony path to the cemetery gates. As they crossed the street he held her hand, but let go when they reached the other side.

'I don't know yet what will happen, Amy,' he said. 'I shall think about it. Very seriously.'

A tram cluttered by. The sun had gone now, and dusk would fall quite quickly.

12

'You look feverish to me,' Gladys said, viewing the typewriter and the blue cloth-backed manual with suspicion. 'Was it cold up the cemetery last Sunday night?'

'No, it was quite warm as a matter of fact.' To cover her confusion Amy dropped a sheet of typing paper to the floor and bent down to pick it up.

'Mrs Rakestraw saw you coming out of the cemetery gates. With a man. She didn't get a proper look at him because she was on the top of a tram, but she was sure it was you.' As a concession to the unseasonable heatwave Gladys had come out without either a coat or a hat, and looked somehow unfinished in the brown crêpe-de-Chine dress that had seen far better days. 'I'm not going to ask you who it was, but you ought to watch your good name. Mrs Rakestraw has a tongue on her like a sozzled parrot.'

'We had been for a walk,' Amy said, despising herself for feeling she needed to explain. 'He's just a friend.'

Gladys's nostrils twitched fiercely to the left with the force of her sniff. 'There's no such thing as a friend if he's a man. Married women don't have friends of the opposite sex. A man who isn't your husband is only out for one thing. You must know that.'

Amy knew nothing. Since Bernard had left her at her door four days ago she had done little else but try to unravel the woolly skeins of her thinking, alarmed at the way her mind swung her up to the heights of excitement, then down to the depths of depression. He had said he would do the thinking for both of them, and a thousand times she had decided to walk the few yards down the street to his house, and a thousand times her pride had stopped her.

'Wesley will come back to you,' her mother was saying. 'Especially now he knows which side his bread is buttered on.'

'You mean now I've got this house?'

'Well, it's bound to have made him think.'

'Think what?' Amy wanted to weep tears of humiliation, hot scalding tears of anger. Lifting the typewriter in her arms she banged it down on to the sideboard, then twitched the cover over it. 'Do you imagine,' she said slowly, 'that I am just waiting for the day when Wesley walks back through that door? To forgive him for what he's done to me? To go on as if nothing had happened?'

Gladys didn't turn a hair at that kind of talk. Amy had been like it since a child – hard, secretive, keeping everything from her mother, yet confiding it all to her father. She caught a glimpse of the top half of herself in the fluted mirror, and thought how much she'd aged recently. What had she ahead of her but years of living by herself, making ends meet, going to the Co-op for a bag of broken biscuits or a few pieces of bacon off-cuts, if she was lucky. Daughters were supposed to be a blessing to their mothers, a comfort in their declining years, not sly like *her* daughter, telling her nothing, keeping all her doings to herself.

'It would be your duty to take Wesley back if he came.' She nodded her head up and down. 'He might not be perfect but a bad husband's better than no husband. If your father was still with me I wouldn't be in the position I am now, with nothing ahead of me but the workhouse.' She saw her reflection again and winced away from it. 'Sitting with a row of toothless women at a long table, eating a basin of pobs.'

'The workhouse is a hospital now, Mam, and I can't see that a bad husband is preferable to no husband. Far from it. Anyway, what makes you think I'd have Wesley back? Maybe I've had time to think about things since he went away.'

Gladys couldn't get over what Amy was saying. 'You've a short memory, madam. I can see it as if it was yesterday – Wesley's father coming round to our house and telling your dad and me that he'd see to it that their Wesley did the right thing by you.'

'Mam! I've spent the last twenty years of my life being grateful to him for that. I didn't know it, but I have. Even if he did come back, which he won't, would I be expected to welcome him with open arms?'

'Yes!' Gladys thumped her fist on the table. 'You stood with him in the sight of God and made promises to stay with him. For better or worse.'

'But *he* left me, Mam, not the other way round.'

'He wasn't brought up like us. His sort act different, have funny moral standards.'

The brown dress was making Gladys say things she knew she'd regret. She'd forgotten to tack the half-moon-shaped sweat protectors in last time she'd washed it through and she knew there'd be two black-wet patches showing underneath her arms. She'd take it off and stuff it in the dustbin when she got home, and never mind how many more years of good wear there were in it. She folded her arms over her one-piece bosom.

'One man, one woman. Like it says in the Bible.'

'Where in the Bible?'

Gladys didn't know, so she went, leaving Amy drained and exhausted, thinking she might go and stand on the front-door step and never mind how common it was supposed to be – just in case he came by.

'Are you looking for anyone in particular?' Bernard said, appearing at exactly the same time, coming down the street to smile and talk to her. 'You have an air of joyful expectancy about you.'

'My mother's just gone. I was seeing her off,' Amy lied, flustered, thinking how his eyes were the exact shade of a pearl-grey April sky. 'She thinks Wesley will come back to me one day and that when he does I should welcome him with open arms.'

'Even though you know you belong to me?'

'Don't say such things!' She put out a hand to him, then drew it back. 'You bamboozle me!'

'I intend to,' he said smoothly. 'I will make your life so complicated that you can bear its complexities no longer, and there will be only one way to simplify it.'

'Really?'

Mrs Rakestraw was peering round her curtain, but Amy didn't care.

'In what way will that be?'

'By walking the few paces to my door,' he said, his eyes twinkling. 'But before that day comes you must be very, very sure.'

He turned to go and she found she couldn't bear it.

'Mrs Rakestraw is watching us, and she'll know now that it was you she saw me with on Sunday evening, coming out of the cemetery gates. My reputation will be in shreds, but won't you come in for a while?'

He came back to her and lowered his voice to a whisper. 'If I come inside I will want to make love to you, but the time is not yet. You have a lot of mind searching to do. Making love is not the most important thing there is, although I know how pleasurable it would be with you, Mrs Battersby.'

He grinned at her embarrassment, lightly touched the tip of her nose with a finger, then turned and bowed politely at the twitching curtain across the street before walking quickly away, going into his own house and closing his front door behind him with a decisive click.

Amy wanted to tell Dora about the way things were between her and Bernard, but as she was far from sure herself, what could she have said? Besides, Dora seemed preoccupied these days, giddy with happiness one minute, down in the dumps the next. Something was going on, Amy was sure of it, and if Charlie hadn't stopped calling round since that last awkward meeting Amy would have asked him straight out.

'Charlie's wife's been round to the house twice lately,' Dora was saying. 'She's still got masses of clothes there and she keeps sorting through them, chucking things out, telling me to send them to a jumble sale. Good stuff that I'd keep for myself if she was my size, if she wasn't such a funny shape. She's got bosoms on her like melons. I looked at the size in one of her brassières the other day and guess what it was?'

'Thirty-eight C cup,' Amy said at once, with professional certainty.

'Men like big chests,' Dora said, squinting down at her almost flat front. 'I bet Charlie Marsden does. I caught him eyeing me up one day when I was bending over the washing machine. I expect he was wondering if I'm a man in disguise. Men like big bottoms as well – big bottoms and big bosoms.'

Amy laughed. 'So where does that leave us?'

Dora turned away, drooped against the wall, defeated, dejected.

'Tell me what's really wrong?' Amy asked softly. 'I know something is.'

'I think Charlie's wife is planning to come back to him,' Dora said in a rush. 'I think all this about sorting through her clothes is an excuse to come to the house.' She gave a shuddering sigh. 'I've noticed she only comes when she knows Charlie could be home from work.'

Amy sat down suddenly. 'If you're right and she and Charlie get together again, that could mean that Wesley . . .'

'Will come back to you.' Dora started off down the lobby. 'You've always known he would; you must have realized it was only a matter of time.'

'Dora! Come back!'

Amy's voice stopped Dora in her tracks. Slowly she turned and walked back into the living room.

'What have I said now? Husbands always go back to their wives after they've had their little flings, just as wives always go back to their husbands. It's common knowledge.'

Amy ignored her. 'You'll still have your job at Charlie's house, Dora. You'll still be housekeeper there. Busty Bertha doesn't do a hand's turn. She's as much good as a chocolate fireguard round the house.'

Dora flung her arms wide. 'You honestly expect me to carry on washing Charlie Marsden's shirts, mending his socks, cooking his meals, being a substitute mother to his daughter, cutting his hair – oh yes, he likes the way I make the most of what he's got . . .' She dropped her arms dramatically to her sides. 'Have you no finer feelings, Amy Battersby? Do you think I'm made of wood?'

'You mean you love Charlie?' Amy shook her head from side to side. 'Oh, dear God, what a mix-up. What a terrible thing to happen.'

205

'It's a wonderful thing to happen! Can't you see? Me and Charlie were meant for each other. We laugh at the same things – we laugh all the time. And what's more, he treats me like a lady, did you know that? He fills the coal scuttle before he goes off to work. "That's no job for a lady," he says. To think that not that long ago I was lugging eight buckets of coal up a flight of stone steps to the mill offices, after carrying eight lots of ash down to the bins in the mill yard. Charlie cherishes me, don't you see? He brings the heaviest of the shopping home in his van, he appreciates what I do for him. He cut his chin shaving the other day and I wanted to lick the blood away for him. He drank too much beer another time and I told him off, and do you know something? He almost cried. Nobody has ever cared for him in a down-to-earth practical sense like that, certainly not madam with her bottle-blonde hair and her big titties.'

'Oh, Dora, Dora.' Amy motioned her to a chair by the fire. 'Shall we smoke the last of Wesley's Russian fags and drink the last of his whisky? I found half a bottle hidden in the cupboard over the hotwater cistern yesterday. Why he felt the need to hide it I don't know.'

'Because he was playing some sort of silly game with himself all the time, that's why!' Dora looked a lot better for her outburst. 'The sad thing about me and Charlie is that, given a bit more time, he would have begun to love me back. I could have made myself indispensable to him, shown him what real loving can mean. He's such a blessed man, Amy, but because he's always joking no one ever takes him seriously.'

'I know that,' Amy said, lighting Dora's exotic cigarette and pouring her a drink. Trying not to remember what she had said to Charlie when he had expressed his admiration for her.

'You're not the right shape for a Romeo,' she had said.

Half an hour later Dora got up to go. The small amount of whisky she had drunk had loosened her tongue even more.

'I'm not going to give up without a fight. I know what's best for Charlie and I'm going to see that he knows it too.'

'Maybe you're wrong about his wife planning to come back. What makes you think he'd want her, anyway?'

'He doesn't want her, that's the tragedy of it. But he married her, didn't he, and to someone like Charlie a vow is a vow. He's one of nature's gentlemen, Amy. If there's a heaven that's where Charlie is sure to go. He'll have her back because that's the kind of saint he is.' She turned at the door. 'Just as *you* will have Wesley back. Because that's the way you're made too. But if you think that virtue has its own reward, you're flamin' wrong. Because it doesn't!'

When the door closed behind Dora, Amy threw her half-smoked cigarette into the fire. She risked setting herself alight by standing on the raised tile hearth and having a good look at herself in the mirror.

Love was certainly blind if the normally cynical Dora looked at Charlie and saw a saint. Amy drew her eyebrows together and made a face at herself. Why did everyone take it for granted that she would have Wesley back, prepared to carry on as if nothing had happened? Was she as loyal as that? Loyal to the point of idiocy? Was she so steeped in religious dogma that she would honour the promises she made on her wedding day in the cold, bare chapel, a child bride with a safety pin in her skirt where it was already failing to meet?

Did 'for better or worse' include a constant tolerance of infidelity? Would a kind and merciful God really expect that of her?

'People are saying that Wesley will come back to me one day soon. Dora tells me that she sees signs that Charlie's wife will be going back to him.'

Amy had met Bernard in the street – accidentally on purpose – and this time they turned their steps towards the park to sit on a bench just inside the side gate overlooking the duck pond. The rhododendron blooms had shed their pink and white petals on the grass like giant confetti, and a weeping willow tree spread feathery skirts of green. Soon it would be dark and all the tennis players had given up and gone home, carrying their tennis balls in string bags looped over the handles of their rackets. The bowling greens were equally deserted, no click of ball against jack, no muted sound of rubber mats being skimmed across well-mown grass. Even the lake was as smooth and motionless as spread silk.

'What will you do,' Bernard wanted to know, 'when that day comes? When your husband returns to you?'

Amy answered his question with another. 'Wouldn't it be my duty to have him back, knowing that I married him in the sight of God?'

'Are you afraid of God?'

Amy looked startled. 'I'm not afraid of the wrath of God, if that's what you mean.'

'So what are you afraid of?'

'Many things, I suppose. Of the war that people are saying will come one day. Of noises in the night when I'm alone. Of terrible things happening to those I love. Of Dora banishing herself from Charlie's house if his wife comes back to him.'

'Of allowing yourself to love me,' Bernard added, the creases round his eyes deepening as he smiled at her. 'But I am everlastingly patient. I can wait.' He held out his hand to pull her to her feet.'What has made you so afraid of happiness? Whoever taught you has taught you well.'

'But I've never been really unhappy, that's what I can't understand.' They walked back to the gate together, hand in hand. 'These days I don't know what's happening to me. I have a feeling that there's a curtain in front of me, one of those long beaded curtains, and if only I could bring myself to stretch out a hand and part the strands, I would stop being afraid, stop always feeling I should do the right thing.'

'The right thing for you is to come to me.'

'No matter who I hurt in the process?'

'The only person you will hurt if you deny your feelings for me is yourself,' Bernard said, walking so quickly now she had to lengthen her own stride to keep up with him. 'And me of course. But I have survived before and I will no doubt survive again.' He let go of her hand. 'But I hope you won't deny this special love which has come to us like a miracle. It's so very, very rare.'

'You're bamboozling me again,' Amy told him. 'I'm in no state to make any kind of decision. It's an obsession I've got, and don't tell me it isn't. I know an obsession when I've got one!'

'Good,' Bernard said as they reached the door. 'Then we're getting somewhere.'

'I really feel,' Ethel confided in Amy, as they stood together whispering in the shabby kitchen of The Cedars, 'that I'm getting somewhere fast with her. I let her have a small drinkie in the morning and another around half past five before we have our tea. Before we go up to bed I give her a wee dram to make her sleepy.'

'She's barmy,' Phyllis said in her normal voice when Amy went through into the drawing room. 'But she means well.'

Amy had got into the habit of calling in to see her mother-in-law about twice a week on her way home from Mrs Green's spotless house, where that particular day she had spent an hour and a half in the bedrooms cleaning the bedsprings with a small painting brush. After the pristine sparkle of the house she'd just left, the shabby comfort of the drawing room and the kitchen, where nothing was streamlined and where even the wooden spoons were stained with the colour of jam made long ago, almost made her want to cry.

Bernard had taken a few days' leave to walk in the Ribble Valley, to climb Pendle if the weather held, he had said.

'My father used to take me for walks,' Amy told him. 'He had a hermit friend who lived in a trailer halfway up Whalley Nab. And another friend who lived in the Ribble Valley. My mother can't bear the countryside, so she was glad to send us off on our own. We used to bring wild flowers back and press them in between sheets of blotting paper in books. My father showed me how to mount them in scrapbooks and write a description of them underneath.'

'Come with me,' Bernard had said, smiling as he waited for her to refuse.

'Your mind seems to be elsewhere today,' Phyllis was complaining.

Amy couldn't take her eyes off her. Since Cousin Ethel's arrival Phyllis had gradually lost the puffy look around her eyes. The fear had gone from her expression, the lonely bleakness quite eradicated. Since Ethel had moved in with her missionary zeal, determined to make herself indispensable, Phyllis was more or less her own self again.

209

'Wesley is far from happy,' she was saying now. 'Has he been to see you lately?' She nodded at Ethel staggering in under the weight of a large old-fashioned mahogany tray. 'I'm telling Amy how worried we are that life doesn't seem to be going right for Wesley.'

'We think the Will may have upset him,' Ethel dared to say.

'More likely his new friend isn't looking after him properly,' Phyllis said.

'Hardly a friend, Mrs Battersby.' Amy was surprised to find herself on the receiving end of a furtive wink from Ethel who was passing Phyllis a cup of tea, sugared and stirred.

'Do let me press you to a sultana scone, dear.' Ethel shook out the folds of a tiny linen napkin and laid it across Amy's knees, pulled up one of a nest of tables, asked Amy twice was she sure she could manage, then sat slightly behind them on a humble-looking chair. 'We wouldn't be at all surprised to see him walk through that door any minute now,' she added archly. 'He did hint that he might . . .'

'Then I'll be going.' Amy stood up, scattering scone crumbs, almost knocking over the table. She stared around her with a wild expression, trying to remember where she had put her coat and hat, and immediately Ethel rushed to fetch them from the cloakroom where she'd hung them tidily away.

'Sit down, Amy! Come back, Ethel!' There was no disobeying Phyllis when she used her committee voice. She took a sip of tea, holding the saucer against her chest in case of spills. 'You mustn't be embarrassed about the house, dear. I'm sure my husband knew exactly what he was doing when he left it to you.'

Amy perched on the edge of her chair, watching the window for the sight of the familiar black car. 'He did?' she said, wondering what was coming next.

'He did it so that Wesley would see how silly he was for carrying on this little tiff between you.'

'And how highly his father thought of you,' Ethel agreed at once.

Amy got to her feet, this time with no intention of sitting down again. She clenched her hands by her sides. They were as red and mottled as potted meat, and her knees were sending shafts of agony down to her ankles. Before Amy dusted the bedsprings, Mrs Green

210

had asked her to roll up the oilcloth in the walk-in pantry and scrub the floorboards underneath with hot water, bleach and an egg-cup of Jeyes fluid. The oilcloth had cracked and Amy had felt at that moment as if something inside her had cracked too.

She hated working for Mrs Green. She wasn't cut out for slaving over what she considered to be unnecessary jobs. She was meant to go to work dressed decently, with a clean white collar tacked in the neck of her dress every single day. She would have got her Higher School Certificate if she hadn't been seduced by Wesley. She could have been a teacher, a top-flight secretary, a civil servant in a government department. But for Wesley Battersby sweeping her off her feet when she wasn't ready to be swept anywhere, she could have been anything she chose to be.

'Wesley didn't walk out on me because of a little tiff,' she said, holding her head up and speaking loudly. 'He left me to live with the wife of one of his friends, and he's going to marry her when the divorces come through.'

'Divorce isn't a word we use, dear,' Phyllis said.

Amy ignored her. 'I think that Mr Battersby left me the house because he wanted me to have something, something of my very own, for the first time in my life. He was trying to give me the security that Wesley never could.' She felt the tears coming and tried to choke them back. 'I know that what I'm going to say will embarrass you, even make you squirm, because feelings are like divorces – they're dirty words .' Her breath caught on a sob. 'Before Wesley went away I couldn't have talked to you like this. I couldn't see that down all those years since I married him he had taken my mind and made it his own.' She lifted her head. 'Now I can tell you how much I loved Mr Battersby, and I hope and pray that he knew it, too.' The tears were running down her cheeks but she made no move to brush them away. 'An' I hope that somehow, somewhere, he can know of my gratitude and of my joy in the marvellous thing he's done for me.' She picked up her hat and coat. 'He was . . .' She had been going to say what a lonely man she had found him to be, but stopped herself in time.

The black car was drawing up outside and she was so determined not to see Wesley, especially at that moment, that she rushed from the room and let herself out by the back door.

Closing it just in time to hear Wesley's voice greeting his mother: 'How are my two lovelies today?'

She could picture him breezing in, coat flying, dark eyes laughing at them, bringing them instant *joie de vivre*, making them feel they were his own precious ones, that he was the most wonderful man in their world – in the entire world.

'Oh, Wesley, Wesley . . .' she whispered softly, finding herself running down the road, running so hard she felt her heart would burst.

Wesley found Arnold Porrit in charge of the shop when he arrived back at Preston.

'Five Woodbines, please.' A boy of about eight years old pushed two pennies across the counter. 'They're for me dad,' he said quickly, spotting Wesley coming through the door.

'An' the same for me,' his mate said, standing on tiptoe to push the coppers at Arnold.

'For *your* dad?' Wesley asked.

'No, sir. For me mam. She's got bronchitis and she says they clear her tubes.'

Arnold watched the slightly bigger of the two boys palm a box of book-matches from the counter, but said nothing. All he wanted was to get away to catch his train to Bamber Bridge, have his tea, then go playing football down the fields with his mates. If he was lucky he might get away before his boss began asking questions – awkward ones, like where was Mrs Marsden?

Arnold went through to the back for his empty lunchbox and his cap. 'Night, Mr Battersby,' he shouted. 'I'm off!'

But his boss was running up the stairs, calling her name. 'Clara? I'm back. Where are you? Clara?'

Arnold closed the shop door behind him and set off down the street towards the station. He knew where she was all right. He'd seen her getting into that old man's car, showing her legs and a lot more besides. She'd said that Mr Brown-Davies was kindly giving

212

her a lift to the library. A likely tale, in Arnold's opinion. Just who did they think he was, imagining they could fob him off like that? A ruddy Ovaltiney?

'I wasn't born yesterday, love,' Dora, told Lottie, when she found the tweed cap behind the sofa. 'You have him round every time your father goes out in the evenings, don't you?' Dora sniffed at the cap and got a strong whiff of lavender-scented Brilliantine, the solidified type, she guessed. 'How does he know you're on your own? Do you hang a flag out of the window?'

'Oh, no. I just ring him up and tell him the coast is clear,' said Lottie.

Dora felt her mouth drop open with the shock of hearing Lottie tell her what was obviously the truth. She sat down at the kitchen table and motioned to Lottie to do the same.

'I think it's time you and me had a bit of a serious talk, don't you?'

'If it will make you feel better.'

Dora gave the cap a furious skim across the table. 'You're not talking to your mother now, madam. It's me, Dora, sitting here. Dora, who wasn't born yesterday. Dora, who cares what happens to you. Who doesn't want to see you get yourself into a mess and spoil the life you haven't started to live yet.' She groped in her apron pocket for a handkerchief and blew her nose. 'I couldn't bear to see you go the way of . . .'

'My mother?'

'I didn't say that!' As a matter of fact, it had been Amy whose name had popped into Dora's mind. Amy, who had once admitted that what her mother had told her about sex could have been written on a pin-head and still left room. Amy, who looked like being bound for life to the wonderful Wesley, a man who wasn't fit to tie her shoelaces. Dora took a deep breath. 'I know you understand the mysteries of the human body, because I've seen your biology drawings.'

'The vagina,' Lottie prompted.

'Yes.'

'And the womb,' said Lottie helpfully.

'Stop it!' Dora reached for the cap being cradled tenderly in Lottie's arms and flung it across the kitchen. 'You think you're God-Almighty clever, don't you, madam? You think you know it all! Well, let me tell you something – you know nothing! But you'll listen to what I'm going to say if I have to sit on your head to get some sense into you. You will listen hard and if you still go on and get into trouble, it won't be because no one cared enough to explain.' To her surprise Dora needed the handkerchief again, this time to wipe her eyes. 'You're upsetting me, madam, and I don't upset easily,' she sniffed.

Lottie's face was a study. Reaching out across the table she laid a hand on Dora's bare arm. 'Jimmy and me haven't done anything dirty,' she whispered. 'Honest.'

'I never said it was dirty!' retorted Dora, only to be shushed into silence by a squeeze of Lottie's hand.

'Jimmy and me are courting strong, but he respects me. We're saving up to get married when I'm seventeen. Jimmy's father has promised him a stall of his own in the fish market when he's eighteen, and I've started a bottom drawer off with two tea-towels and four yellow dusters. I'll show them to you if you like.'

'Sometimes people can get carried away,' Dora said carefully, still determined to have her say. 'Especially boys of Jimmy's age.'

'That's what happened to Mrs Battersby, isn't it? She was still at school like me when she had to get married, wasn't she? So Mr Battersby never really respected her. No man respects you if you give him your body before you're married. Jimmy says my mother has no respect for herself, that's why she goes with men. Jimmy says that something in her past must have made her feel worthless.'

'He's got an old head on young shoulders,' Dora said faintly. 'I'd like to meet him one day.'

'He can gut a herring quicker than you can bat an eyelid.'

'That's worth knowing.' Dora smiled. 'I'm liking him more by the minute.'

'You do believe that we intend to wait till we're married before we think of going the whole way?' Lottie's young voice was unsteady.

Dora gazed deep into the troubled dark eyes. 'I believe you, love.

Implicitly,' she said, meaning it too. 'But I think you should invite Jimmy round when your father's in, so you can introduce them.'

'You do?' Lottie looked doubtful.

'I'll have a word with him first.' Dora got up and went to get the ironing board from the cupboard. 'I must get on, or you won't have a clean blouse to wear in the morning. Why they have to have a box-pleat down the back I don't know. They're a real sod to get right.'

'I wish you'd been my mother,' Lottie said, going pink in the face and rushing from the room.

Leaving Dora reaching in her apron pocket for the handkerchief again.

Amy told Dora that Charlie had once asked *her* to have a quiet word with his daughter.

'A birds and bees word?'

'Yes.'

'And did you?'

'No. I never got the chance. I haven't seen much of Charlie lately.'

'I wonder why?' Dora said dreamily, not caring one way or the other.

Charlie had started persuading her to stay on and have a meal with them instead of going home at six o'clock. 'It's only right when you've prepared such magnificent food. I bet the King wouldn't turn his nose up at this hotpot,' he'd said.

'We're having red pickled cabbage with it,' Lottie had told him, and they'd sat there, the three of them, tucking in and laughing, like a proper family.

'Wrap yourself round that, Charlie,' Dora had said. 'It'll put hairs on your chest, that will.'

'He's only got one at the moment,' Lottie confided, shaking the HP sauce over her plate.

'An' I knot that one so it can't escape,' said Charlie, setting them off laughing again.

Amy could hardly bear to see the shining happiness on Dora's face. If Mrs Battersby was right, and Wesley was looking fed up, then he and Clara weren't getting on with each other – so Clara would go back to Charlie, Dora would leave her job and would never ever again look as she was looking at this moment. As though all her ships were coming into harbour at once. She would be back to running from one job to another. She would shrivel up again, become exhausted and ill. She would probably die. It wasn't fair! Amy felt like crying.

'Life itself isn't fair,' her father had told her years ago. 'Once you've learnt that lesson you're halfway there.'

'I'm making spotted dick pudding tomorrow,' Dora was saying. 'Charlie's had to let his belt out two notches.'

The next day Wesley came without his key, which he could have sworn was in the glove compartment of his car. Where the hell was Amy? He stood fuming on the pavement for a good five minutes before going back to his car to sit drumming his fingers on the steering wheel.

Obviously in a paddy, Mrs Rakestraw decided, watching him through her lace curtains.

'Your husband was here, but I told him you always went round to your mother's on a Friday.' Mrs Rakestraw all but fell off her doorstep in her haste to pass on the news to Amy. 'He was sat in his father's car for ages before he drove off. How is your mother? She's a bad colour lately, isn't she? I haven't seen her in Sunday school for a while. Has Mr Dale been on his holidays? I saw him coming past with a case not half an hour ago. He's caught the sun on his face. It's as brown as a pickled walnut.'

13

'I knew you were back because Mrs Rakestraw told me,' Amy said. 'She saw you, and I bet she'll be watching us now. I think she fears the worst.'

'She has the picking eyes of an old woman who sleeps badly,' Bernard said.

'Or of one who strains them peering through her lace curtains.'

He looked so different with his brown face and his open-necked shirt with the collar laid neatly over his sports jacket that Amy couldn't resist telling him.

'Mile upon mile of open moorland. Wild flowers, running streams, the sound of birdsong, heather-clad hills . . .' Bernard shook his head. 'No one where I come from would believe it. To the majority of Londoners, Lancashire is all mills and muck and rows of terraced houses, flat caps and whippets, flat vowels, and men who would kill if you insulted their football club.'

'That last part's true,' Amy said.

They were walking towards the centre of the town and, because it looked like rain, Bernard had brought an umbrella with him. Already Amy was calmed by his nearness, warmed by his solicitude, happy to be with him, and never mind who saw them together. Outside the Majestic Cinema they stopped to stare at a framed still of Greta Garbo, bare-shouldered and glamorous, and Bernard said how glad he was that Amy had left *her* eyebrows where they were.

'Wesley came today.' Amy dragged her feet a little. 'But I wasn't in.'

'Mrs Rakestraw told you?'

She nodded. 'I gave his mother a piece of my mind while you were away. She doesn't think that Wesley is at all happy at the moment.'

'And that bothers you?'

They were on the Boulevard in front of the railway station. Behind them Queen Victoria stood on her plinth staring sternly at the soot-blackened buildings.

'I can't be glad he's unhappy,' Amy said at last. 'I know I don't want to see him or talk to him, but you can't live with someone for all those years and then just cross them from your mind.' She bit her lips. 'I suppose it's because he dominated me so much. I feel I'm just waiting for him to order my life again, even though I know I would never let him influence me again.'

Bernard was very pointedly ignoring her. 'Look at the semi-circular arches and triangles of that building across there.' He pointed with the umbrella. 'Some people find Victorian architecture pretentious and over fussy, but I don't.'

'I just wish I didn't feel so married! I wish I was better at casting off inhibitions. I wish I didn't always feel guilty – even when I'm as innocent as a flamin' newborn lamb!'

'All that detail in stone symbolizes an age to me when wealth and the flaunting of it wasn't considered to be a sin. I would quite like to have been a mill owner going off to exploit my workers for all my worth.' He grinned down into Amy's serious face. 'Wearing a red carnation in my buttonhole.'

They walked through the cathedral grounds, and because no one was about Amy took his arm, pressing it into her side.

'The Inn of the Lord,' she said softly. 'That's what this church was called hundreds and hundreds of years ago.'

'The Inn of the Lord. I like that,' said Bernard. Then he brought the conversation down to earth by saying that he hoped the war he could see coming wouldn't put a stop to the huge building project planned for the cathedral.

'I refuse to discuss the possibility of another war.' Amy withdrew her arm and began to walk more quickly. 'I won't look back. Not at anything. From this moment I have no past, not even a single memory. I have decided that I only began from the time I've known you.'

Bernard took her hand. 'But you *are* your past, lassie. Just as I am

218

mine. What has happened to us has made us the persons we are. The sad things, the glad things – we measure what is to be by them. Can't you see that?'

'I'd like to tell you about my babies some day,' Amy said suddenly. 'Because they are part of me.' She hesitated. 'As Anna is part of you.'

As he left her at her door she told him, 'I think I know what I'm going to do. I think that time is almost here.'

'I'm glad to hear it,' he said, walking away from her with the rolled umbrella looped over his arm. Like a city gent, Amy thought fondly.

Ethel would never have believed that Wesley could speak to his mother like that. Not after the way she'd always thought the sun shone out of him, not after the way they'd paid for him to go to the Grammar School. To give him a place in the sun, as Phyllis had been fond of saying.

'All three shops will be yours eventually, dear,' Phyllis told him. 'But Mr Thomson thinks . . .'

'Mr Thomson? Harold po-faced Thomson? I might have known. Father primed him well, didn't he? Can't you just see the old codger taking instructions from Father, giving advice to Father? He never liked me.'

'Their friendship would have nothing to do with anything legal. You know better than that, Wesley.'

'Stop playing God! Try and see things my way for a change!' His face twisted into a sneer, and when Ethel moved towards the door he called her back. 'Listen well, Ethel! You may learn something about this family that will surprise you.' He rubbed his finger and thumb together, in what Ethel thought of as a very vulgar motion. 'It's cash I need, Mother, not bloody promises.'

As he leaned over Phyllis's chair she cowered back as if she was afraid he might be going to hit her, and for one heart-stopping moment Ethel had thought the same. She looked at his features contorted into ugliness with the force of his emotions and she shrank back herself from the popping hatred in his eyes. In that moment she decided that it was just possible, probably even more than possible that her cousin's blue-eyed boy might not be quite right in the head.

'Two hundred to the church extension fund!' he shouted. 'Two hundred to the Oddfellows and various other charities, and the same to my wife. Only she isn't my wife now, is she? The only wife I have lives with me in two dreary rooms with packing cases instead of furniture, a spluttering gas fire and a camp bed that wasn't even good enough for the Scouts' last jumble sale. I was sure,' he yelled, stabbing his finger at his mother, 'that things would improve for me from now on. I promised Clara that we'd move. I promised and promised her that we'd move. Even before Father died I was sure he'd come up with a loan, but instead of that he hands over my house to Amy!'

To Ethel's horror he threw himself down on his knees by his mother's chair and laid his head in her lap. Ethel stood transfixed with disgust.

'Mother, darling Mother . . . I have to get my hands on some money *now*. She'll leave me if I don't get her out of that terrible room.' His voice was a drawn-out wail. 'It's diabolical what my father's done to me. He's deliberately left me out – left me skint, penniless, humiliated me.'

'The Preston shop could be a little gold mine.' Phyllis's hand was on her son's dark head in a gesture of motherly concern. Ethel held her breath. Couldn't she see that Wesley was play-acting? Just as he'd play-acted all his life. If she fell soft and gave him money or made promises, Ethel would walk out. Or say something she might regret.

'How do you know the Preston shop could be a little gold mine?' Slowly Wesley raised his head.

Like a snake preparing to strike, Ethel thought.

'I thought you never discussed business with my father?' Wesley stood up. 'He told you I wasn't running the shop properly, didn't he? He suspected me of filching part of the takings. Didn't he?'

Ethel thought that Phyllis looked just like Queen Mary sitting there, upright in her chair with her waved hair as perfectly ridged as corrugated cardboard. Only a slight twitch beneath her left eye betrayed her agitation.

'I'm beginning to think that a lot of what your father kept from me was for what he imagined to be my own good.' Phyllis met Wesley's angry gaze unflinchingly. 'Because he knew I would be more than likely to take your side against his. That's something I'm beginning to realize day by day.'

'But my father is dead! He's influencing you from the grave!' Wesley snatched up his trilby from the chair by the door. 'I'll come back when you're feeling better, when you're seeing things the way they are.' He glared at Ethel, standing harmlessly by the door. 'I don't suppose you could. . .?' He brushed past her, almost knocking her over. 'Oh, God, forget it. You're two stupid women who can't see further than the ends of their noses!'

'I think we'll have a little drinkie, dear.'

Ethel thought that Phyllis needed something to pull her together. She seemed to have shrunk, to have shrivelled to half her size, to have aged twenty years, but already she was enjoying the sherry, even though she was drinking it far too quickly. It was the first time Ethel had seen her cousin looking vulnerable and the sight choked her up.

Plunging in where angels should have been terrified to tread, she said: 'Wesley had no right to speak to you like that. He's not brought you a lot of joy, has he? No, you've not exactly had an easy life, Phyllis. I mean to say, I know Edgar was a good husband, but he was wrapped up in his shops, either working on his papers when he was at home or asleep in his chair.'

'He and Wesley never saw eye to eye, Ethel. I thought Edgar was too strict with him, and he thought I was too soft.' Phyllis held up her empty glass, narrowed her eyes as if examining it for flaws. 'You don't understand, dear. How could you be expected to when you've never had a child? Never even had a man.'

Battle lines were drawn. Ethel wasn't going to stand for a nasty remark like that. 'Everybody knows you spoiled him rotten. The whole family knew.'

'One of us had to! What chance did the boy have being forced to marry when he was only just twenty?'

'How old was Amy?'

'Still at school. Seventeen.'

'She had two stillbirths, didn't she?'

'And more than one miscarriage. Her mother revelled in the details, but her sort would.'

'Her sort?'

'Her class, Ethel. You know full well what I mean.'

'I like Amy's mother.' When Ethel raised her voice it came out as a squeak. 'From the first time I saw her it was like calling to like. The one in the pinny, always in the kitchen – let's send for Ethel – just as I suppose it was always Amy's mother with her hands in hot soapy water when a dirty job needed doing.'

Second sherries had been poured and were being knocked back.

'I wish I hadn't been so sharp with Wesley.' Phyllis was feeling awful about it, wishing Ethel hadn't been there as a witness. And why was she imbibing when it was common family knowledge that Ethel could get tipsy on a spoonful of cod-liver oil?

'Does Amy know that Wesley was expelled from school?' she was saying now. 'From nursery school? He had a vicious streak in him right from the beginning.' Another sip, and worse was to come. 'Does Amy know he was sacked from his job on the railway for being caught with his fingers in the till?'

Phyllis's thin mouth was slack with shock, but Ethel hadn't finished yet. Draining her glass, her head thrown back like a Russian general at his regiment's annual dinner, she hurled it into the fireplace.

'You may have slept with a man, Phyllis Battersby, but, by God, I bet you've never let rip enough to do that!'

Clara was upstairs in the room that had once been her bedroom before she left Charlie. She was waiting for Wesley to pick her up and in the meantime she was packing a few things into the small case she'd brought with her.

She had no fancy to go downstairs to where Dora Ellis was

222

queening it in the kitchen. The spare little woman, seen close to, was better looking than Clara remembered. No oil painting, but fuller in the face, rosier, younger somehow. Perhaps she'd had a perm? Clara leaned towards the triple mirrors on the dressing table to pout her lips and fluff out her hair.

'Dora told me you were here.' Lottie drooped against the wall, lank-haired, ink-stained, school tie askew. 'Don't you get tired of looking at yourself in the mirror? Nothing's changed as far as I can see.'

'Oh, Lottie . . . Lottie . . .' Clara picked up her case. 'I'm going in a few minutes and goodness knows when I'll see you again. Must you hate me as much as all that?'

Lottie closed the door and slitted her eyes in a way that made Clara wince. 'Why do you keep coming back? There's no room for you here. You're not wanted.'

To Clara's amazement the remark was like a stab through her heart, hurting for a second then flaring into instant anger.

'You don't need to worry, Lottie. I won't be coming back. This is the last time, I promise.' She snatched up a black velvet theatre coat from the bed and looped it over her arm. She motioned to Lottie to let her pass, then something in the girl's expression held her still. 'I'm sorry,' she heard herself say, 'I'm sorry – sorry – sorry.' Then she was running down the stairs, calling out to Dora that she was going, taking a letter from her pocket and putting it on the hall table, crashing the heavy front door behind her.

As soon as she got into the car she could see that Wesley's anger matched her own. He drove badly, wrestling with the gears, crouching over the steering wheel. Already he was regretting speaking to his mother the way he had. He would ring her up after they'd eaten, sounding so apologetic, so contrite she'd be forced to laugh. Tomorrow he'd send flowers, masses of them. Clara needn't know. She wouldn't understand.

Feeling more relaxed, he reached for her knee and squeezed it. 'We'll be out of the flat very soon now, darling. Things are moving slowly, too slowly I admit, but you know how long these things take.'

A glance at Clara's set expression told him that she didn't know and wasn't prepared to understand. He frowned, the fear creeping towards him again. She seemed to have distanced herself from him lately, to have moved a pace or two away, to have stopped listening properly to what he was saying. Almost as though she wasn't interested.

'I'm not going back there again,' she said at last, breaking the silence growing and lengthening between them. 'Charlie's got quite a cosy set-up going for him, with Amy's friend in his kitchen, and like as not in his bed.'

'No chance of that.' Wesley laughed and swerved right, frightening the life out of a woman driving a little Austin Seven. 'Dora Ellis has been past it for years. She'd run a mile if a man snapped his braces at her.'

'Is that meant to be funny?' Clara was wetting a piece of hair and bringing it forward on to her cheek. 'You're grinning like a butcher's dog.'

She was gone from him again, into some far-off place where he couldn't reach her. Feeling murderous again, Wesley pressed his foot down hard on the accelerator.

A temper like Wesley's needed watching, Ethel told herself as she got her things together in Phyllis's guest room. But she ought not to have said the things she had, unforgivable things that Phyllis would never forget. Folding a lock-knit nightdress, she laid it in the bottom of her case. The drink had done its worst, leaving a lump where her stomach used to be, so she sat down on the bed for a while, holding her manicure set in one hand and her furry slippers in the other. Her hair was slipping down at the back, but what did it matter?

The thought of going back to her lonely house set in an avenue of other lonely houses, where people either went out to work or shut themselves away behind their lace curtains, appalled her. Since her parents had died Ethel had felt unwanted, not needed. She had waited on them hand and foot, cherished them, preserved them like bottled fruit, not letting the wind blow on them if she could help it.

Ethel rolled up a pair of grey lisle stockings and tucked them down the side of her case before laying her bottle-green velveteen after-six dress on the bed and filling the folds with tissue paper. She was a good packer and always had been.

She could still hear her mother's voice: 'You're a good packer, Ethel. There's never a crease when the case is opened at the other end.'

The memory of her mother brought tears to her eyes. One plopped on to the green velvet and she wondered if it would leave a mark. She was good at getting marks off things, she knew that too. She had this knack of knowing what to use – bread for a stain on the wallpaper, salt and lemon for ink, soda water for coffee, and blotting paper, then talcum powder for grease.

'No one can remove stains like Ethel,' her father had said. 'There's not much she can't turn her hand to.'

Now her skills weren't wanted because she had done the one thing Phyllis could never forgive her for – she had dared to criticize Wesley. Groping for a handkerchief Ethel cried in earnest, great glycerine tears down her mottled cheeks, running in rivulets down her chin. It was as if all the tears of her life were draining her heart.

From the doorway Phyllis watched her cry. She had been crying herself, and it had suddenly struck her how incongruous it was – two old women in floods of tears, one upstairs and one down.

'Why don't we go away for a holiday? Goodness knows we're both ready for a break. What do you say, Ethel? I like the idea of Rhyl or Colwyn Bay. Do you remember we always went to North Wales when we were children? I can't bear the thought of Bournemouth now Edgar's passed away. We went to the same hotel there year after year.'

Two pairs of red-rimmed eyes met and held. There would be no more mention of what had been said today, Ethel knew that for a fact. Phyllis wasn't waiting for an apology, she was just making it clear that an armistice had been declared.

'Llandudno's nice, too,' Ethel said. 'The last time I took my father there he was in a bathchair. He loved sitting on the front with a rug round his knees.'

'Right then.' Phyllis nodded. 'We'll go downstairs and I'll look

225

hotels up in a book I have.' She pointed a finger at the case. 'You've always been a good packer, Ethel. You can do mine for me when we've decided where to go.' She marched along the landing, stiff as a steel poker. 'While I'm doing that you can make us a pot of Earl Grey if you will. I always find him strangely comforting.'

Ethel followed on, her cup running over, needed. There to make herself useful, a person again.

Wesley was still feeling sick with anger when they got back to the flat. When he went upstairs after checking the till and locking the door behind Arnold Porrit he found Clara in that same strange frame of mind.

'Things are definitely moving,' he told her. 'I reckon that we'll be out of here by the end of the summer, if not before.' He tried to take her in his arms. 'You've been very patient, darling, putting up with all this.' He waved a hand at the rickety table, the cardboard boxes, the sagging sofa. 'There are always bound to be hiccoughs where Wills are concerned. I'll have you in the house of your dreams before you know it.'

Clara closed her eyes so that she would not betray her disgust at the way he repeatedly made promises she knew by now he could never keep.

'I'm leaving you, Wesley,' she said.

He seemed to be pretending he hadn't heard her. He was still half smiling, still putting on what she had come to know as his 'endearing' act.

'By tomorrow, when I've smoothed Mother's ruffled feathers, the picture will be different. I played it all wrong today, but tomorrow . . .'

'There won't be any tomorrow, not for you and me, Wesley.' She was looking more animated than he had seen her for a long time. Behind her the rain pebbled the window, and already the room had darkened, but her blonde candyfloss hair stood out round her head like a nimbus.

'I'm going to live with Colonel Brown-Davies,' she said. 'As his

226

housekeeper, for the sake of gossip, but as soon as my divorce from Charlie comes through we'll be married.'

The breath left Wesley's body as if he'd been winded. He bent to light the gas fire without any conscious volition, totally unaware of what he was doing. When it plopped into life he swung round.

'Do you mind saying that again, because I can't believe what I think I heard. You and that old man? Him touching you, making love to you? He's been married at least twice before. Do you know that?'

'Yes, he told me. His first wife died in childbirth and the second after being in a nursing home with consumption for years and years. He's a lonely man, a kind man, and he doesn't make promises he can't keep.'

'And you love him?' Wesley's voice was a sarcastic sneer.

'As far as I'm able to love anyone, yes, I care for him.'

'The fact that he's worth half a million at least has nothing to do with it?'

'I would say it had more than a lot to do with it.' Clara smiled at the thought of the mink stole she'd been promised, feeling already the touch of the soft fur at her throat. 'I know how to make him happy, you see.' She looked Wesley straight in the eye. 'As for what you're thinking about, he might need a little help, but he's far from past it.'

'You little . . .' Wesley raised a hand, then as quickly lowered it. What she was saying, what she was inferring, made him sick to his guts. He could hardly bear to look at her, so he covered his face with his hands, ashamed to find that he was shaking, hoping she wouldn't notice.

'Look, Wesley.' She actually came to sit beside him. 'I've never pretended to be other than I am. You think back and you'll realize that's true. You've given me a wonderful few months – God, they must have been wonderful for me to stay in this dump!' She touched his arm. 'Have you stopped to think what it's been like for me day after day in this room? Helping that halfwit in the shop when it was busy. There were days when I even considered going back to Charlie – but there's Lottie, and just to look at her makes my flesh crawl.'

227

'Your own daughter . . .' Wesley sounded very old and very ill. 'Charlie's daughter.'

'But she isn't, you see. Lottie's the result of four or five minutes' stupidity on the way home from a dance. I didn't even know his name.' She jumped up. 'For God's sake, Wesley, which part are you playing now? King Lear? Hamlet? You've known the way I am since the first time you kissed me. You said you'd never met anyone like me and I don't suppose you ever will again. I'm a sod, Wesley, through and through. If there's a hell I'll go straight down to it, straight into the flames of burning hellfire.'

'Don't say things like that!'

'Go back to Amy. She's cared for you all down the years and she'll go on caring for you. She's frightened of hellfire, you see. She'll feel married to you till the day she dies. You had pure gold, Wesley, and you threw it away.' She sat down near to him again and touched his arm. 'I told you when all this began that I hated upsetting Amy. I couldn't laugh the way she does if I'd gone through what she has. I saw her one day, you know. She was outside the library in Blackburn talking to a tall thin man with straight brown hair blowing in the wind. He left her and went into the Education Office, and there was something – I don't know what it was – but there was something between them. They should have seen me, but they didn't.'

'You can forget that. I know who it was and he's a jessie. Reads poetry and bakes his own bread. He was probably giving Amy a recipe for date and walnut loaf. The last time I saw him was the night we came here to live together. I was on my way to pick the taxi up and meet you, and he was on the other side of the street. Striding along in the pouring rain to his cup of cocoa by the fire. Amy wouldn't look twice at him. She wouldn't look twice at anybody but me.'

'Why?'

'Because she wouldn't, that's why. She's religious for one thing, so once married she'll stay married; and for another she's not that way inclined.'

'What do you mean?' Clara had moved closer and was stroking

his arm. He had calmed a little now, but she could still feel the trembling of him, still sense the effort he was making not to pull her to him. 'You mean she doesn't enjoy doing the things we've enjoyed? Are you trying to tell me that she's frigid?'

Wesley's arm jerked upwards so suddenly that she fell back against the sofa cushions. When he turned to look at her, the expression in his eyes made her recoil.

Moving away as quickly as she could, she ran across the tiny landing into the bedroom, took her packed case from its hiding place and crept to the top of the stairs, then slowly, slowly down each creaking step into the shop, lifting the counter-flap and sliding the bolt on the front door.

It was a full twenty minutes until the time she was being picked up, but she was no fool. An innate sense of self-preservation had got her out of many a tight corner before, and what she had seen in Wesley's eyes had been murder. Not premeditated, but the swift and total loss of control of a man who didn't know how to cope with his anger.

Trembling herself by now, she glanced up at the square of light above the shop, and darted down a narrow back street to stand shivering in the shadow of a cold wet wall, feeling the rain beating down on her uncovered head.

Wesley heard the car draw up outside and the slam of the doors. He had no idea of how long he had sat there, unmoving, staring straight ahead, feeling the rage gathering inside him, choking his throat, pounding his heart. Five, ten minutes, or longer?

Picking up the cushion by his side, he tore at the braid and found that it came away easily in his hand. It was the same with the cupboard door – when he wrenched at it that too came to pieces, to loll drunkenly from its hinges. The chair he smashed against the wall splintered like dry firewood, and the card table crumpled like tissue paper.

He cried aloud without knowing who to. How dare Clara leave him? He was always the one to leave, his the exit line. First his mother, then Clara, deserting him when he needed them most. He sat down and buried his face in his hands.

*

Charlie had Clara's letter in his hand as he came into the kitchen. Dora could see at once that something had happened. He was half smiling, half serious, walking about with his hat on the back of his head, going over to the window to read it again because he wouldn't wear his glasses, yet needed the light.

'She's coming back, isn't she?' Dora hadn't a discreet bone in her body, so saw no reason to conjure one up now. It had always been like this with Charlie. Say what you were thinking right out, no messing about, just straightforward talk. 'So this is where I hang up me pinny and do a bunk, isn't it? Because there's no room for her and me in the same house. Do you think I could carry on working here, seeing the way she put you down and ignored Lottie? I'd throttle her with the tea-towel, and swing for it gladly.'

All the time she was talking Dora was rolling out the pastry crust for a steak and kidney pie. The meat was steaming away in its brown dish, the gravy thick, dark and brown, bubbling slightly, straight from the oven. The rolling pin went thump thump along with Dora's heart, but she wasn't going to do any touting for sympathy from this lovely little fat man staring at her from the other side of the table.

'Have you finished, woman?' Charlie threw the letter to one side and leaned on the table, getting all floury but not noticing. His cheeks were flushed and a bead of sweat glistened on his upper lip. 'By 'eck, woman, but you don't half go on! Stop that flamin' rolling till I've had a chance to get me speak in.'

'She's claiming half the house.' Dora was too upset to keep quiet. 'She had your Lottie near to tears – the poor little lass hasn't come down since – but did she come in here and tell me she was off? Not on your nelly! Too jumped up for the likes of me.'

'Stop it, Dora! Do you hear me? Shut up!' Charlie snatched the rolling pin and hurled it from him. 'This letter is to tell me that my dear wife is leaving Wesley Battersby and going to marry a chap with a double-barrelled name. She wants the divorce speeded up so they can marry. She encloses a forwarding address and hopes that I will be as happy as she knows she is going to be.'

230

'Just like that?' Dora said, when she'd got her breath back.

'Just like that,' Charlie agreed. 'But this time my guess is she's serious. My guess is this chap is loaded. Money has always been Clara's god. Wesley must have spun her a good tale to lure her away from the material comforts she had here.'

'A little palace,' Dora said. She rubbed her hands down her apron. 'I'm sorry I jumped in too quick. But ever since she went, and Lottie wouldn't come downstairs, I've been telling myself that she was coming again, the next time for good. And being you, you'd have had her back, wouldn't you?'

Charlie pretended to think for a minute. 'Well, I wouldn't exactly have seen her go short of a bob or two, but there's no place for her in my house again. I never thought to see Lottie so happy – she can go two days at a stretch without lying now.' He picked up the letter from the table. 'I'd best go up and talk to her, and you'd best get that crust on yon pie if we're to eat at a decent hour.'

Yon pie . . . Dora smiled to herself. Charlie often lapsed into dialect when he was particularly happy. It was as though the soft words of long ago were a cover-up for the reticence he felt at talking soppy. Lovingly she laid the pastry lid over the meat, fluting the edges and, quite carried away by her own euphoria, shaped a couple of leaves complete with veins from the left-over bits.

'It seems silly you having to go home at this time every night as soon as you've done the washing up,' Charlie said later. 'Don't you think?'

Dora thought. But only for a minute. Only a little while ago she had thought the gates of heaven were closed against her. She had seen herself going back to her shabby house with carpets so thin you could see the nicks of the floorboards through them, and an emptiness that was beginning to drain the very life from her. She went on scouring out the brown pie dish, careful not to turn round.

'Are you suggesting that I move in here? Be a living-in housekeeper?'

'Yes, I am.' Charlie sounded aggrieved, as if already someone had challenged his decision. 'What's wrong with that?'

'You mean me to give up my own house?' Dora scraped away at

a burnt-on bit of kidney. 'You mean move in here lock, stock and barrel?'

'Every lock, every stock and every flamin' barrel.'

'You'd have to marry me of course,' said Dora, squeezing her eyes tight shut and sending up a fervent prayer. 'When the divorce comes through.'

He was so close behind her she could feel him through her skin. She loved him, every inch of him, including his little twinkly eyes, his two chins and not forgetting his beer belly. He wasn't a bit like Ronald Colman or Robert Donat, there was neither of them a patch on him. He was cuddly, funny, with a sense of the ridiculous to match her own, and she loved him in a way she had never thought to love again.

'Art thou proposing to me, lass?' she heard him say, 'because if thou art, then I accept.'

When she turned round she was enveloped in a hug that took the breath from her body, and when she looked into his eyes they were filled with tears.

'I'll look after you,' Dora whispered fiercely. 'And Lottie, and that lad she's going out with, and anybody who comes into this house. Everyone will be as welcome as the flowers in May. I'll fill the tins with cakes and I'll polish the sideboard till you can see to shave in it . . .'

There was no controlling her. The dam of Dora's unhappiness had burst; she was transported into a realm of such delight that it threatened to overwhelm her. The only time she calmed down a little and grew serious was when she tried to talk to Lottie about her feelings for her mother.

'When you stayed upstairs after she'd gone I thought she must have upset you, love. I'll never try to take her place, I promise.'

Lottie's dark eyes flashed scorn. 'I stayed in my room because I wanted to be quiet. I knew she was telling the truth when she said she wasn't coming here any more, and I wanted to dwell on it.'

'Dwell on it?'

'Let it sink in that I never needed to try to make her like me again. Mothers are supposed to love their children, aren't they? So I never gave up the hope that one day my mother might look at me and like what she saw. Now she's gone for ever and I don't need to try any more. As far as I'm concerned she's dead.' The hardness in the dark eyes suddenly softened. 'But *you* won't go away, will you, Dora?'

'When the time comes for me to leave for good I'll be in me box,' said Dora, making Lottie laugh out loud.

'Jimmy says you're a card,' she said.

'Good thinking there,' said Dora, going through into the sitting room to tell Charlie that she was going now, that it would take a week or more to clear her house and wind up her affairs.

He offered to get out the van and run her home, but she refused. She wanted to see Amy, to tell her the wonderful news and break it to her that she wouldn't be living next door for much longer.

'Do you and Amy tell each other everything?' Charlie looked a bit worried, though Dora couldn't for the life of her see why.

'She's been seeing a lot of Mr Dale, though she hasn't told me that. Amy can be very secretive when she wants to be.'

Charlie looked relieved. 'But you have a feeling that Wesley will be back soon?'

'A definite certainty, Charlie. Now that Clara's leaving him, the wonderful Wesley won't stop on his own for long. He has to have a woman fussing round him like his mother used to do.'

'Am I like that?'

'Not a bit like that.' Dora was quite firm. 'I wouldn't have let myself be persuaded to marry you if you'd had the slightest resemblance to Wesley.' She came further into the room, closing the door behind her. 'My opinion of Wesley was formed one day when he came into my house and tried to kiss me.' She shuddered. 'Well, more than kiss me. He almost tore my blouse off before I got my knee to him.'

Charlie couldn't help a small smile lifting the corners of his mouth. The thought of his little Dora biffing Wesley Battersby where it would hurt the most struck him as being hilariously comical, though what she was telling him now wiped the smile clean away.

'In the house next door, in the living room on the other side of my wall, Amy was lying on the settee trying to get over her third miscarriage. I'd just been in to see her and the look on her face was still with me. She was heartbroken, Charlie, and yet she was trying to laugh. The thing about Amy that's so upsetting is she always tries to laugh when the rest of us would be having a good old scream. She'll have Wesley back because she's not hard enough to send him packing, though it won't be long before he's off with some other woman – that's the way he is. There are some women who are born mugs where men are concerned and Amy's one of them, I'm afraid. He'll turn up with his case one day and she'll forgive him because that's what they tell her to do at Sunday school.' She turned back for another hug. 'Oh, Charlie me darlin', I'll see you tomorrow.'

'And tomorrow, and tomorrow, and tomorrow,' he said in a deep throbbing film-star voice, making her laugh once again.

Her face ached with smiling so much, she told herself as she walked along, wanting to get to Amy and tell her the unbelievable news.

14

'Did you like Shakespeare when you were at school?' Bernard asked, as they fell into step.

'Not the way we acted it,' Amy said. 'The way we said the words parrot-fashion made them seem meaningless. When I first heard *As You Like It* performed by Shakespearian actors on the wireless I couldn't recognize it. At school we got the wrong rhythm to the words somehow.'

She knew there was a reason for his question so she waited, walking along by his side, turning up the familiar road leading to the park, wanting to take his hand but not quite liking to. She marvelled at the ease of their conversations, the way she felt she could say anything she wanted to him, be herself, not have to sound happy when she felt sad, not feeling she should match her mood to his, as she had with Wesley.

'What never ceases to amaze me is the way Shakespeare first said almost everything that's worth saying.' He took her hand, holding it tightly in his firm warm grasp. 'Give sorrow words,' he whispered softly. 'The grief that does not speak whispers o'er the fraught heart and bids it break.'

Amy pulled away from him. The rain had left the air smelling fresh and green. The evening clouds had parted and rolled away, the wind had dropped and soon there would be stars.

'Tell me about the babies,' Bernard said. 'It's time, you know.'

'I can't,' she said, unwilling to try to release the pain held so secretly inside her for so long. 'It's not a subject I care to talk about.' She began to walk more quickly. 'What right have you to intrude on my private thoughts?'

'Tell me,' he said again, leading her to their favourite seat by the duck pond. 'I'm waiting.'

She sighed. 'The words are stuck in my heart. It hurts me to try to say them.'

'That's because they've gone rusty,' he said.

'You're not my doctor, you know.'

'True.'

'Nor a psychiatrist.'

'Correct.'

'I don't have to . . .'

'I agree.'

'My own mother never asked me any questions.'

'I can't believe that.'

Amy's hands were balled into fists. When she began to speak her voice was filled with anger, raw with pain.

'People think, if they think at all, that the first baby, the one born perfect but dead, must be the one I grieve for most. Because he was finished and whole, you could count the nails on his tiny fingers and toes. He was so beautiful, you see.' She was quiet for a while. 'What they don't understand is that each time I miscarried it was like losing a baby just the same. To me, maybe because of that first one, a conception, a first realizing I was carrying again, was like a birth merely waiting to happen. I would get out the baby clothes again, buoyed up with hope, sure that this time . . .' Her voice faltered. 'One day I overheard my mother talking to a neighbour: "Our Amy's had another 'miss', but she's only stopped off work one day this time. She's not one to make a fuss." And each time she would assure me that what was happening to me was all for the best. Once she caught me lying down on the settee and told me that she remembered women weavers in the mill standing at their looms with blood running down their legs, but still there, working, not giving in to it.' Her voice rose. 'My mother isn't a cruel woman, not at all. What was happening to me, not once, but time and time again, was beyond her grasp. In her book a miscarriage was like a bad cold, to be got over as quickly as possible and then forgotten. Certainly not mentioned in company. Or in private, either.'

She sat up straighter, lifting up her chin. 'Wesley's mother was ashamed of me. Disgusted would be a truer word. You'd have thought I was doing it on purpose, but all her sympathy was for Wesley. By some twisted quirk of her imagination, losing an unformed baby was common, something only ignorant women do. Though Mr Battersby always asked me how I was, without putting into words what he was referring to, of course.'

'And Wesley?'

'Oh well, he did try and help.'

'In what way?'

'He got the address of a birth control clinic in Manchester. You can find them if you know where to go.'

'And?'

'Well, he suggested it might be a good idea if I went. So I caught the train one morning and though I was scared stiff, it wasn't as bad as I expected. You waited in a big bare room. I was surprised to see quite young women there. You went behind a curtain into a cubicle and a lady doctor examined you and asked a few questions. She passed no comment on anything I told her, it was just like having a normal conversation. She gave me . . . she explained to me . . .'

'It's all right, lassie. You don't need to tell me any more.' Now *he* was angry. Amy could hear it in his voice, sense it in the way he sighed deeply. 'Couldn't your mother have gone with you?' he asked.

'My mother?' Amy's eyes widened with horror. 'I couldn't tell my mother! She doesn't know such places exist.'

Bernard picked up a loose pebble and skimmed it clean across the grass verge and the railings into the water. He was imagining her sitting in the train alone, with the address in her handbag, shelled in her own anxiety, fearful of what to expect.

'Dora?'

'She was always so busy, every moment to account for. Anyway, Dora doesn't like Wesley. I wouldn't have put it past her to shout at him and ask him what he was doing to get me pregnant so often when he knew what was almost bound to happen.' She turned to him. 'Is all this shocking you?'

'Yes. It's shocking me all right. But not for the reasons you think. Oh, Amy, Amy, wasn't there one person you could turn to during all those years? Not one person who would understand? There comes a time when everyone needs to take an outstretched hand.'

As he had stretched out his hand to Dora, Amy thought, without being able to stop the words coming into her head.

'I understand that,' she said softly. 'Once I wouldn't, but now I do.'

He pulled her into his arms and kissed her, gently at first then with passion.

'If someone sees us,' Amy whispered.

His answer was to kiss her again, so that she clung to him uncaring, feeling the rain beginning again and not caring about that either.

'You mean you went with Mr Dale for a walk in the park? In the rain?' Dora said, coming in and catching Amy drying her hair on a towel. 'I'll be thinking there's something going on between you.'

'I'll tell you some day,' Amy said from inside the folds of the towel.

'But not tonight?'

'Not tonight.'

In a way Dora was glad. Her own news was so thrilling, so momentous, she wanted the stage to herself without anything to steal her thunder. She went to sit in the wonderful Wesley's chair, dangling her thin legs because it was too big for her.

'Charlie has asked me to marry him!' she burst out, only slightly embroidering the truth. 'So I'm moving in with him and Lottie sooner than later.'

Amy's response was even more than she had imagined it would be. The damp toffee-brown hair swung forward as Dora felt the kiss land somewhere near her ear.

'That's the best news I've heard since the Co-op put their divi up!' Amy couldn't conceal her delight. Charlie and Dora. Perfect. Absolutely definitely perfect. 'Do you remember that time we went to the pictures to see Deanna Durbin in *Three Smart Girls* – the night you met Charlie to speak to for the first time?'

Dora clasped her hands together. '*Two* smart girls, he said, sweeping his hat off and bowing to me. I couldn't get over how lovely he was then.'

'And do you remember how we sang all the way home? Linking arms and singing.' Amy threw back her head, sparkled her eyes like Deanna Durbin's, made her mouth into the same pouting shape. 'Will there be someone? Someone to care for me?'

Dora waited till she'd finished, then joined in at the end, totally out of tune: 'Will there be happiness for me?' she carolled, flinging her arms wide.

'Yes! Yes!' Amy cried. 'Oh Dora, can I be your bridesmaid?'

'In purple satin with shoes dyed to tone?'

'Oh yes, please.' Amy sat down and they beamed across the sunrise rug at each other. 'This calls for a drink,' Amy said, going through to see what she could find.

'I'd gone off whisky, anyway,' Dora told her, sipping the dandelion and burdock. 'You can have too much of a good thing, I always say.' She looked straight at Amy. 'You haven't asked me how I can be so sure that Charlie's wife won't want to move back with him.'

'Because she's going to marry Wesley one day when the divorce is through.'

'Have you seen any divorce papers, Amy?' Dora put her cup down on the floor beside her chair. 'Has Wesley asked you to go to a solicitor?'

'No.'

'Well, Charlie's got his papers through. He told me tonight. I'll be named as co-respondent I imagine, but who cares?'

Amy was a bit perplexed. 'But Charlie isn't the guilty party. Clara left him.'

'He's a gentleman, Amy. You know that.'

'There's something else, isn't there?' Amy frowned into her cup. 'You're holding something back, aren't you?'

'Clara's left Wesley,' Dora said in a rush. 'She's gone to live with an old geezer with pots of money. She came to Charlie's house today and left a letter spelling it out, giving him a forwarding address.'

239

Amy went first white then red. There was too much emotion going on inside her to properly take in what Dora had said.

'I don't believe it,' she said at last. 'You can't just . . . I mean to say, how could she?'

'If you say poor Wesley, I'll clock you one,' Dora warned.

But Amy said she wasn't going to say anything of the sort. 'I never understood how he could take her there in the first place. That flat is awful. It was only meant for the odd overnight stay. Wesley used to sleep there sometimes when it was stock-taking time, or if he wanted to work on the books.'

Dora's lip curled. Oh yeah? she said in her head. 'That must have been jolly convenient,' she said aloud.

Phyllis had let lucky with her holiday arrangements. The Grand Hotel at St-Annes-on-Sea had two single rooms vacant and would be pleased to welcome Mrs Battersby and Miss Tunstall for two weeks' stay. The lady next door, who had turned out to be quite charming since Edgar's death, had promised to see the milkman and explain.

'There are times, Ethel, when there's no shame in letting a neighbour know one's business.'

'As long as they don't get too familiar, dear.'

Ethel was doing lots of packing, following the list that Phyllis had given her and saying nothing, even though she couldn't see when a full-length evening dress would come in at St-Annes-on-Sea. For herself, the bottle-green, calf-length velvet would do nicely, worn with her crystal beads and her silk evening bag with the tortoiseshell clasp.

She knew full well, though she wasn't saying anything about that either, that Phyllis was in effect running away from another confrontation with that son of hers. Another scene like that and Ethel wouldn't give a tuppenny bun for Phyllis's heart. And *she* hadn't helped either, shouting and chucking her glass into the fireplace. She would never touch another drop of anything stronger than sarsaparilla for as long as she lived. She burned with shame when she thought about it.

'I ought to ring Wesley,' Phyllis said about half-past nine. 'He'll be coming to see me to apologize and I wouldn't like him worried when he finds the house locked up. He'll be sorry for the way he behaved. Do you remember when he was a little boy how he would go out into the garden and pick a flower for me when he'd been naughty? I'll have Mr Thomson round when we come home to detail something out for him. I'm sure Edgar wouldn't have wanted him to feel so cast down.' She handed Ethel a pair of sandals which should have gone at the bottom of the case, but in her contrite state her cousin said nothing, just took them from her and reached for the tissue paper.

Phyllis went into her own bedroom and picked up the telephone receiver. Ethel stopped rustling paper to listen.

'Hallo, dear, this is Mother. Have you got a cold coming on? You sound a bit hoarse. Yes, dear, I know you're sorry, and I am too. People do get heated about Wills. Yes, I know, dear. But I won't be in tomorrow. No. Me and Ethel are going away for two weeks to St-Annes-on-Sea, staying at the Grand Hotel on the front. The one not far from the pier. I'll send you a card, dear, so you'll know we're all right. Wesley? You do sound peculiar. You mustn't take things so much to heart. Well, if you really want to see me . . .'

'Put the receiver down!' Ethel urged in a fierce whisper from the next room. If Phyllis Battersby cancelled their holiday so as not to disappoint her precious son, Ethel would . . . she would take to drink again! 'Put it down!' she hissed, knowing that she couldn't be heard but praying there was something in thought transference. 'PUT IT DOWN!'

'I'll have to go now, dear,' Phyllis was saying. 'There's someone at the door.' The receiver went down with a click that brought tears of relief to Ethel's eyes.

'God forgive me.' Phyllis looked shattered when she came through. 'I just told Wesley a white lie because I didn't want to go on talking to him. I told him there was someone at the door.' She sat down on the bed, looking so shriven and worried that Ethel went to sit beside her and put a comforting hand on her arm. 'Am I doing the right thing?' Phyllis whimpered. 'I'd walk to hell and back on hot

241

coals for that boy, and yet now when he's sorely troubled, when he needs me, I run away.' She turned an anguished face to Ethel. 'I *want* to run away, you see. I just don't want to face him. Does that make me a bad mother?'

In all her years Ethel had never heard her Cousin Phyllis talk about feelings like this. Never heard her question herself. She swallowed hard. 'You've been a marvellous mother. Too good, that's been your trouble, dear. Now he's playing on your sympathy, though I don't think for one minute he'd allow you to cancel your holiday just for him.'

'But he would!' Phyllis cried. 'He would. Don't you see, Ethel? That's why I have to be strong and go away . . .'

'And enjoy yourself, even if it kills you,' Ethel said, taking no notice when Phyllis took a lace-edged handkerchief from her sleeve and wept gently into it. 'What time is the taxi coming, dear?'

The next day being a Saturday Amy went with her mother on the market. She had been doing this every week since Wesley went away and the routine was always the same. First they would each buy a quarter of loose lettuce leaves from the stall by the Market House, then a quarter of tomatoes from the stall opposite because they were cheaper and local grown. Gladys liked talking to the shrimp women who came from Southport and sat in the open cobbled space. No matter how cold or how warm the weather, they wore long full skirts and flowered cotton sun-bonnets, selling their shrimps from wide baskets covered with check cloths.

Amy hung back while her mother passed the time of day and remarked on the weather for the time of year with the fattest of the four stout ladies.

'Two pots of buttered? Yes, me love, the shrimps is lovely today, pink and tender as a baby's toes.'

'Let's be extravagant and go in the Market House for a cup of tea,' Gladys said when the shopping was done, 'and if we're careful not to let anyone see us, we can eat one of the eccles cakes you've just bought with it.'

'Mam!' Amy said, following her inside, stopping for a moment at the covered button stall, which had always fascinated her. In you could go with a few buttons and a piece of material and come out with them covered so neatly they would make a homemade dress look as if it had been made by a professional dressmaker. She was always thinking she would make something just to see it covered from neck to hem with a row of exquisitely covered buttons.

'There's an empty table over there,' Gladys said, pushing her way to it, bemoaning the fact that they wouldn't be able to eat their eccles cakes because they were in full view of the ladies presiding over the tea urns and the plates of iced fancies. 'I just felt like an eccles cake,' she grumbled, settling her shopping on the floor by her chair. 'You haven't been putting rouge on, have you? Your cheeks look a bit red to me. I wish you'd tell me what's going on, because something is. I can feel it in my bones.'

'Wesley is on his own again. Clara Marsden's leaving him,' Amy said casually. 'But that's not making my face red. I just happen to be hot. It's always hot in here.'

Beneath the little round felt hat Gladys's face sharpened visibly. 'She's lucky her husband will have her back. From what I've been told she's been in and out of that house more times than the neighbours can keep count. They say she has a case ready packed for when the next man comes along.'

'She's not going back to Charlie. She's going off with someone else. An elderly man with pots of money.'

'No fool like an old fool,' Gladys said quickly. Amy could almost see her mind ticking over, weighing up the situation, thinking what to say for the best. 'So Wesley will be coming back to you,' she said at last.

Amy finished drinking her tea and put the thick white cup back in its saucer. 'What shall I say to him, Mam, if he does come back?'

She had that closed sly look on her face that Gladys had never been able to fathom, but she said what needed saying: 'You tell him it's all best over with and forgotten, then you carry on like you were before.'

'How were we before, Mam?'

Gladys felt the familiar sense of not getting anywhere coming

243

over her. They were on opposite sides of the fence, always had been. It was like talking at a brick wall. She reached down to her basket for a pair of grey cotton gloves and wrestled her fingers into them.

'How you were, lady, was a married couple. Man and wife living together like God intended you to.'

'Even unhappily?'

Gladys snorted. 'What's happiness got to do with it? Your trouble is you've been going to the pictures too often. Life's not like that. You live it and get on with it, not forever bothering about being happy.' She glanced at the next table and lowered her voice. 'You don't know how lucky you've been. I know women with husbands who beat them, or drink their wages away of a Friday night, or make unusual demands on them, and they still stick with them. Wesley did wrong, but he's a man. I've not told anybody about it, and though there may have been rumours they'll die down when folks see you together again. You can put the whole thing behind you.'

'What would you say, Mam, if I told you I've fallen in love? Really deeply in love, for the first time in my life. With a man who cares for me in just the same way. A good, kind, honourable man who would never ever hurt me.'

Gladys stood up. 'If we stop here any longer we'll have to fork out for another cup of tea. I think we'd best go home.'

She didn't speak again until they reached the house. She trudged along, carrying her basket, sweating gently because whatever the weather she would never go into town without her hat and coat on. What was niggling at her was the look she had seen on Amy's face when she talked about the man she said she was in love with. Gladys couldn't get over it. It was as though the years had dropped away, leaving the young Amy she remembered, a pretty girl with shining eyes and a lovely softness in her expression. How long since she'd looked like that? Dear, dear God of mercy, how long?

'I won't come in, Mam.' Amy was trying to smile. 'I'm sorry I've upset you so much. I'd like to tell you more about him, but I know you can't . . . I know you won't.'

244

Gladys inserted the heavy key into the lock. 'There's one thing I will say. You're storing up a might of trouble for yourself.'

She went inside and closed the door. Took her shopping through to the back scullery, then sat in her rocking chair by the empty grate, staring into space in the room where even in mid-summer the sun did no more than briefly touch the backyard wall. She sat there thinking for a long time, still wearing her hat and coat, and the grey cotton gloves.

Wesley came about five o'clock, and this time he rang the bell.

When Amy opened the door, he drooped against the wall and, in a weary humbled voice, asked if he might come in. He looked haggard, exhausted, with a stubbled chin and dark smudged shadows beneath his eyes. When he sat down in his chair he put a hand to his forehead as if to stem a stab of pain.

Amy stood by the sideboard, waiting for him to speak, waiting for him to tell her that Clara had left him. She felt strangely aloof, almost unconcerned, as if she was watching him acting a part in one of his plays.

'What do you do,' he began at last, speaking in a low tremble of a voice, 'what do you do when you realize one day that you've made a mess of your life? That you've made a terrible mistake, a terrible, terrible mistake?' Wearily he moved his head from side to side. 'You know what I've come to tell you, Amy, don't you?'

Still she waited, wanting him to tell her in his own words.

'I want to come home, Amy,' he said, holding out a hand to her. 'I want to be given the chance to make amends, to spend the rest of my life on my knees before you, begging for your forgiveness, seeing you smile again.'

'And Clara?' Amy watched him carefully. 'What about Clara? What does she have to say about this?'

Wesley shrugged his shoulders. 'What Clara says is no concern of mine. You're the only woman in my life from now on.' He stared down at his hands. 'You always have been the only one, Amy, but I was too much of a fool to realize it. I'm crawling at your feet, can't you see? If pity is akin to love, then pity me now, I beg of you!'

'Have you told Clara you're leaving her?' Amy's eyes never left his face. 'Does she know you want to come back to me, Wesley? Have you told her?'

His face flushed. 'I don't want to talk about Clara. That's done with, finished. Why do you keep bringing her into it? You and me are what matter now. Just you, and me. No one else in the whole wide world. Oh, Amy, don't stand there so far away from me. Come to me and let me feel your arms around me and the warmth of your forgiveness. I ache for you, with every beat of my heart, I ache for you.'

'Stop it! Just stop it!'

His mouth dropped open. He couldn't believe what she was saying.

'Clara has left you, Wesley. She's gone off with someone else, and the only reason you've come here today is because you want me to think it was the other way round.' Amy couldn't get the words out fast enough. 'Oh, you knew I would find out eventually, but by then you hoped you'd be settled back here.' She made a dismissive movement with her right hand. 'Of all the despicable things you've done in your life, this must surely be one of the worst. You wanted me to think you had left her for me, Wesley. Didn't you? You never had a change of heart, never felt sorry. Clara has left you, so you come crawling to me. Why don't you admit it?'

Dora . . . It came to him right away. He'd forgotten about Dora working for Charlie, forgotten that Clara had been there yesterday.

'So you see,' Amy was saying, 'there's no hope for you and me, Wesley. I don't think there has been right from the beginning. In fact, I think the best thing you ever did for me was to walk away on that New Year's Eve, carrying your case and leaving me a note.' She pointed a finger down the lobby. 'Oh yes, I've seen the case. You were so sure I would welcome you back, you didn't even bother to leave it in the car. You think these past months haven't made any difference to me, don't you?'

'You've changed. I'll say that much.'

'Of course I've changed! I've found out for one thing that I could manage my life on my own.' She nodded at the typewriter on the sideboard. 'I've found I can do things I'd only dreamed about, that I can make my own decisions, be myself, not merely a continuation of you.'

'I've never heard such rubbish!' He was recovering from the shock, blustering now. She could hear it in his voice. The hangdog look had gone, the little-boy-lost expression faded. He was getting up from his chair, he was coming towards her.

'If you touch me I'll scream,' she said clearly. 'If I scream Dora will hear me, because she's just the other side of that wall.'

Ignoring her, he took a step forward.

'Wesley!' She knew it was important that she didn't move. If she backed away he would come after her, she could see it in his eyes. 'Go now! I never want to see you again. If you touch me I'll be sick.'

It was the worst thing she could have said to him, and yet in another way it was the best. The insult to his self-esteem, the affront to his sexuality, froze him where he stood.

'You'll regret this,' he mumbled. 'Some day you'll realize what you've done.'

'Go now, Wesley,' she repeated. 'And close the door behind you, please.'

His mother had said that, or something similar. They were turning their backs on him, the two women in his life. He stumbled his way down the lobby and picked up the case. But he'd show them. He'd make them eat their words. One day they'd come crawling to him, and he'd snap his fingers in their faces. Like that!

As he started the car, as he drove away, he saw, in his driving mirror, Amy coming out of the house. Just to show her, he increased his speed, turning the corner almost on two wheels. He knew exactly where she was going – next door to talk about him to Dora Ellis, with her sparrow's body and her nitpicky eyes.

Dora, the best friend – he held her responsible for a lot of this.

But Amy turned right, not left, and by the time Wesley was halfway into town, driving the car like a madman, she was knocking on Bernard's door.

He'd been reading. His glasses were in his hand and he had the

247

bemused look about him of a man who can lose himself in the music of words.

One look at Amy's face told him all he needed to know. Gently, as gently as on the night Wesley had left her, he led her into the house.

'I've sent him away,' she whispered. 'I never want to see him again. It's over, Bernard, and I'm glad.'

His book was lying open on the little wine table by his chair. Slowly he closed it and put his reading glasses back into their brown leather case. He was an orderly man, a man who knew what he wanted, but a man of patience who was prepared to wait for as long as it took.

'Come here, bonny lass,' he said.

His arms around her were a coming home, a knowing that she was being held safe, a quiet certainty that from now on all sadness would be shared, all happiness gloried in together. His kiss left her shaking, clinging to him, murmuring his name, sighing against his lips.

'We're the lucky ones,' he told her, a long time later. 'To find each other like this. To love like this . . .'

'To love like this,' she whispered, holding him even more tightly, lifting her face again for his kiss.